T0334290

CRITICAL FRONTIERS OF THEORY, RESEARCH, AND POLICY IN INTERNATIONAL DEVELOPMENT STUDIES

Series Editors
Andrew Fischer, Giles Mohan,
Tanja R. Müller, and Alfredo Saad Filho

Critical Frontiers of Theory, Research, and Policy in International Development Studies is the official book series of the Development Studies Association of the UK and Ireland (DSA). The series profiles research monographs that will shape the theory, practice, and teaching of international development for a new generation of scholars, students, and practitioners. The objective is to set high quality standards within the field of development studies to nurture and advance the field, as is the central mandate of the DSA. Critical scholarship is especially encouraged, within the spirit of development studies as an interdisciplinary and applied field, dealing centrally with local, national, and global processes of structural transformation, and associated political, social, and cultural change, as well as critical reflections on achievingc social justice. In particular, the series seeks to highlight analyses of historical development experiences as an important methodological and epistemological strength of the field of development studies.

Advanced Praise for *Philanthropy and the Development of Modern India*

Arun Kumar has written a fascinating archive-based study of Indian philanthropy over the course of the twentieth century. The book shows in great depth and detail how Indian elite philanthropies—from Bombay Parsis, Marwaris in Calcutta, and Ahmedabad's textile industrialists—forged their ideas of modernity and development within colonial India and after independence. Those elites' caste and religious identities ensured disagreements and debates on the meaning of development and modernity, yet played a profound role in the development of key development concepts such as self-reliance. This comparative approach is one of the most fascinating aspects of this landmark, ground-breaking study. There are few such in depth and detailed original studies of Indian philanthropy—Arun Kumar's book has set a very high bar for future scholars.

Professor Inderjeet Parmar, City, University of London,
author of *Foundations of the American Century*.

This is a remarkable inter-disciplinary work straddling cultural studies and development studies, bringing together a concern with the nation-form into conversation with post-Independence discourses of modernization. Drawing on little-known archival material from the 19th century onwards, Arun Kumar demonstrates how wealthy Indians forged a connection through new kinds of philanthropy with emerging ideas of the national-modern. By bringing the nation into focus, and often working closely with nationalist political leaders, the philanthropists—from the early twentieth century capitalists to the twenty-first century IT billionaires—promoted a discourse of self-care and responsibility. In doing so, they were able to foster a circumscribed modernity that side-stepped older caste hierarchies. Himself a former development consultant with a major philanthropic organization, Arun Kumar provides compelling insights into how the seemingly universal imperative of development is entangled with contentious histories of colonialism, nationalism and modernity.

Professor Tejaswini Niranjana, Lingnan University,
author of *Musicophilia in Mumbai and Mobilizing India*.

Philanthropy and the Development of Modern India

In the Name of Nation

ARUN KUMAR

OXFORD

UNIVERSITY PRESS

Great Clarendon Street, Oxford, OX2 6DP,
United Kingdom

Oxford University Press is a department of the University of Oxford.
It furthers the University's objective of excellence in research, scholarship,
and education by publishing worldwide. Oxford is a registered trade mark of
Oxford University Press in the UK and in certain other countries

First Edition published in 2021

Impression: 1

Published in the United States of America by Oxford University Press
198 Madison Avenue, New York, NY 10016, United States of America

British Library Cataloguing in Publication Data

Data available

Library of Congress Control Number: 2021942712

ISBN 978–0–19–886863–7

DOI: 10.1093/oso/9780198868637.001.0001

Printed and bound in Great Britain by
Clays Ltd, Elcograf S.p.A.

For my dad, Ashok (1943–2021).
For Kabirji; and for my Kabir

Acknowledgements

devaliyā mein dev nāhi,
jhālar koote garaj kasi.

In one of his poems, '*Thāra rang mahal mein*' (In your colourful palace), Kabir cautions us:

> There is no god in that temple,
> So what's the point in beating the gong.[1]

As I turned the words over and over again, I wondered if the elites' philanthropic pursuit of development throughout twentieth century India that I outline in this book was also not a bit like that? Constructing opulent 'temples' of modernity that were always distant; where the poor and impoverished had little chance of finding a god—that is, the salvation of development—no matter how often or how loudly they beat the gong. What, then, was the point of those temples of modernity, after all? As I researched and wrote about those 'temples of modernity', to borrow from that peculiar Nehruvian term, I kept thinking to myself what, indeed, was the point of me talking about them? After all, development must be about the poor; except that it often isn't.

In writing about development and the 'temples of modernity', I have accumulated many debts. I owe an intellectual debt to many people—those who read and commented on different chapters and versions of the book; those who suggested references and pointed me to different archives; and those who have gently reminded me to either finish writing the book quickly or take as long as I needed to. I thank Fahreen Alamgir, Anindita Banerjee, Amon Barros, Brian Bloomfield, Martin Brigham, Sally Brooks, Colin Brown, Gibson Burrell, Indira Chowdhury, Bill Cooke, Shane Hamilton, Shirish

[1] Translated by Linda Hess and Shabnama Virmani; see Ajab Shahar, 'Thara Rang mahal Mein', posted 22 July 2019, https://www.youtube.com/watch?time_continue=260&v=cApx92qpFks&feature=emb_logo.

Kavadi, Daniel Lacerda, Leo McCann, Raza Mir, Tanuja Kothiyal, Tejaswini Niranjana, Nidhi Srinivas, Kevin Tennent, and Pete Thomas variously in Australia, the United Kingdom, France, Hong Kong, India, and the United States. I have also presented parts of the book in different forms at Ahmedabad, Anaheim, Anand, Exeter, Frankfurt, Glasgow, Lancaster, Loughborough, Newcastle, virtually at 'Vancouver', and York—thank you to the audience for their comments, indulgence, and questions. I thank the interlending services at Lancaster and York's J. B. Morrell libraries for sourcing books, book chapters, and articles not already available.

I also want to thank Adam Swallow and Henry Clarke at OUP for their patience and support; the series editors and three reviewers for their comments and suggestions—most of all, to focus on the central argument and sharpen it.

I owe a different kind of debt to my parents, Rani and Ashok for their quiet forbearance which I could never quite learn. I am certain no one would have been prouder that I have written a book than my father, that he passed away without quite knowing makes me sad in ways that I will always struggle to overcome. My son, Kabir and partner, Nivedita have assured me, read drafts, made suggestions, asked difficult questions, proofread, interrupted, stopped me from writing without saying so, reminded me about the book, and helped me forget about it from time to time—for all that and more, I thank them. There is a book-shaped hole in my weekends and in my future annual leaves—when I wrote much of this book—that I promise to spend with you now.

*

I am grateful to the Economic History Society for the Carnevali grant, which helped me do archival research in London, New Delhi, and Mumbai, as well as financial and administrative support from my departments at Lancaster and York which helped me travel to London, Mumbai, New Delhi, and Pune. Some of the material presented in chapters 3, 4, and 5 was published in a very different form in *Development and Change*: 'Pragmatic and Paradoxical Philanthropy: Tatas' Gift-giving and Scientific Development in India', 49, 6 (2018): 1422–46.

Contents

List of Abbreviations

AES	Ahmedabad Education Society
ATIRA	Ahmedabad Textile Industries' Research Association
BHU	Banaras Hindu University
BITS	Birla Institute of Technology and Science, Pilani
CINI	Central India Initiative, Tata Trusts
CSR	corporate social responsibility
DCTR	Demographic Centre for Training and Research, Bombay
ICRC	Indian Cancer Research Centre, Bombay
IIM	Indian Institute of Management (here, Ahmedabad)
IISc	Indian Institute of Science, Bangalore
KEF	Karmakshtera Educational Foundation, Ahmedabad
MIT	Massachusetts Institute of Technology, Cambridge
NGO	nongovernmental organization
PRL	Physical Research Laboratory, Ahmedabad
RSS	Rashtriya Swayam Sevak Sangh
RWB	Rural Welfare Board
SBI	Sukhi Baliraja Initiative, Tata Trusts
SDTT	Sir Dorabji Tata Trust
SRTT	Sir Ratan Tata Trust
TACEB	Tata Agricultural and Rural Training Centre for the Blind, Vapi
TACO-AN	Tata-Cornell Initiative in Agriculture and Nutrition
TCL	Tata Chemicals Limited, Mumbai
TIFR	Tata Institute of Fundamental Research, Bombay
TISS	Tata Institute of Social Sciences, Bombay
TMH	Tata Memorial Hospital, Bombay
TRC	Tata Relief Committee

Note on Sources

GA	Godrej Archives, Mumbai
IOR	India Office Records, British Library, London
LSEA	Special Collections, London School of Economics and Political Science, London
NAI	National Archives of India, New Delhi
KL	Kasturbhai Lalbhai Papers
NMML	Nehru Memorial Museum and Library, New Delhi
JB	Jamnalal Bajaj Papers (1st and 2nd Instalments)
PT	Purshottamdas Thakurdas Papers
1043	Birla-Nehru Correspondence. Files 1–5, Accession number 1043
TCA	Tata Central Archives, Boxes 174–212
	Box number precedes the file number and document details in Notes
TNA	The National Archives, London
UCL-SC	Papers of Travers, Robert M. W., included in Ramsay Papers; RAMSAY/ 67-106/82-101, Special Collections, University College London
WLA	Archives and Manuscripts, Wellcome Library

1

Development, Modernity, Nation

An Introduction

Writing from Nasik Central Jail on the eve of his forty-first birthday, the founder of the Bajaj Group of companies, Jamnalal Bajaj (1889–1942) made seven promises to his god.[1] Seeking the blessings of Mohandas Gandhi, Bajaj pledged to contribute to: removal of untouchability by 'opening' at least one Hindu temple and five water-wells to entry for Dalits; remarriage of a child widow across sub-castes within the same *vrna*; and convincing at least two women to abandon their *ghoonghat*.[2] Further, he promised to: make a lifelong friend, preferably someone who was either a Muslim, an 'untouchable', Parsi, or a Christian Englishman; financially help at least one family that earned its

[1] Born to a peasant family in Sikar, Bajaj was adopted by a rich businessman Seth Bachhraj of Wardha when he was five years old. He attended school from the ages of six to ten; and was married two years later to Jankidevi Jajodia. Following Seth Bachhraj's death, Bajaj inherited 6 lakh (or 600,000) rupees and took over the reins of the family businesses of moneylending and the cotton trade, which Bajaj expanded rapidly. He was known for his principled business practice and affluent lifestyle, unlike the thrift associated with his *Vaishya* caste. His early charity in famine relief and education led to honorary awards of a magistrate and later Rai Bahadur, both of which Bajaj subsequently renounced. Bajaj was actively involved with the Congress party and was one of the leading patrons and followers of Gandhi and his constructive programme. On his death, Jankidevi renounced her share of Bajaj's wealth (approximately Rs. 250,000) for Gandhi's cow-service programme; see Nanda, *In Gandhi's Footsteps*, 360.
    The Bajaj Group was founded in 1926. In 1931, they established the Hindustan Sugar Mills Ltd., before diversifying into the production of cement, electrical appliances, and scooters when Kamalnayan Bajaj took over the reins of the Group following Jamnalal's death in 1942. In 1972, the former's son Rahul Bajaj became the managing director of Bajaj Auto, leading the company to significant commercial success. For an extended discussion on Rahul Bajaj, see Piramal, *Business Maharajas*, 85–133.
[2] Bajaj's promises, it is worth pointing out, upheld the sanctity of the caste system and maintained the pollution-purity norms on which the *chaturvrna* system is based by avoiding marriage across *vrnas*. It was part of Gandhian reform of Hinduism from within, which Ambedkar has criticized extensively, see for example Ambedkar's *Annihilation of Caste*, Ambedkar's Writings and Speeches (henceforth AWS), volume 1, 41–2, 67–9.
    The *chaturvrna* (or four *vrnas*) system, on which the caste-Hindu system is based, comprises of the Brahmins (the so-called priestly castes), *Kshatriyas* (warrior and ruling castes), *Vaishyas* (traders, merchants, and moneylenders), and the *Shudras* (those who engage in manual labour). Dalits, literally meaning those who are oppressed or broken, are outside the four *vrnas* and considered untouchable by caste-Hindus.
    Ghoonghat refers to the practice of covering the heads, and sometimes faces, among caste-Hindu women.

Philanthropy and the Development of Modern India: In the Name of Nation. Arun Kumar, Oxford University Press.
© Arun Kumar 2021. DOI: 10.1093/oso/9780198868637.003.0001

livelihood honestly; and encourage at least one household to commit itself to the service of the Indian nation.

Bajaj's modest but strangely specific list—with its commitment to 'reforming' untouchability, widow remarriage, alleviating poverty, and contributing to national service—can be read as a contemporary, 'cosmopolitan' manifesto for *development*, broadly defined. Although not extensive or inclusive in any way, it mirrored the particular concerns and desires of caste-Hindu elites in Indian society, then. In the reform of which, Bajaj promised to make gifts: of money, influence, service, and friendship. His gifts, Bajaj clarified, were not motivated by any personal desire for glory, recognition, or rewards. On the contrary, he hoped to overcome any such lingering desire in his self. However, such rewards were not to be eschewed altogether, Bajaj cautioned. If they opened avenues for further service, he noted, then it was well worth pursuing them diligently.[3] Philanthropy, therefore, was not simply a means for acquiring or consolidating further cultural, reputational, or symbolic—and ultimately, economic—capital.[4] Instead, in Bajaj's formulation, it served as the strategic means to a different end—reforming society and one's own 'self'.

What such reform meant and how it could be attained though differed significantly, I outline in this book, both among contemporary elites and over time. Like Bajaj, India's economic elites have led a long and concerted effort to reform and modernize Indian economy and society in the name of its *development*. From cotton, jute, and opium traders and later mill-owners from Bombay and Ahmedabad in the nineteenth century, industrialists and merchants from the twentieth century, to software moguls in Bangalore and Hyderabad from the turn of the twenty-first century, India's economic elites have used their philanthropy extensively and influentially to sponsor and support development in the country. In so doing, they made extensive and generous gifts: of time, expertise, technology, capital, land, and material.[5] Contrary to twenty-first-century claims which have tended to present Indian philanthropy as a 'laggard' when compared to its Western counterparts then,

---

[3] Bajaj's letter to Naraindas Gandhi dated 3 November 1930, Correspondence: Gandhi, Naraindas, Jamnalal Bajaj Papers (henceforth shortened to JB; 1st inst.), Nehru Memorial Museum and Library, New Delhi (henceforth NMML).

[4] Andrew Carnegie's philanthropy, Harvey et al. argue, helped him consolidate his wealth by converting cultural, reputational, and symbolic capital into economic capital and building momentum by entering into a self-reinforcing growth cycle of capital; see Harvey et al., 'Carnegie and Entrepreneurial Philanthropy', 429–30.

[5] For an insightful history of modernization of philanthropy in India including the transition from Mughal to early colonial India, see Haynes, 'Tribute to Philanthropy', 339–60. Also see Pushpa Sundar's *Beyond Business, Business and Community*, and *Giving with Thousand Hands* for a historical overview of Indian philanthropy.

Indian economic elites' philanthropy has exerted a significant—occasionally acknowledged but often left unproblematized or poorly theorized, one might argue—influence on development in India, historically.[6] Although not 'a' history of Indian philanthropy as such, the book draws on their philanthropic history to interrogate elites' imaginings of development. I focus on what can only be termed as the 'long' Indian twentieth century—witness to British colonialism, various nationalisms, post-colonial nation-building, Nehruvian socialism, neoliberal globalization, and diverse social movements.

*

In 2009, I travelled to a tribal village in Khirkiya, Madhya Pradesh on a commissioned consultancy with the Sir Ratan Tata Trust (SRTT), one of India's largest and leading philanthropic organizations. A group of Gondi *adivasi* young men and children had gathered round, waiting patiently for the meeting to begin. We sat on tarpaulin sheets under the cover of darkness to discuss the potential areas of involving youth in a children's education programme, implemented by a local non-governmental organization (NGO) with support from the Trust. The NGO ran programmes for improving children's education outcomes through academic support (using teaching-learning material and through the deployment of para-teaching staff in government schools), and by catalysing community involvement (primarily through oversight and social accountability mechanisms). Our meeting ended with community facilitators from the local NGO singing a song in Hindi—it emphasized unity and the need for collective organizing for the benefit of the Gondi youth and children.

On our way back, I asked the NGO's community facilitators about their choice of singing songs in Hindi and not Gondi. I was told that the facilitators did not know any; most of them, although from the area, were not *adivasis* themselves and did not speak or understand Gondi. I wanted to know more on the place and significance of Hindi—predicated in particular conceptions of post-colonial linguistic nationalism and difference—in the lives of Gondi *adivasis*.[7] Singing such songs in Hindi, they reasoned politely, was useful in

---

[6] Contemporary status reports on Indian philanthropy tend to see it as a 'laggard' compared to its global counterparts: in scale, ambition, mode of *doing* philanthropy, its professional management, and 'scientific' evaluation, etc. For example, Blake et al., term it as 'broken'; see 'Giving in India', 6. Elsewhere, I have argued that scholarship on Indian philanthropy can be classified into three different types of narratives: modernizing, nationalist, and managerialist. Scholarship on contemporary twenty-first-century Indian philanthropy is narrated, by and large, using managerial vocabulary; see Kumar, 'Pragmatic and Paradoxical Philanthropy', 1424–5.

[7] To clarify, I use two distinct but commonly recognized variations of the term. When used as a temporal marker, I use 'post-colonial'. Elsewhere, following Leela Gandhi's caution, I use 'postcolonial'

cultivating collectivism among the Gonds. But more importantly, they pointed out, learning Hindi was useful for the Gonds—it helped them fill forms for various governmental welfare schemes and sell their produce in the weekly bazaars, where much of the business was transacted in Hindi and not Gondi. Hindi, therefore, was the language of development—with the state and in the market; Gondi, on the other hand, was rendered a relic of their pre-modern past. This, I was to discover later during the course of my association with the Trust, was the archetype of contemporary development supported by it, where developmental philanthropy had come to assume, by and large, a pedagogic role for itself. A large part of the development work supported by the Trust, then, was directed at *educating* the poor about becoming and being modern, a theme I interrogate further in chapter 5.

Development and modernity, therefore, was not only about teaching the poor new skills and languages relevant for the changing structure and demands of capitalism and its markets, but also transforming attitudes: of becoming responsible citizens, aware, organized, and engaged. Disregarding collective organizing within Gondi society, contemporary development hoped to replace it with new, modern, one might argue now neoliberal, forms of organizing: self-help groups, oversight committees, interest groups, producer companies, etc. Needless to say, such an imagination of development as a break away or rupture from the past is hardly new. It can be understood as the arrival of the 'modern moment', which 'creates a dramatic and unprecedented break between past and present'.[8] As we are all too familiar with now, this transformative promise of development is yet to be realized in much of the postcolonial world. Instead, the dualisms that colour our conceptualization and descriptions of development and modernity—traditional versus modern, man versus machine, artisan versus industrial workers, etc.—are plagued by discrepancies and ambivalences in the postcolonial world. Writing about specificities of dualism and modernity India, the noted sociologist Satish Deshpande argued that the 'most obvious differences in Indian accounts of dualism have to do with the social units in which tradition and modernity are located and their mutual articulation.' Tradition and modernity in India, he argues, 'are not only segregated into separate

---

to designate the condition which did not begin with the end of colonialism, i.e. its aftermath, but from its coming and therefore should not be understood simply as a 'post-' condition. See Gandhi, *Postcolonial Theory*, 3.

[8] Appadurai, *Modernity at Large*, 3. Elsewhere, Dube suggests understanding it as a rupture which 'brings into view a monumental narrative—the breaching of magical covenants, the surpassing of medieval superstitions, and the undoing of hierarchical traditions'; see Dube, 'Enchantments of Modernity', 729.

personalities…but are also apt to occur, in comparable Indian accounts, as integral parts of *the same personality*.[9]

The ways by which tradition and modernity are entangled *within* the same Indian personality, however, are far from static. They can be understood, I suggest, as a particular, historical formation of modernity in India and possibly other postcolonial locations. It is these shifting and changing careers of modernity—and so, development—that I interrogate in this book.

Writing the Nation in

Bookending these two philanthropic gestures—from Bajaj's commitment to reforming his self and society in colonial India to Tata Trusts' support to NGOs in educating market-ready, and one might argue development-ready, citizens in twenty-first-century neoliberal India—was Indian elites' desire to transform India into a 'modern' and 'developed nation'. Here, I am conscious of the dangers of collapsing different forms of economic and social change into a singular category of 'development'. But interrogating these broad socio-economic changes alongside each other, I would argue, serves a range of crucial analytical purposes. First of all, it enables us to plot the continuities and disjunctures between the more familiar development landscape from the second half of the twentieth century and the earlier colonial and nationalist forms of social welfare and economic advancement. For example, ideas of 'self-care' and 'responsibility' that are more commonly associated with neoliberal capitalism from the 1990s, have a much longer historical trajectory that emerged not just from post-independence nation-state's desire to project its independence and autonomy but were also—as I outline—part of nationalism's critique of colonialism.

Secondly, interrogating them alongside each other enables us to view how formulations of development in India have vacillated between modernity and modernization. Both *modernity* and *modernization*, the historian Prakash Kumar astutely points out, are used for distinct purposes in South Asianist readings. Modernity, he notes, is used conceptually to challenge and criticize the colonial civilizational claims and to call out its limited explanatory potential given its Western mooring. On the other hand, modernization is used to criticize the violence unleashed by the extension of the global industrial complex in the region and the attendant emphasis on expertise and bureaucracy

---

[9] Deshpande, *Contemporary India*, 36, italicized in original.

often associated with post-war international development.[10] The shifts between development as modernity (during colonialism) and modernization (post-colonialism) were not simply sequential, chronologically, but, as I go on to discuss, have existed alongside each other. Such connections become evident only when one reads nationalist, socio-economic reform alongside post-colonial development. Relatedly and thirdly, irrespective of their historical relation to colonialism (during or post-), formulations of development throughout the twentieth century were—I argue below and throughout the book—commonly indexed within the national question in India. Social reform in colonial India, for example, was often justified in the name of national 'advancement' or 'progress'. Equally nationalist economic programmes such as the Gandhian 'constructive programme' were similar to or shared many common features with community development programmes that followed. There are still other similarities. Elites' philanthropy, for example, has remained moored to patronage-based politics even if the nature of state had changed drastically, and served their own narrow class interests, as I argue in the coda.

Examples of how modernity, development, and the 'nation' were entangled in India can be found in several places. Hagiography and even public histories, for example, have tended to attribute elites' philanthropy for development to their love for the country and its leaders. Jamsetji N. Tata's philanthropy (1839–1904), founder of the Tata Group—India's leading global conglomerate, for example, was said to be driven by his love for his country and Bombay city.[11] He acted—in his industry and philanthropy—out of 'compassion for a citizenry labouring under the twin realities of oppressive foreign occupation and overwhelming poverty'.[12] If received accounts are to be believed, colonialism, patriotism, and the poverty of their fellow citizens have shaped the

---

[10] Prakash Kumar, 'Agrarian Development in India', 2.

[11] From Behroze Cursetjee's talk delivered at the Tata Staff College on February 22, 1956; from File no. 174, Tata Central Archives, Pune (henceforth TCA).

Founded in 1868 by Jamsetji N. Tata, the Tata Group now comprises of over thirty operating companies, with operations in more than a hundred countries. The Tatas made their early wealth trading in commodities such as cotton and opium, followed by the Empress Mills founded in 1877. The Group has since developed extensively with business interests in aviation and automobiles, chemicals, telecommunications, steel, etc. Since the 2000s, the Group has also acquired a number of large businesses overseas, including Tetley in 2000; Daewoo in 2005; steel giant Corus in 2007; and Jaguar and Land Rover brands in 2008. The Group currently operates in over a hundred countries and employs over seven hundred thousand people.

For a discussion on the Tata Group, see Lala, *Creation of Wealth*; Witzel, *Evolution of Corporate Brand*; Kuber, *The Tatas*; and Sen, *House of Tata*.

[12] Tata Group, 'The Giant who Touched Tomorrow', accessed 25 June 2013, http://tata.com/aboutus/articles/inside.aspx?artid=AapOEYsYNwI=.

Tatas' philanthropy, then and since. On the other hand, Bajaj's philanthropy was shaped to a large extent by Gandhi's personal influence over Bajaj and his 'constructive programme' with its inter-linked criticism of exploitative colonialism, and its positive counter-narrative of nationalism and village industries' revivalism. Related examples of elites' commitment to nationalist leaders can also be found in the gifts made in memory of various Indian leaders following their demise. In 1948, for example, Ghanshyam Das Birla (1894–1983) and Kasturbhai Lalbhai (1894–1980) were charged with overseeing collections for the Gandhi Memorial Fund from within the private sector to build a suitable memorial.[13] A target of Rs. 5 crores was set with industry-wise quotas assigned. Birla and Lalbhai signed letters in appeal and wrote personally to their associates and extended networks urging them to contribute. Following their efforts, a total of Rs. 5.27 crores had been collected by April 1950.[14] Similarly following Nehru's demise in 1964, a Memorial Fund was launched under the leadership of J. R. D. Tata. Inviting tax-exempt contributions, the Fund's leaders hoped to raise 5 crores again to establish an institute of advanced studies in the country.[15]

Development in India, therefore, was closely indexed simultaneously within particular formations of modernity and modernization; and that of the nation, both rhetorically and otherwise. This, one suspects might be true for a range of other locations from the Global South too, albeit their formulations would have been distinct; and possibly manifest itself in different sites and in different order from what I present here. In interrogating this coupling

[13] Born to Baldeo Das and his Yogeshwari in Pilani, Rajasthan, Ghanshyam Das Birla was the third of four sons. He was sent to live in Calcutta at the age of nine to pursue his education and later to Bombay to learn English and bookkeeping. He moved back to Calcutta at the age of sixteen to work in the family business. In 1911, he launched the G. M. Birla Company to trade in jute, before moving on to cotton once the World War I ended. In the early 1930s, the Birlas joined the sugar industry before diversifying into textile machinery, automobiles, bicycles, plastics, and insurance and banking. Birla frequently moved in and out of politics and business, but returned to take over in 1977, with the assets over Rs. 1,065 crores; rising to over Rs. 2,500 crores when Birla died.

For an extended discussion on Birla's life, business, and politics, see Piramal, *Business Legends*, 1–153; and Medha Kudaisya's *G. D. Birla*.

Kasturbhai Lalbhai was born to an economically and socially prominent family of Ahmedabad's *nagarsheths* in 1894. The Lalbhais made their wealth as moneylenders, landowners, jewellers, and traders. Following his father's demise, Lalbhai joined the family business of cotton textile mills at the early age of seventeen. He went on to establish Arvind Limited in 1931, and soon rose to prominence as one of the country's leading textile industrialists. Throughout his life, Lalbhai remained a prominent educationist founding various institutions in the city of Ahmedabad, and was actively associated with various leaders from the Congress party. As chair of the Anandji Kalyanji Trust for fifty years, Lalbhai oversaw the renovation and maintenance of various Jain temples throughout western India.

For a biographical discussion on Lalbhai, see Piramal, *Business Legends*, 295–324.

[14] Kudaisya, *G. D. Birla*, 271–2.

[15] Press statement issued on 8 January 1965 by the industrialists' committee of the Nehru Memorial Fund, Kasturbhai Lalbhai Papers, NMML (henceforth shortened to KL).

of development with modernity and the national question, I turn to political histories of nationalism from India. In *The Nation and its Fragments*, Partha Chatterjee has outlined the imbrication of post-colonial national development in India within its earlier nationalist movement. By the early 1940s, the dominant argument of nationalism against colonial rule, he argued, 'was that the latter was impeding the further development of India: colonial rule had become a historical fetter that had to be removed before the nation could proceed to develop. Within this framework, therefore, the economic critique of colonialism as an exploitative force creating and perpetuating a backward economy came to occupy a central place.' And further that even if the economic logic of exploitation were to be proved incorrect through empirical investigation, hypothetically speaking, it did not in any way reduce the nationalist claim. Nationalism, therefore, was not premised only along the primordial difference of race or religion, instead it was provided with the positive content of national development. Colonialism was, Chatterjee noted, 'illegitimate not because it represented the political domination by an alien over the indigenes: alienness had acquired the stamp of illegitimacy because it stood for a form of exploitation of the nation (the drain of national wealth, the destruction of its productive system, the creation of a backward economy etc.).'[16]

For India to develop then, following nationalism's developmental logic, it needed to govern itself as a matter of historical necessity. Development of the nation, therefore, was colonialism's counter: a positive intention as against colonialism's destructive forces. In its quest for legitimacy, the post-independence nation-state dedicated itself to the enormous task of social justice. Social justice, however, could not be attained within the old, colonial, institutional framework. Nationalism now required new institutions, which reflected the 'spirit of progress or, a synonym, modernity'. By way of development, nationalism in post-colonial India came to be translated into nation-building; its ideology was now that of the nation-state; and the pursuit of social justice—or more generally questions of development—the source of its legitimacy.[17]

How might we, then, describe, interpret, and theorize postcolonial development and its relationship with modernity and modernization on the one hand, and the national question on the other, in twentieth-century India? Working my way through three schematic histories of development—universalizing

---

[16] Chatterjee, *Nation and its Fragments*, 203.   [17] Chatterjee, *Nation and its Fragments*, 133.

international development; its counter: local or participatory development; and finally national development—each with their own specific relation to and scale of modernity and their respective criticisms, I argue that we need new ways to think about development's entanglements with modernity and the national question.

Development Histories

Modernity, according to Richard Fox, is 'the Enlightenment project—the Western Truths of alienated production and bureaucratic rationality and secular progress, and the associated practices of science, technology, humanism, productivity, development, and management'.[18] While compelling, Fox's attribution of modernity to the West re-inscribes a hierarchical geopolitical order between the modern West and those living in countries and communities outside it—a dualism on which development is framed. It consigns those living outside it to languish—eternally—in what the writer Pankaj Mishra poignantly called 'the waiting room of history'.[19] Overcoming this 'lag' or 'deviation' among those residing in the periphery and in relation to those 'ahead' of us in the so-called First World became the primary burden of the post-World War II international development era.

Evidence of this can be found extensively in development literature in the accounts of the under-developed subjectivity of the poor who resided in the so-called Third World. The poor were characterized by and represented through their 'powerlessness, passivity, poverty, and ignorance, usually dark and lacking in historical agency, as if waiting for the (white) Western hand to help subjects along and not infrequently hungry, illiterate, needy, and oppressed by its own stubbornness, lack of initiative, and traditions.'[20] To them, post-war international development offered science, planning, technology, and international organizations as its key tools. Together, these universally applicable and seemingly neutral tools of overcoming poverty offered a linear, pre-determined, predictable, and sequential path to development to the then so-called Third World countries.[21] Framed along the modernity-tradition dualism, modernization—dressed as development—offered the

---

[18] Fox, 'Communalism and Modernity', 237.
[19] Mishra's 'History's Waiting Room.' *The Guardian*, 28 February 2015.
[20] Escobar, *Encountering Development*, 8.
[21] Seth, Gandhi, and Dutton, 'Postcolonial Studies', 8.

complete erasure of the past stubbornly residing in the Third World, and replacing them with thoroughly modern societies.

Driven by universal and universalizing formulations of the modern, international development and its characteristic US-led modernization was—according to some of its critics—imposed from the outside in. It undermined, the latter argued, the sovereignty of post-colonial Third World nations and unleashed extensive violence on people, communities, and their ecologies.[22] This central criticism about the imposed narrative of universal-modern development, however, does not quite fit the Indian context, and one suspects other Third World locations too, in any meaningful way. Helleiner, for example, in his revision of received accounts of the Bretton Woods institutions (that are known to have championed Truman-era international development) has argued that several so-called Third World countries, especially those from Latin America, were enthusiastic participants at the 1944 conference. Their eager support, he adds, has probably been written out of historiography as the Bretton Woods institutions—shortly after their inauguration, scaled back financial assistance turning attention towards European Reconstruction—came to adopt more conventional free market policies, and as the influence of domestic proponents of the New Deal that championed 1930s Latin American developmentalism, waned.[23] Still others have demonstrated persuasively and in different ways that development was not simply imposed from the outside but actively desired by the subaltern masses, such as the Dalits in India, on which more later.[24] Also relevant to us, universal-modern development and its criticisms assigned passivity to Third World elites. Escobar, for example, inaccurately notes that they actively 'pledge[d] allegiance to the banners of reason and progress' and agreed to all forms of imposed development.[25] This is patently false as I demonstrate in this book that postcolonial elites from the Third World have actively engaged in fashioning their own forms of, and challenges to, modernity as part of development.

*

Foremost among those challenging the universal-modern development from above, was post-development studies, which has provided an influential but misplaced critique of international development and its neutral, desirable,

---

[22] See for example, Escobar, *Encountering Development*; and Rahnema, *Post-development Reader* for an overview of their critique of post-war era's international development.
[23] Helleiner, 'Reinterpreting Bretton Woods', 961–3.   [24] Guru, 'Dalits', 123–36.
[25] Escobar, *Encountering Development*, 31.

and universally applicable tools and technologies of development.[26] Their criticisms are premised on international development's 'discovery' of poverty in the so-called Third World, whose peoples were universally labelled with characteristics such as those that Escobar lists, and the undermining or bypassing of local communities and their knowledges. As a grand theory and developmental approach, modernization with its attendant universalism, linearity, and sequencing of development, became a Western imposition on the Rest of the World.

Hoping to see off the demise of development as its name suggests, post-development studies offered indigenous, community-centric, and local visions of development as possible alternates to the universal modernity of the post-war international development. Activist-scholars such as Vandana Shiva and Claude Alvares, for example, challenged universal and universalizing modernity's destructive force and championed calls for the re-instatement, variously, of pre-developmental, local, indigenous, traditional, etc.[27] Drawing our attention to communities living in modernity's aftermath (particularly capitalist science and technology, heavy industry, and mechanization), which international development was meant to be helping in the first place, they articulated localized visions and scales of development. The decades long work of Practical Action, itself inspired by Schumacher's classic *Small Is Beautiful*, advocated for intermediate technology as a suitable alternative to modernization's violence.

The case for local also comes to us from another direction. Premised in a related criticism of experts and their decontextualized knowledge, scholars of participatory development have also been calling our attention towards the local: specific, embodied, and community-led. Its proponents included various practitioner-scholars such as Robert Chambers, Rajesh Tandon, and Anil Agarwal.[28] Instead of blaming the poor, that is the recipients of development, for its failures, they called for an inversion of power relations in development. Exemplified through the subtitles of Chambers's books 'Putting the Last First' and 'Putting the First Last', they invited the re-ordering of development policies and practices. Although influential, the proponents of local development have not been without criticism. Nederveen Pieterse, for example, has argued that such criticisms have 'underrate[d] the dialectics and complexity of motives

---

[26] See Crush's edited *Power of Development*; Ferguson, *Anti-politics Machine*; and Rahnema, *Post-development Reader*, among others.

[27] See, for example, Alvares, *Science, Development and Violence*; and Shiva, *Staying Alive*.

[28] Chambers, *Whose Reality Counts?*; and *Rural Development*. Also see Knight et al.'s *Reviving Democracy*.

and motions in modernity and development'.[29] Others such as Marc Edelman have pointed to their singular failure in taking into consideration development that has risen from within: where the peasants' organizations and its leaders and activists have insisted on 'their aspirations for improved economic and social well-being', which they happened to term development.[30] Still others, such as Arun Agrawal, Uma Kothari and Bill Cooke, in different ways, have challenged proponents of local or participatory development for essentializing and/or romanticizing the local or traditional communities; limitations in their conception of indigenous or community knowledge; and their concealment of the power structure of and within local communities.[31]

The second schematic history of development then was that of local development, which was variously a denunciation, rejection, or invitation to move post- or past- development. In training its attention on what I have designated as the universal-modern above, local development was both a challenge to the neo-colonial global order and its use of international development in doing so. But more importantly, here, it offered a radically different engagement with modernity. For those of us residing in the aftermath of modernity, it offered a return to the past—to pre-modern forms of society, technology, economy, and knowledges.

Proponents of local or participatory forms of development—impelled by their rejection of modernity, and development itself—are, however, unable to account for the Indian masses' desire for modernity. The subaltern desire for *particular* infrastructures, codes, and technologies of modernity provides them with an emancipatory route out of their oppression. This desire for modernity and its assemblages can be witnessed variously in: learning the English language; connecting to the digital; accessing 'modern' education and healthcare; belief in rationality, logic and reason as against caste-based belief and superstition, etc. Leading Dalit scholars, for example, have noted that modernity promised a breakaway from the 'language of obligation' under the Hindu feudal order, but also the pursuit of inclusion based on 'modernist credentials (skills, abilities and excellence)'.[32] Although this emancipatory promise of modernity—in terms of its rupture from the Hindu social order of the past—has remained unfulfilled for Dalits, it remains a powerful draw and one

---

[29]   Nederveen Pieterse, 'After Post-development', 183.
[30]   Edelman, *Peasants against Globalization*, 190.
[31]   See, for example, Edelman and Haugerud, *Anthropology of Development and Globalization*, 49–50; Agrawal, 'Indigenous and Scientific Knowledge;' and Cooke and Kothari, *Participation: The New Tyranny?*
[32]   Guru, 'Dalits', 123.

that is hardly accounted for by the proponents of local development as well as those from post-development studies with its attendant focus on rejections of universal modernity.

*

A third schematic history resides *between* universal-modern international development and local development, both in terms of scale but also conceptually, as it synthesized elements from each. Large-scale (mostly) organized projects of national development, a wide variety of which were on display in the post-colonial nations of the Third World, were frequently seen either as deviations or context-specific pursuits of modernity, which were not universal but attentive to local conditions, requirements, and resources. It vacillated between high modernity—James Scott's *Seeing Like a State*, for example, brilliantly chronicled post-colonial national development's authoritarian pursuits of modernity—and less-spectacular, but no less-organized, smaller-scale projects such as the community development projects in India from the 1950s.[33] Emerging in the middle of the twentieth century, according to its proponents, it offered liberation from dependency for previously colonized nations in the so-called Third World. Informed by the work of dependency theorists, national development projects, therefore, promoted autonomous growth through raising trade tariffs and barriers, import-substitution industrialization at home, and reducing reliance on imported raw materials.[34]

Paradoxically, national development shared features of both universal-modern modernization as well as those of local, participatory development. Tracing the intellectual legacies of national development in the twentieth century, Immanuel Wallerstein argued that national development was the mechanism by which Third World countries from the periphery were integrated into the world-system. Beginning from 1917, Leninism and Wilsonianism, he argued, presented two different paths to national development that were ultimately aimed at the Third World's integration. In the post-colonial developmentalism from the post-war period, although the two routes to national development seemed distinct, they shared several common features: they were driven by nation-states' objectives of increasing national wealth, modernizing their infrastructure, and optimism in achieving development. In

[33] Scott's *Seeing Like a State* chronicles examples from Brazil, India, Soviet Union, and Tanzania among others.

[34] Closer to time when national development projects were at their peak, Alejandro Portes identified three different sociological perspectives on it: as social differentiation, enactment of values, and liberation from dependency; for a full discussion see Portes, 'Sociology of National Development'.

short, national development according to Wallerstein was premised in modernization's universal-modern that I discussed earlier, where Third World countries played 'catch up'.[35]

Still others have plotted how national development in the post-colonial Third World did not simply imitate modernization as Wallerstein suggests but provided alternate conceptions and trajectories of national development, synthesizing elements of the universal-modern with those of the local. Starting from the Ruvuma Development Association's funding by Oxfam in 1960, the *Ujamaa* villages in Tanzania are one of the leading examples of such national development projects. Designed around the expectation that 'working together' locally would translate into 'living together', the *Ujamaa* village development model represented the 'kind of society, that Oxfam supporters would like to see everywhere'. Although initially promising, the project soon ran into difficulties as the villagization project turned increasingly authoritarian leading to forced resettlement from the late 1960s onwards.[36] Epitomizing the ways by which the post-colonial nation-states of the time tended to assume the authority to know and speak for the peasantry in their countries, projects such as the *Ujamaa* revealed the contradictions between democracy and participation that played itself out in many Third World countries of Africa, South and Southeast Asia.[37] National development, therefore, shared features of both universal-modern international development and with local or participatory development visions. One way of thinking about national development's relationship with modernity would be to think of them as hybrid formations of modernity.

*

The three schematic histories that I have chronicled above share a particular relationship with modernity and operate at distinctive scales from each other. From international development's enthusiastic embrace of the universal-modern to local and post-development's denunciation, challenge, and even rejection of modernity, to national development's more sophisticated responses to it (or what one might call hybrid modernity), as pure types they help order and understand development's entanglements with modernity. For different reasons, each of these—I would argue—are limited in their usefulness when it comes to understanding the nature of postcolonial development.

---

[35] Wallerstein, 'Concept of National Development', 521–4.
[36] Cited from Jennings, 'Almost an Oxfam', 512.
[37] Schneider, 'Freedom and Unfreedom', 372.

In discussing the reasons, it might be helpful to outline what I think might, ultimately, be helpful in interrogating and theorizing development in a range of postcolonial locations such as that in India; as it helps pinpoint the limitations of the received conceptual vocabulary drawn from the three schematic histories discussed previously.

To return to my earlier question then, how might we understand postcolonial development in the long Indian twentieth century? Together, the entangled forms and formations of development, modernity, and the national question in a range of Third World locations can be helpfully understood, I suggest, as the autonomous developmental realm of the *national-modern*.[38] I borrow the term from cultural studies scholar, Tejaswini Niranjana. Probing the new nationalisms in the aftermath of the Mandal Commission and the Babri Masjid demolition from 1990 and 1992 respectively, Niranjana invites us to think of the then-present as 'post-national-modern'. Different from the widely known postmodern and postnational, the unwieldy term, she suggests, can be used to interrogate how different social groups access and negotiate the emergent formations of the national-modern (that is, how modernity has been inextricably linked to the national question in various Third World locations). In a way, then, this book interrogates the formation of the post-condition that Niranjana invites us to think about. While the remainder of the book is dedicated to plotting and explaining the shifting contours of national-modern— that is what it looks like and why, it is worth clarifying upfront how national-modern is distinct from the three development schemas outlined above, the importance of thinking of postcolonial development as not simply derivative or indigenous, and the significance of looking at Indian elites' philanthropy, historically.

Unlike universal-modern's unbridled faith in modernity: science, technology, capital, polity, and institutional infrastructure (or modernization to be more precise), the national-modern was marked by its ambivalence towards modernity in Third World locations such as India. This ambivalence was a result of the historical context in which it emerged. 'The same historical process that has taught us the value of modernity,' Chatterjee notes, 'has also made us the victims of modernity. Our attitude to modernity, therefore, cannot but be deeply ambiguous. This is reflected in the way we have described our experiences with modernity in the last century and a half.' 'But this ambiguity,' he adds, 'does not stem from any uncertainty about whether to be for or against modernity. Rather, the uncertainty is because we know that to fashion

---

[38] See Niranjana, 'Nationalism Refigured', 141.

the forms of *our own* modernity we need to have the courage to reject the modernities established by others.'[39] Through their philanthropy, India's economic elites have engaged in fashioning, I would argue, not *our* (as Chatterjee suggests) but *their own* modernity, which I have designated as the national-modern. It was based, sometimes, in the similar rejection of others' modernity (that of the colonizers'); and at other times, in its ambivalent embrace, different from that propagated by US proponents of modernization.

Equally it would be inaccurate to designate the national-modern as somehow lesser than the universal-modern or even a deviant. 'Assiduously plot[ting] against the horizon of a singular modernity', Dube notes, modernity's diverse and distinct formations and practices in non-Western locations begin to appear 'primitive or progressive, lost or redeemable, savage or civilized, barbaric or exotic, ever behind or nearly there, medieval or modern'.[40] Such a plotting of against the universal works only, incorrectly so, to re-emphasize the dualism of East/West, modern/traditional, colonial versus nationalist modernity, and so forth. Instead, I suggest that thinking of national-modern in this way permits us to theorize the specificities of development in a range of postcolonial locations in and of itself, instead of having to reference or gesture towards Western formations and representations of modernity.[41]

National-modern is also distinct from post-colonial national development in its relationship both to colonialism and to early twentieth-century nationalisms (the latter of which has received relatively lesser attention in development studies). Of historical necessity, national development followed colonialism—as a post- condition. Like its predecessor nationalism, national development—or nation-building to use its Indian equivalent—was also compelled to articulate its difference from colonialism as a regenerative and productive force unlike colonialism's destruction and extraction.[42] National-modern, on the other hand, did not have to bear such a burden. It borrowed freely from colonial forms of modernity. Jamsetji N. Tata's philanthropy, for

[39]   Chatterjee, *Empire and Nation*, 152; emphasis added.
[40]   Dube, 'Enchantments of Modernity', 731.
[41]   In *Asia as Method*, the cultural studies scholar Kuan-Hsing Chen invites us to move past the impasse arising out of the mutual entanglement of 'Western' imperialism, colonialism, and the Cold War from which there is little respite for those of us from and writing about 'other' locations.
[42]   See Chatterjee, *Nationalist Thought* for a detailed discussion on nationalism and nation-building relationship with colonialism.

example, conveniently acknowledged the superiority of 'Western' modernity and sought to replicate it into the Indian context.[43]

Differently from post-colonial national development, national-modern shares a prior, on-going, and more complicated relationship with colonialism. It worked alongside and/or within, and not necessarily against or after, colonial development and administration. Speaking at a meeting to discuss the transfer of power from British rule at Chatham House in London in 1933, Purshottamdas Thakurdas (1879–1961), for example, made national-modern's relationship with colonialism—in India's economic elites' conception—clear.[44] That Indian [elites] were now in a position to govern its own masses, he noted, was the logical outcome of colonial forms of development. Referencing Macaulay, Thakurdas concluded his remarks: 'if the granting of an English educational system to India meant that in course of time Indians would claim to govern themselves, that would be the proudest day in the history of England.'[45] National-modern, therefore, can be understood as what Bhabha has designated as 'postcolonial contra modernity' which may be 'contingent to modernity, discontinuous or in contention with it, resistant to its oppressive assimilationist technologies'.[46] However, to make clear how the national question was written *into* postcolonial development in the Third World, I prefer to use the term *national-modern*. Equally it helps me work through its vacillations between various forms of modernity and modernization.

*

To clarify, though, I do not wish to reclaim the national-modern as a more desirable or even less virulent form of development or even suggest that we turn to it in our search for alternates. It was—and still is—*not* simply a

---

[43] Tata, his biographer Frank R. Harris noted, was not narrow in his commitment to India unlike some of his contemporaries. Instead he was quick to acknowledge what the West had to offer and sought to replicate in the country as I show in chapter 4. See Harris, *Tata: A Chronicle*, 251.

[44] Born in a Gujarati *baniya* family in Girgaum, Bombay, Thakurdas was first enrolled in the Mumbadevi Municipal School and then at Tejpal Anglophone Vernacular School, before joining the Elphinstone High School. Having lost his parents at a young age, Thakurdas was raised by his uncle. Trained as a lawyer, he joined his uncle's firm, Narandas Rajaram and Company, as an apprentice before becoming a partner in the firm in 1907. Thakurdas soon came to be known as the 'cotton king' and was nominated to the Bombay Legislative Council in 1916. He served on several public committees, some of which I discuss later in the book, and between the 1930s and the 1940s held the post of director in over sixty companies. He was also one of the authors of the Bombay Plan.
See Moraes, *Thakurdas*; also see Nayak and Maclean, 'Co-evolution, Opportunity Seeking, and Institutional Change', 29–52.

[45] Thakurdas's remarks at a meeting at Chatham House, London on 4 July 1933, file 1, Purshottamdas Thakurdas Papers (henceforth shortened to PT), NMML.

[46] Homi K. Bhabha, *Location of Culture*, 9.

counter to or the opposite of development's empire-building desires. Instead, it is used throughout the remainder of the book as an analytical category: as a way of interrogating development's entanglements with modernity, colonialism, nationalism, nation-building, and capitalism in the postcolonial world.[47] The designation of autonomy, here, is also considered: in that the making of the national-modern was driven by the elites' desire to mark off their conceptions of modernity as somehow distinct from other formulations of modernity, and including their occasional (but not always) rejection of it. The constitution of an autonomous realm of the national-modern, I argue therefore, worked both to legitimize development but also to justify the exclusions and dispossession it caused. Put another way, it became the object whose pursuit enabled the economic elites to selectively engage with specific, circumscribed formations of modernity, while excluding others. It was also used to explain away the fallout of development itself. With industrialization, for example, rural and urban communities were evicted and moved into programmed social and economic units, but these were deemed acceptable—indeed necessary—as they ultimately served the larger objective of nation-building. In doing so, Indian economic elites worked frequently with and sometimes against, I argue, the contemporary governing regimes—be they colonial, nationalist, or the post-colonial nation-state.

*

Over the following four chapters, the book interrogates the national-modern and explains its shifting formations. Drawing on the history of India's economic elites' philanthropy, I argue that the constitutive *imaginaries* of national-modern emerged as a particular formation of capital, caste, gender, modernity, modernization, nationalisms and later nation-building, religion, 'tradition', etc. Following Elta Smith, I understand *imaginaries* as 'a particular, often complex view of the world that comes to shape agenda, research trajectories, projects, and policies' in development.[48] The following chapters: on civil society, community, self, science and technology cover a significant *site* of doing development and as an *object* at which their philanthropy was directed. To clarify, those were not the only *sites/objects* of their philanthropy.

---

[47] Ferguson, 'Decomposing Modernity,' 166–7 makes a similar suggestion on probing modernity as a folk or native category.

[48] Imaginaries, Smith argues, are 'normatively loaded visions not only of what should be done "in the world" but also how it should be undertaken and why'. They refer, therefore, to ideologies, social factors, and practices; and are made up of scientific, technological, economic, political, and cultural imperatives; see Smith, 'Imaginaries of Development', 462.

For example, the elites tried to imagine a different kind of national-modern Indian economy. I have not covered them, or in the breadth that archival material I have gathered thus far would have enabled, here as I do not possess the disciplinary expertise to deal with them, meaningfully. I must also add here that given that it is less a history of Indian philanthropy from the twentieth century, I have organized my argument thematically, and not simply chronologically or even by philanthropists, one at a time. I understand that this means I move forwards and backwards in time across different chapters, which can be distracting; but this was the only way I could work across sites and themes and point to connections in development imaginaries. Within each section, though, I have tried to present my material, chronologically, as far as possible, without compromising the argument.

The book's focus on economic elites' philanthropy is significant for two reasons. Interrogating development's entanglements with modernity in the postcolonial world is hardly new, these interrogations have been written, by and large, from the standpoint of the subaltern (developmental subjects) or the post-colonial nation-state.[49] Despite their political and economic influence, relatively little is known about postcolonial elites and their role in development, beyond their mischaracterization as captors of power, scarce resources, and anti-development.[50] Moving past the problematic conflation of their interests with those of the governing regimes, and collapsing elites into a singular social class with shared interests and behaviours, the book contributes to growing and renewed interest in studying elites and their philanthropy within development studies, and more widely still.

Relatedly, the role and contributions of the Indian economic elite to the country's industrialization and their tumultuous relationship with contemporary political regimes are well known in business and economic histories of India.[51] However, comparatively less is known about their role and motivation to contribute to India's development through their philanthropy. Among those probing economic elites' philanthropy and development, there exists a historical gap as scholars have tended to focus, separately, either on philanthropy during colonialism, particularly in the nineteenth or early years of the

[49] Gupta's *Postcolonial Developments* and Ferguson's *Expectations of Modernity* come to mind given their meditative interrogation of 'messy' modernity in the postcolonial world. Relatedly, Scott's *Seeing Like the State* is an exemplar of rich but state-centric accounts of postcolonial development and modernity.

[50] See Amsden et al.'s edited *Role of Elites* for a useful review but also an insightful call for engaging with and not bypassing elites in development studies.

[51] See for example, Kudaisya, *Anthology of Business History*; Roy, *Business History of India*; and Tripathi and Jumani, *Indian Business*.

twentieth century. Where they have focused on economic elites' philanthropy and its role in nation-building, it has been restricted to, by and large, individual business groups or specific institutions endowed by them. There are also, as I have mentioned previously, evaluation and status reports on twenty-first-century Indian philanthrocapitalism, which, I have argued elsewhere, are largely managerial—that is, inclined towards promoting more philanthropy, uncritically, without interrogating its deleterious consequences.[52]

Before moving on, it is worth discussing the history of Indian elites' philanthropy from earlier centuries briefly as it has had a formative influence on Indian philanthropy in the twentieth century; and clarifying the choice of elites and specific philanthropic gestures I focus on, given the wide variety of gifts and gift-making they have engaged in, next.

Elites and 'Organized' Philanthropy

Since the seventeenth century, the Indian mercantile elites have used philanthropy both for building their reputational capital (within their own kinship-based groups by funding community infrastructure) and for fostering ties with the ruling class. The form of their philanthropy for the latter, however, changed under colonialism as gifts given to political rulers as tributes were rendered illegal. The incoming colonial bureaucracy put in place new—one might say, 'modern'—regimes of governing charity, which sought to separate the pursuit of profit from charity. Colonial law on charity distinguished the pursuit of private profits and altruistic philanthropy, more rigidly than before. Such moves at re-constituting charity reflected, the historian Ritu Birla notes, 'the "disembedding" of the abstract market from the fluid vernacular capitalist context of gain and giving that saw self-directed action (or profit) as always already within broader communities...and so always other-directed.'[53]

[52] Prior historical studies of Indian philanthropy have focused on the shifts in economic elites' philanthropy from pre- to colonial rule and how they navigated the latter in nineteenth-century India; see for example, Haynes, 'Tribute to Philanthropy', 339–60; Palsetia, 'Honourable Machinations', 55–75 and 'Merchant Charity', 197–217; and White, 'Crisis to Community', 303–20. Studies of Indian philanthropy in the twentieth century have focused, to a large extent, on colonial India; see Mukherjee, 'New Province, Old Capital', 241–79; Ramanathan and Subbarayappa, 'Indian Institute of Science', 871–926. Still others have focused on the endowments to individual institutions; see for example, Bassett, *The Technological Indian*; Chowdhury, 'Fundamental Research', 1095–129; Kavadi, 'Lady Tata Memorial Trust', 69–74 and 'Tata Memorial Hospital', 282–4. All of these have been helpful in developing the argument I have presented here.

For an overview of scholarship on Indian philanthropy, see Kumar, 'Pragmatic and Paradoxical Philanthropy', 1438–40.

[53] Ritu Birla, 'C=f(P)', 136.

Philanthropy, then, came to be orientated differently under colonialism. It was directed towards a newly imagined *public*: good, utility, or welfare. It soon became, the historian Douglas Haynes noted, drawing on more than three centuries' history of philanthropy of Surati *sheths*, one of the available means by which the Indian economic elite demonstrated their shared concern (with the colonial bureaucracy) for the masses and their willingness to invest in social reform of the latter. Seeking to ensure a secure commercial and political environment for themselves, the Surati *sheths*' philanthropy adopted a new idiom of giving: secular, civic-orientated philanthropy for the public benefit, displacing their earlier tributes to rulers and charity within their own communities.[54]

Leading this 'imitation' of the imperial idiom of philanthropy in their search for political titles, influence, and power were the Anglophile Parsi business leaders from Surat and Bombay on the western Indian littoral. Sir Jamsetji Jejeebhoy (1783–1859), a leading Parsi businessman and philanthropist for example, used 'modern' philanthropy strategically with the objective of creating a collaborative ruling community with the British, which included a place of significance for himself. Reflecting imperial values, his patronage of art and architecture and his gifts in the form of modern medicine not only afforded him political recognition and prominence, but also constituted an emerging medium of transmission of modernity *to* the masses.[55] Alongside colonial attempts at implanting modernity (through the establishment of an abstract 'public purpose' as the objective of philanthropy, or propagating newer realms or subjects, or even new modes of gift-making), the Indian economic elite continued to use philanthropy more creatively and strategically than before. They developed a sophisticated and strategic twin-track approach to philanthropy (another reminder of the importance of studying non-Western philanthropy differently and on its own terms, and not just in

---

[54] Haynes, 'Tribute to Philanthropy', 339–60.

[55] See Palsetia's 'Honourable Machinations', 55–75 and 'Merchant Charity', 197–217 for a discussion on Jejeebhoy's philanthropy. Like Jejeebhoy, other contemporary and earlier Parsis also used their philanthropy, strategically, to consolidate their collective economic and social standing. The historian David L. White, for example, has outlined how the Parsis financed community infrastructure in Bombay, enabling fellow Parsis to join them in various economic activities in the newly colonial trading city, see 'Crisis to Community', 183–203. For a general but important insider account of the history of Parsi philanthropy up to the nineteenth century, see Karaka's *The Parsees*, and *History of Parsis*.

In addition to their trading roles, the Parsis, more than other communities of the region, came to be seen, and saw themselves, in the important in-between role of business intermediaries. In this role, they came to be characterized by their progressiveness, rationality, and civilized masculinity. It is instructive to note that the Bombay Parsis—as a community—believed themselves to be distinct from the 'Pure Natives' via their Westernization in the form of charity, racial purity, and emphasis on truth; for more see Luhrmann, *The Good Parsi*.

relation to the West). Such philanthropy not only responded to the colonial attempts at modernizing charity but also continued to rely on their earlier vernacular forms of charity directed within their own religious or caste-based communities. Its continued use enabled the mercantile elites to accumulate *ābru*, or reputational capital, which not only helped consolidate their economic networks and credit-worthiness but also their social standing.[56] Thus, even as the Indian economic elites assumed a frontier role in the transmittal of modernity to the masses, they did not abandon their own 'traditional' forms of charity, which were aimed at accumulating reputational capital and building trustworthiness within their own communities.

Characterisitcally pragmatic, remarkably responsive to their historical contexts, and in their desire for building alliances with and within their contemporary political and economic regimes, elites' engagement with modernity adopted, therefore, a simultaneous embrace and side-stepping of colonial modernity, depending on philanthropic recipients and audiences. Thus, their philanthropy was neither simply imitative of the imperial idiom, nor was it 'traditional' in the narrow sense that some contemporary commentators allege.[57] Emerging histories of Indian elites' philanthropy seem to agree with this. Seeking to extract the charge of 'imitation' on rapidly modernizing philanthropy in nineteenth-century South Asia from the stigma associated with imitation in nationalist thought and the anxiety it is riddled with in postcolonial thought, Brian Hatcher has argued that the then incipient 'modern' philanthropy in early colonial Bengal was a complicated outcome of local elites' intimate relations with Europeans. He argues that the elites borrowed, appropriated, and re-tooled a wide range of ideas (of association, society, civil society, community, etc.) and practices (rules, norms, artefacts, rituals, etc.) to fashion their own forms of modernity. Instead of seeking a singular source of this shift to modern forms and expressions of philanthropy, Hatcher invites us to 'ponder instead the messy and vibrant mingling of multiple traditions'.[58] Following Hatcher, the book is also committed to pondering the intermingling of different and sometimes even contradictory traditions that have shaped Indian economic elites' philanthropy over the twentieth century. But more importantly, this attention to different contemporary traditions and

---

[56] Haynes, 'Tribute to Philanthropy', 339–60.

[57] In *Business and Community*, for example, Pushpa Sundar invokes an unbroken, uniquely Indian 'tradition' that connects its economic elites' charity from the past to the present forms of philanthrocapitalism, without acknowledging the wider social and intellectual forces that have formed and challenged it, including that of colonialism.

[58] Hatcher, 'Imitation, Then and Now', 98.

how they interact with each other, from colonialism to nationalism and later nation-building, religion, caste, capital, etc., helps us read the careers of development and modernity in the postcolonial world.

*

The rich and influential historiography of Indian elites' philanthropy from the seventeenth to nineteenth centuries has provided extensive accounts of the modernization of their philanthropy itself and its use as a channel for transmitting modernity in pre-, early, and colonial India. It has focused on some of the leading trading communities, such as Parsis from present-day Gujarat and Mumbai and the *baniāns* from colonial Calcutta.[59] Similar historical accounts of philanthropy from the twentieth century, however, are few and far between. Those that are available have been restricted, by and large, to the first half of the twentieth century only—that is during colonialism.[60] These, as I go on to demonstrate in the remainder of the book, constituted only a small part of the wide spectrum of motivations and ways by which Indian economic elites' philanthropy engaged with questions of development and modernity from the twentieth century.

A notable exception to the lack of historiographic attention to economic elites' philanthropy from twentieth-century India is Pushpa Sundar's *Beyond Business* (2000), its updated and revised edition *Business and Community* (2013), and her more recent work *Giving with a Thousand Hands* (2017; which focuses on twenty-first-century philanthropy in India). Starting from the middle of the nineteenth century onwards, Sundar has traced the contribution of corporate and individual philanthropy to society. Her approach, however, suffers from a number of drawbacks as I have outlined elsewhere, including the conceptual conflation of CSR and philanthropy, for example, and her inattention to the influence of colonialism on Indian philanthropy despite historical evidence and historiography to the contrary. Still others take issue with her conclusions, for example, her undue optimism in business leaders' trusteeship as Sundar makes a case *for* ever more CSR, without discussing holding corporations and large corporate houses to account over their failures to contain—leave alone contribute to development

---

[59] In addition to the historiography of Indian philanthropy, also see the special issue of the journal *Modern Asian Studies* on 'Charity and Philanthropy in South Asia' (2018). It does not, however, engage explicitly with the questions of development per se.
[60] See, for example, Mukherjee, 'New Province, Old Capital', 241–79.

meaningfully—the pollution of lands and water, displacement of *adivasis* in the tribal heartland, and corruption.[61]

The similarities and differences in the nature, mode, objects, and motivations of Indian elites' philanthropy across the colonial and post-colonial periods from the twentieth century, therefore, deserve greater historical attention. The shifts, from various nationalisms in the first half of the twentieth century to different regimes and rhetorics of nation-building from the second half invite us to provide new ways of thinking and theorizing philanthropy, and therefore development itself. The shortcomings of scholarship on Indian philanthropy should not, however, detract from the point that the Indian economic elite have played and continue to play a significant but problematic role in the country's development. Serving the frontiers of modernity in India in the twentieth century, their philanthropy has been constitutive of a range of development imaginaries and influences, while their financial capital and networks provided means for conducting these.

Among others, the book draws, mainly, on the philanthropic histories of the Bajaj, Birla, Lalbhai, Sarabhai, and Tata families, and Purshottamdas Thakurdas. From the post-1990s period which saw the rise of neoliberal global capitalism in the country, I focus on Sunil Bharti, Shiv Nadar, Nilekanis, and Azim Premji.[62] The choice of economic elites' philanthropy has been shaped by a number of reasons, both historical and historiographical. The historical reasons relate to size, scope, and relevance of their philanthropy to development and modernity, while the historiographical reasons include availability, access, and conditions of access to archival material, and language

---

[61] For a detailed discussion of some these issues, see my review of her work; 'Review', 563–6. The Indian business historian, Dwijendra Tripathi, also does not share Sundar's enthusiasm over trusteeship and its futures; see Tripathi, 'Book Review', 334–7.

On a related note, Ranajit Guha in *Dominance without Hegemony*, 62, argued that trusteeship was a mere mask. 'On the side of the indigenous elite,' Guha wrote, 'we have an emergent capitalist class keen on masking its role as a buyer and user of laborpower by pretensions of trusteeship with regard to the labor force.'

[62] In Sundar's classification, twenty-first-century Indian philanthropy is comprised of eight sources. Of which, donors of older family businesses and new entrepreneurs from IT and related fields are the focus here. Others in her classification include celebrities, non-resident Indians (NRIs), CEOs and professionals, corporate CSR foundations, foreign (mainly US) foundations, and community foundations. See Sundar, *Giving with Thousand Hands*, 148–9.

Both the Azim Premji and Bharti Foundations were started in 2000. Rohini Nilekani launched Pratham Books in 2004, Arghyam in 2005, and EkStep with her husband and tech-entrepreneur Nandan Nilekani in 2014. First among the so-called 'new age' philanthropy was the Shiv Nadar Foundation, launched in 1994, but which only expanded more extensively into primary and higher education, research, arts, leadership, etc. from 2003 onwards. Despite belonging, chronologically and discursively, to the twenty-first century, such 'new age' philanthropy built on and drew from national-modern imaginaries of development from the earlier century. The discussion of such initiatives, though, is deliberately brief.

of archival material. The sometimes heavy emphasis on the Tatas is, in many ways then, hardly unexpected—again for reasons both historical and historiographical. Not only were they the first business house in the country to organize their archives and make them publicly available, they also possess a long-standing and extensive history of philanthropy: from endowing institutions of science, social science, and performing arts, to sponsoring the higher education of Indians abroad, and partnering with NGOs in areas such as education, health, livelihoods, arts and crafts, natural resource management, etc. The 'unbalanced' narrative, I believe, tells its own story about their complicated relationship with the national-modern.

As I plot and probe their use of philanthropy for development, I focus on 'organized' philanthropy, on which a short explanation follows.

*

In their widely cited formulation, Robert Payton and Moody define philanthropy as a multiplicity of voluntary giving, voluntary service, and voluntary association.[63] In this book, I focus on all three forms of philanthropy, that is, Indian economic elites' gifts of cash and time, their service in the form of expertise and extended networks, and their involvement with voluntary associations such as NGOs. Gifts made by the Indian elites came in various forms: from the Tatas' early adoption of trusts to organize their philanthropy to Birla's disorganized but on-going and frequent contribution to Nehru's Prime Ministerial Relief Fund on various pretexts (both personal and public), and finally to Purshottamdas Thakurdas' philanthropy, where he not only gave away his own money, but also his gift of raising resources through his business and personal contacts, and chairing appeal committees and commissions, starting with the Famine Relief Fund from 1912 and the Bombay Presidency's War and Relief Fund started in 1914.[64] Bajaj, on the other hand, frequently hosted India's nationalist leaders at Bajajwadi at Wardha, where he diligently looked after their sleeping and eating arrangements. Nehru, Bajaj's biographer Nanda recounts, preferred buttered *chapatis* and boiled potatoes and liked to live on the first floor of the main building, an outsized bed was arranged for the tall Abdul Ghaffar Khan, and C. Rajagopalachari preferred *rasam*. Many of them also relied on Bajaj's expertise to manage their personal

---

[63] Payton and Moody, *Understanding Philanthropy*, 6.

[64] Elsewhere, I have outlined how the Tatas' early efforts to systematize their philanthropy drew more on US foundations' experience, and less on British charity in ways that were quite paradoxical, historically; see Kumar, 'Pragmatic and Paradoxical Philanthropy', 1438–40. See file 26 (Parts I and II), PT for Thakurdas's involvement with famine and war funds; also see Moraes, *Thakurdas*, 19–23.

finances.[65] Each was purposive and strategic, both in elites' individual careers and the career of the national-modern. However, the focus on the three forms is not even or continuous in the book as elites' *mode* of doing philanthropy changed over their own lifetime.

It is also worth distinguishing between philanthropy and corporate social responsibility (or CSR). I have decided to focus solely on philanthropy and not corporations' CSR divisions or foundations, which are of relatively recent provenance in India. Following an amendment to the Companies Act in 2013, India has seen a burgeoning of CSR in the country. Many corporate houses have established separate foundations which engage both in onward grant-making and implementing their own programmes.[66] The initial endowment of such foundations did not come from elites' personal wealth but from corporate profits. Such foundations often operate separately from elites' philanthropy. Tata Trusts, for example, often have little or no relationship with the CSR activities of individual corporations within the Tata Group. Such CSR divisions and corporate foundations like the Infosys Foundation, I believe, deserve to be scrutinized separately. Their relationship with modernity, religious belief, nation-building, caste etc., tends to be more diffuse and carries less of an imprint of their leaders' imaginaries of development. They are also more recent and do not, therefore, lend themselves to historical study, as such.

The book focuses on elites' *organized* philanthropy, notwithstanding the slippery notions of the term. By *organized*, I do not refer simply to gift-making by formal philanthropic organizations (such as a Trust or a Society, the equivalent of American foundations); but to planned and systematic philanthropy, impactful and mostly large scale or even if small scale, it was at least recurring or sustained over reasonably longer periods of time. Thakurdas, for example, made numerous small grants and donations for day and boarding schools in Bombay Presidency. When reminded to make payments to the Kathiawad Boarding School that he promised previously,[67] Thakurdas responded that all promises and arrangements for payments needed to be recorded on paper, otherwise 'people would get nervous of promising

---

[65] He looked after Rajendra Prasad's family finances; helped purchase the family home of C. Rajagopalachari in Madras, and so forth; see Nanda, *In Gandhi's Footsteps*, 251–6.

[66] As per Sec. 135 Chap. IX, sub-sections 1–5, any company with a net worth of Rs 500 crores or more, or with an annual turnover of Rs 1,000 crores or more, or with an annual profit of Rs 5 crores or more, must constitute a committee which will oversee its CSR policy, which must have an outlay of at least 2 per cent of the average net profits from three preceding years.

[67] Thakurdas had promised to pay Rs. 2,500 annually for five years to a boarding school in Kathiawad; letter from Harilal G. Parikh to Thakurdas dated 14 May 1925; file 33/1923–27, PT.

donations'.[68] Similarly, working as the honorary general secretary and treasurer of the Bombay Central Famine Relief Fund, Thakurdas raised 10 lakh lbs. of fodder for cattle, affected by famine in the summer of 1912 in the Saurashtra region.[69] Responses to reports circulated by Thakurdas are particularly demonstrative of notions of 'organized' that I refer to. One response, for example, noted his 'systematic and business like methods', which had been instrumental in 'saving endless lives amongst the cattle'.[70] J. Booth Tucker of the Salvation Army, for example, wrote that he was impressed with the way the fund had been administered. 'Bombay,' he wrote, 'has the good fortune to possess large-hearted and successful business men, who take their philanthropy into their business and their business into their philanthropy, and thus make a success of each'.[71] Thakurdas was actively involved in famine relief efforts throughout the late 1910s.[72] Like Thakurdas, Lalbhai was known for bringing in organization to the administration of charity, including those of religious trusts. As the chair of the Anandji Kalyanji Trust that oversaw the renovation and maintenance of Jain temples across western India, he introduced strict budgetary systems. He also ensured that board meetings were no longer organized around the 'sweet will' of the board's chair but were held regularly and scheduled in advance.[73]

Notwithstanding the current calls for further systematizing, organizing, and managing Indian philanthropy in the twenty-first century, responses to Thakurdas's report of the famine relief committee's work are revealing of how long-standing the notion of using business-like approaches to doing philanthropy, particularly in the realm of development, has been.

Even though I steer clear of individual charity—much of which was driven by elites' religious beliefs—I recognize that even their organized philanthropy remained inflected by their religious-beliefs, subscription to caste-based norms, and conception of gender-relations. Ignoring these as remnants of 'tradition' or constitutive of a hybrid modernity would have been a mistake. In a recent review of the scholarship on South Asian philanthropy, Filippo

---

[68] In his response dated 16 May 1925 to Parikh, Thakurdas mentioned that per arrangements, the boarders were to be called after his late father's name and the school send their total numbers to him, file 33/1923–27, PT.

[69] From letter to Thakurdas dated 27 March 1912; file No. 4, PT.

[70] Addressed to Thakurdas, it is hard to decipher the signatory of the letter dated 2 September 1912 which was sent on the letterhead of Lyon, Lord & Co. Ltd. of Bombay; file no. 4, PT.

[71] From Booth Tucker's letter to Thakurdas dated 30 September 1912; file no. 4, PT.

[72] More than money, Thakurdas gave freely of his own time and networks. A persuasive and respectable figure among the cotton merchants, mill-owners, and financiers in the Bombay Presidency region, Thakurdas mobilized his networks to raise money for famine relief, see file no. 19/1919–20, PT.

[73] Piramal, Business Legends, 305–6.

Osella makes a similar point. Instead of making a clear distinction between religion-minded charity of the past (such as *dān* and *zakat*) and 'modern' forms of secular philanthropy that followed it, he reminds us to be mindful of confining philanthropic practices to the narrow realms of tradition and modernity, exclusively.[74] Therefore, instead of disregarding 'traditional' charity that is frequently driven by beliefs, I have chosen to study them *alongside* or *as part of* their attempts at constituting the national-modern, where useful. This has been particularly productive as it has opened ways into discussing how social vectors of religion, caste, class, gender, and ritual became central to particular formulations and formations of national-modern development.

---

[74] Outlining how religion has also continued to play an influential role in Western philanthropy, Filippo Osella notes: 'Historically, then, the worlds of charity, economic practice, and political calculation have seldom been apart'; see Osella, 'Charity and Philanthropy', 12. In the same issue, Birla, 'C=f(P)', 134 also explores how cultural conceptions of charity, *dān* and *zakat* are folded into contemporary market society.

2

Community

In Nation's Name

Shortly after the demise of his father Baldeo Das, Ghanshyam Das Birla wrote a letter to Nehru remembering him and outlining his views on charity and modernity.[1] Orthodox in some ways and having retired from public life to Banaras, he possessed the 'most advanced views on all modern problems… [and] was completely non-communal in his outlook'. He spent his life and money 'helping the poor. His charity was mostly old-fashioned, viz., giving alms, food, clothes etc to hundreds of poor people every day.'[2] In 1899, for example, Baldeo Das opened relief centres, a free canteen, and a cheap grain store to feed the poor in Pilani, then suffering under a severe drought. Again in 1905, he spent Rs. 10,000/- constructing wells following another drought.[3] It was left to his children, Birla noted, to look after modern charities which 'inspired me to put up greater and greater services'.[4]

Like the Birlas, the Tatas too had a long and prior history of charity, largely restricted to their own communities.[5] Nusserwanji Tata, father of the Tata

---

[1] In 1879, Shivnarain and his son Baldeo Das set up a *gaddi*, an independent firm of sorts, named after themselves. In 1911, as Baldeo Das retired from active business, Ghanshyam Das joined his brother in Calcutta to establish his businesses. Even as the brothers continued their traditional broker- age and trading work from the *gaddi*, Ghanshyam founded a new firm with his brother-in-law to launch his own business career. Like the Tatas, the Birlas also made their early wealth trading in opium before moving on to cotton and jute, and still later in textiles, aluminium, cement, and chemicals.

By 1945, the Birla Group comprised twenty companies, which grew into India's largest corporate group in 1977 with assets worth Rs. 1,065 crores. By 1983, when G. D. Birla died, the Birla Group had over two hundred companies, assets over Rs. 2,500 crores and sales over Rs. 3,000 crores. The Group was formally divided in 1983 with assets divided between Birla's sons and grandsons, and nephews and grand-nephews; see Piramal, *Business Legends*, 135.

In the remainder of this book, Birla is used to refer to Ghanshyam Das only; while other members of the Birla family are referred to by their first or full names and together as the Birlas.

[2] G. D. Birla's letter to Nehru dated 4 April 1956; from file 3, files 1–5, Accession no. 1043, NMML (henceforth shortened to 1043).

[3] Kudaisya, *G. D. Birla*, 11–12. Thanks to his philanthropy, the Lal Ghat in Banaras where Baledo Das lived came to be known as Birla Ghat.

[4] G. D. Birla's letter to Nehru dated 4 April 1956; from file 3, 1043.

[5] The historian David White noted how Parsi elites used philanthropy in the eighteenth century to build community infrastructure in 'new' cities such as Bombay. It both facilitated the community's

Group's founder, Jamsetji Tata (1839–1904),[6] was renowned for his charity: he sponsored the construction of fire temples and towers of silence 'which provide[d] devout Zoroastrian with a key to the gates of heaven.'[7] Differently from their fathers, though, both Birla (Ghanshyam Das) and Tata (Jamsetji) acted swiftly in adopting another—more modern—form of philanthropy at the turn of the twentieth century.[8] Moving away—although not completely, as I go on to argue in the third part of the chapter—from their fathers' charity directed at their own Marwari and Parsi communities respectively, they made numerous generous gifts of cash, kind, service, and association towards India's development. This modernization of their philanthropy involved two inter-linked moves. The first involved the installation of the 'nation' as the object of their philanthropy, which replaced the earlier charity for the welfare of their own kinship-based communities, which I discuss below. The second involved imagining 'new' forms of modern communities, which they argued were inte-gral to the pursuit of development in the country.

Decrying the alms and charity handed out by elites from an earlier gener-ation, Jamsetji Tata outlined his vision of 'constructive philanthropy' in an interview given to the *West Coast Spectator* in 1899. 'There is one kind of charity common enough among us [Parsis],' he noted, 'which is certainly a good thing, though I do not think it is the best thing we have. It is that patch-work philanthropy which clothes the ragged, feeds the poor, and heals the sick and halt.' But it was hardly the best thing. Instead, he advocated making gifts to further the cause of national advancement.[9] Tata's shift away from charity towards kinship-based communities came, first, with the Endowment Fund established in his name. Started in 1892 with the idea of supporting

migration from Surat to Bombay as well as contributed to their rise in public life and fostering their collective identity as Parsis; see 'Crisis to Community', 303–20.

[6] The founder of the Tata group, Jamsetji Tata was born on 3 March 1839 in Navsari, Gujarat into a family of priests. His father, Nusserwanji Tata, was the first member of his family to go into business and trade. Jamsetji went to Elphinstone College in Bombay, from where he graduated as a 'green scholar' in 1858. He went on to join his father's business at the age of twenty. In 1868, he founded Tata and Sons as a trading company, before initiating the cotton, iron and steel, and hospitality businesses, among others. He is said to have travelled widely and read extensively. He passed away in 1904 in Germany.

[7] Harris, *Tata: A Chronicle*, 120.

[8] Like his father, Tata too made numerous gifts from the 1860 onwards to charity. Unlike his father though, Tata's gifts were less sectarian and more public. These included construction of sanatoriums, maternity homes, and memorials to British administrators and educationists who served India with sympathy. He also sponsored disaster relief efforts in India and Italy; from Lala, *Love of India*, 95. Tata's early philanthropy from the second half of the nineteenth century can also be interpreted, following Palsetia's historiography of Jamsetjee Jejeebhoy's philanthropy from the first half of the nineteenth century, as attempts at building a place of significance for themselves within colonial regime; see Palsetia, 'Honourable Machinations', 67–8.

[9] Cited from Lala, *Love of India*, 113.

Parsi students to pursue their higher education abroad, Jamsetji Tata himself amended the remit of the scheme opening it 'to all capable natives of this country'.[10] The advancement of the nation, not their own kinship-communities, thus, became the primary purpose of his philanthropy. Tata's bypassing of the Parsis in his charity caused a stir among the Bombay Parsi community. He responded to their challenge: 'what I ask my-fellow Parsees is: "What difference is it to them whether it is exclusively to their benefit or open to all?"'[11] Similarly, as he was finalizing the location of his Institute of Science (which later came to be known as the Indian Institute of Science at Bangalore, IISc, and on which more later in chapter 4) in 1900, for example, there was considerable opposition to locating the institute outside Bombay. In response, Jamsetji promised to establish it in Bombay provided the city's municipal commission was willing to provide Rs. 100,000 to supplement his additional endowment of Rs. 50,000 each year for the next ten years. The municipal grant, however, would have meant that the institute was secular and open to students of all religions and castes. It was rejected by the Parsi elite in Bombay, since they wanted to draw exclusive benefits from Tata's liberality without having to share it with other communities.[12]

Like Tata and Birla, Walchand Hirachand (1882–1953) believed that philanthropy must respond to the needs of the country. Although not the most charitable of men, even less so than his religious-minded father, elder sister, wife, and cousins, he believed that the country did not need any 'more new places of worship, hermitages, bathing-places, pilgrim shelters, rooms for sacrifice and dharamshalas'. Setting out his modern vision, India's wealth should be invested—according to Walchand—in building 'places of learning, factories, mills, experimental laboratories, tool rooms, and halls of science'.[13] With the nation firmly established as the objective and site of development, India's elites set about imagining new national-modern communities. By the turn of the twentieth century, then, geographical communities: in villages, towns,

---

[10] Jamsetji Tata's will dated 16 December 1896; cited from Lala, *Love of India*, 219–23.
[11] Cited from Lala, *Love of India*, 113.
[12] Jamsetji Tata's scheme for a Research Institute in India. File no. L/PJ/6/554, 2150, India Office Records, British Library, London (henceforth IOR).
[13] Cited from Piramal, *Business Legends*, 164–5.
Walchand was born in a prosperous Gujarati Jain family in rural Sholapur. Having lost his mother shortly after his birth, the family migrated to Bombay where his father had established a moneylending practice. Having initially enrolled in St. Xavier's College, he soon dropped out to join the family's business and later a mill. At twenty-one, Walchand became a building contractor. He entered the shipping industry in 1919 before going on to build India's first shipyard, aircraft factory, and car plant. By 1947, Walchand's Doshi group of businesses were in the top ten business houses of the country. Following a stroke in 1949, he retired from all businesses a year later.
For a detailed discussion on Walchand, see Piramal, *Business Legends*, 155–294.

and cities of poor, 'backward classes' became the new objects of Indian elites' philanthropy.[14] In the name of their development, such poor communities were expected to become self-reliant and responsible—actively contributing towards it through paid and unpaid labour, by raising money within their communities, offering donations of land, or even donating material. Willing and ready, communities of poor were expected to—in the imagining of India's economic elites—focus less on their rights and more on what they could, somehow, provide from their own meagre resources. This tendency has only become more extensive and acute as neoliberal globalization became the dominant development framework at the start of the twenty-first century.

At all times, though, these developmental imaginaries of community were, as I go on to show in this chapter, closely imbricated within the national question. I further argue that notwithstanding claims to the contrary that the move away from kinship-centric charity was part of the secularization of Indian philanthropy in the name of its modernization,[15] Indian elites' reimagining of 'new' modern communities involved the maintenance of close ties with their own kinship-based communities. And that contemporary formulations of modern community remained, at best, circumscribed by the interplay of social vectors of gender, religion, tradition, and most importantly, caste.

Nation, through Community

Addressing his fellow *baniāns* at the Aggarwal Mahasabha in 1926, Bajaj invited leaders of his community to dedicate their wealth to the pursuit of development. Couched both in anti-colonial sentiment of exploitation and draining of indigenous wealth, and nationalist tropes of service and local development, Bajaj called for a revitalization of elites' philanthropy targeted at their geographical communities. 'Our complaint against the British,' he spoke, 'is that they take away wealth from our country…A similar charge can be laid against us.' Although speaking at a caste-based association, Bajaj exhorted

---

[14] A community is typically conceived in one of the three ways—first, on the basis of *interaction* where members share interests (artisans, policy analysts, etc.). Second, *geographical* communities where members belong or reside in the same location or administrative unit (a village, neighbourhood, etc.); thirdly, on the basis of *identity* where members belong to a relatively cohesive social system (a tribe or a clan, for example). See Lee and Newby, *Sociology*, 43.

In elites' imaginings, conceptions of community slipped from one category into other over time but also co-existed alongside.

[15] Palsetia, 'Merchant Charity', 209–12 discusses the adoption of imperial 'cultural idioms' by Indian elites as a crucial part of their strategy to build collaborative governing regimes with the British.

them to rethink their social responsibilities to 'look to the interests of the province, region or society in the midst of which we earn our living and, whenever necessary, we should serve it with all our heart'. Not dissimilarly from Jamsetji Tata's chastising of his fellow Parsis and inviting them to think of the 'national', Bajaj also challenged the Marwaris trading in foreign cloth. 'They cannot resist,' he said, 'the temptation of making money' even when they knew that their actions drained India of its wealth. Their greed, he noted, left hundreds of thousands starving, who might otherwise have benefited from hand-spinning and weaving. Inviting them to be more responsible and bold in their national service, Bajaj outlined the challenge confronting his fellow *banians*: 'If we do our business in accordance with an accepted code of ethics, we will win not only the sympathy, but the respect of the society and the country. The more we are with the people, the less afraid we will be of the officials.'[16]

His exhortation to serve the interests of the proximal 'province, region, or society' manifests itself in his extensive support towards various community-development schemes launched between the 1920s and 1940s. Popularly known as the 'constructive programme', it involved promoting khadi, village industries, a national language (Hindi), basic education, removal of untouchability, etc. In this, Bajaj was drawn to and inspired by, the historian Nanda notes in his biography, 'Gandhi's austerity, self-discipline and voluntary poverty'. In Gandhi, Bajaj had found 'a guide whose actions corresponded with his words'.[17] Moved, Bajaj dedicated himself to the Gandhian vision of *swaraj* in a letter to his wife Jankidevi in 1921. Gandhi, Bajaj recalled, had entrusted him with 'tak[ing] care of the legacy when I [Gandhi] am gone'. 'The more we live with simplicity and in spiritually elevating company the better the progress of *sadhana*,' Bajaj urged his wife. 'Until we get swaraj,' he promised 'we must not think of other things'.[18] Particularly impressed by Gandhi's Sabarmati Ashram, in the construction of which Bajaj contributed Rs. 31,000, Bajaj was taken by its rules and vows: truth, non-violence, celibacy, and manual labour, which guided conduct and not rituals. It became, for Bajaj, an exemplar of the kinds of communities India needed to build on its route to development, with a particular emphasis on khadi, trading in which—he believed—was in the highest interest of the country. He asked people to 'wear

---

[16] Nanda, *In Gandhi's Footsteps*, 145–7.   [17] Nanda, *In Gandhi's Footsteps*, 34.
[18] Letter from Bajaj to Jankidevi dated 22 August 1921; cited from Nanda, *In Gandhi's Footsteps*, 94.

hand-spun and hand-woven cloth made in our villages, in our province, in our country' as an act of patriotism.[19]

Bajaj became increasingly involved actively both as a donor and a leader of various Gandhian community development associations, including the Charkha Sangh, Shri Gandhi Ashram, Meerut, Shri Gandhi Seva Sangh, the Gau Seva Sangh, Satyagraha Ashram, and so on. His philanthropy was complemented by his increasing involvement with the Congress and its auxiliary organizations. Following the special session of the Congress in 1920, Bajaj renounced the Rai Bahadur title bestowed by the British. He soon became an active member of the Congress and served as its Treasurer for nearly two decades. Elected before the Nagpur session of the Congress in 1921 as Gandhi's recommended candidate, Bajaj assumed charge of the former's call to raise one crore (or 10 million) rupees for the All India Tilak Memorial Swarajya Fund by 30 June. Even though only two-fifths of this amount had been collected by 14 June, Bajaj refused to give up. Finally, a total of Rs. 98 lakhs had been raised by the deadline. Gandhi refused to accept this, so Bajaj and fellow treasurer and businessman from Bombay, Umar Sobhani, contributed Rs. 1 lakh each. Bajaj did not stop there. He continued to raise still further donations for the Tilak Memorial Fund. In 1922, he donated a further Rs. 1 lakh to support subsistence allowance to be paid to the lawyers who had given up their practice in protests against the colonial government.[20] Thus, Bajaj became a significant sponsor of various contemporary nationalist organizations.

Most significant among Bajaj's philanthropy from this period were the gifts he made to promote khadi. Premised in the nationalist-developmental logic, the local production and consumption of khadi and the use of the charkha, coupled with the boycott of all trade in foreign cloth, became a crucial site of the national-modern starting from the 1920s onwards. 'Khadi and spinning were aimed at removing rural poverty', while Swadeshi according to the business historian Gita Piramal was 'aimed at removing the British'.[21] Ideas of social reform, economic revitalization, and extension of modern infrastructure in India's villages and towns, soon came to be organized around khadi. Bajaj was first entrusted with the task of leading the boycott of foreign cloth and promoting khadi in 1922 by Gandhi. In a letter to Bajaj, Gandhi wrote: 'unless the merchants dealing in foreign yarn and cloth give up their trade,

---

[19] Nanda, *In Gandhi's Footsteps*, 147.

[20] Nanda, *In Gandhi's Footsteps*, 61–5, 84. Lalbhai also contributed Rs. 10,001 to the Fund and was selected by Gandhi to serve as one of the three trustees; see Piramal, *Business Legends*, 325.

[21] Piramal, *Business Legends*, 357.

and the people get rid of their infatuation for foreign cloth, the greatest disease of the country, viz., starvation can never be cured.[22] It was soon followed by a Congress resolution calling for the 'universal adoption of the spinning wheel and the consequent use of hand-spun and hand-woven khaddar', in order to 'give to millions of Indian homes a steady cottage industry' to utilize spare manual labour and supplement the meagre incomes of 'millions of half-starved poor people'. Congress's efforts at promoting khadi to fight starvation, generate employment, revive India's economic output, and reduce its reliance on foreign cloth led to the establishment of its Khadi Department.

Led by Bajaj, the Department provided loans, technical instruction, and education to individuals and communities across the country to adopt khadi. It had an outlay of Rs. 17 lakhs, which Bajaj had both helped raise and contributed towards. In December 1923 the All India Khaddar Board was founded with plans for establishing similar provincial boards across the country. All Congress workers and volunteers were to be trained in spinning and carding, with the national Board under Bajaj's leadership ultimately responsible for the disbursal of funds.[23] Bajaj's efforts at promoting khadi as part of the Khaddar Board, however, were not particularly successful as it was deemed to be politically motivated. It was soon decided that the promotion of khadi should be separated from the Congress's wider political activities. In 1925, an All India Spinners' Association was launched, again with Bajaj as its treasurer, to continue and expand khadi-related work across the country. In 1927, following his recovery from illness, Bajaj was appointed as the officiating chairman of the executive council of the Association. As part of which, Bajaj toured the length of the country in 1928 promoting the production of khadi. Within a year, the production of khadi had gone up from 24 lakhs to 32 lakhs, and its sales had increased from Rs. 33 lakhs to nearly Rs. 50 lakhs. Soon, there were 260 khadi centres, of which 110 were production centres while the rest were sales outlets.[24]

That khadi was not simply a local livelihood but integral to national-modern development can be gauged from how it was framed and presented to the masses. The case for khadi, Nanda wrote: 'was generally put in economic and political terms as a supplementary occupation in India's villages.'[25] Khadi and village communities thus became sites of the Gandhian

---

[22] Kalelkar, *Gandhian Capitalist*, 50–1; cited from Nanda, *In Gandhi's Footsteps*, 84–5.

[23] Zaidi and Zaidi, *Indian National Congress*, vol. VIII, 497–8; cited from Nanda, *In Gandhi's Footsteps*, 85, 107–8.

[24] Nanda, *In Gandhi's Footsteps*, 120, 155–6.   [25] Nanda, *In Gandhi's Footsteps*, 110.

denunciation of colonialism (via its draining of Indian wealth and exploitation of its resources), India's nationalism (revival of local industry and economy), and developmentalism (in its direct attack on behalf of India's hungry, naked masses and potential to generate surplus). Its imaginings were, however, also modern in Bajaj's ambition to loosen the grip of the pre-modern, kinship-based communities and re-organize them into modern, economically productive (beyond mere subsistence) village communities. These entangled imaginaries of national-modern khadi-producing and consuming villages manifest themselves, more comprehensively, in the work of the All India Village Industries Association, on which more next.

*

Following Gandhi's promise to return to the Sabarmati Ashram only after India had attained Swaraj, he was forced to spend his time when visiting Ahmedabad at the Harijan Sevak Sangh. Without a home now, Bajaj reiterated his earlier promise to Gandhi to raise the land, buildings, and funds for a Gandhi Ashram at Wardha, which had benefited both from Vinoba Bhave's 'constructive work' and Bajaj's organizational acumen. It led to the founding of the All India Village Industries Association in 1934. The Association was dedicated to 'village reorganization and reconstruction, including the revival, encouragement and improvement of village industries and the moral and physical advancement of the villages of India'. Constituted under Bajaj's leadership, the Association received the generous donation of the former's garden-house named Maganwadi and twenty-acre orchard in Wardha. With a view to 'improv[ing] the villages', Gandhi and his colleague, Mirabehn identified Segaon, five miles east of Wardha and which was later named Sevagram. Not only was Bajaj the village's landlord, he also possessed an orchard and farm in the village, which would have facilitated its selection as an exemplar of the 'constructive' development programme.

'I have come to your village to serve you,' Gandhi said outlining his agenda for development work in the region. It included: fighting untouchability, reviving village handicrafts, improving public hygiene and sanitation. As Gandhi experimented with becoming a villager, he was joined, among others, by his wife Kasturba, Abdul Ghaffar Khan, and later Rajkumari Amrit Kaur. Despite their intent, though, they achieved little. Many were soon stricken with illness: cholera, malaria, and dysentery were common during the monsoons. They decided, therefore, to build a dispensary. Shortly after, a small dairy was organized, and then Nai Talimi Sangh (New Education Organization) also moved its headquarters to Sevagram. Untouchability, however, persisted despite all efforts to the contrary, including opening access to a private well that belonged to Bajaj, for Dalits.[26]

With extensive support from Bajaj, Sevagram soon became emblematic of contemporary community development. Sevagram, according to Gandhi, was different from Soviet Russia's centralized planning. It was a response to India's unique development challenges, which Gandhi laid out as follows: 'Have we organized any single village according to our programme? Have we introduced food reform there? Are their roads and their lanes clean and perfect? Have we revived any industries? Have we tackled the problem of drink and vice?'[27] Couched in the familiar Gandhian tropes of revivalism, moral reform, and autonomous economic activities, this mode of community development shared a complicated relationship with modernity: it was modernizing in its renunciation of the pre-modern (caste, for example) and desire to impose order (perfect lanes) but not necessarily enthralled by it. That such community development was framed—expectedly so—as part of the national question can be gauged from the colonial government's suspicion towards Sevagram and the Village Association—which was seen as part of the Congress's latest strategy to widen its base in the Indian countryside. Fuelled by the growing attention, and with a view to place village-based community-development at the centre of India's nationalism, Gandhi convened the annual session of the Congress in 1936 at Faizpur (also in Maharashtra). It led the colonial administration to conclude that Gandhi's hold on 'popular imagination, and particularly on that of peasants,' had become 'as great as ever'.[28]

*

As with khadi promotion and village community development, Bajaj was also committed to Gandhi's 'cow protection' programme. In 1941, he helped launch the Gau Seva Sangh (Organization for the Service of the Cow), met and corresponded with potential donors and workers of the Sangh, and even served as its elected president. Later, he helped organize the All India Cow Conference at Wardha. As with the Village Association, it drew on particular formations of modernity to promote the cow protection programme by synthesizing these with contemporary caste-Hindu beliefs around the sanctity of the cow. The work of the Sangh, which Bajaj crafted with other Gandhian leaders and Gandhi himself, sought to combine scientific principles and

---

[26] Nanda, *In Gandhi's Footsteps*, 210–23.
[27] From *Harijan*, 5 September 1939; Nanda, *In Gandhi's Footsteps*, 223.
[28] Nanda, *In Gandhi's Footsteps*, 213–14.

practical economics for the reconstruction of the Indian rural economy. Challenging the exploitation of cattle through under-nourishment and over-work, it hoped to improve their productivity, ensure veterinary services, scientific breeding, as well as fight off adulteration. Promoting community-production, it encouraged cattle farmers to look after them collectively and then divide the income amongst themselves instead of looking after them as a household, as was common practice.[29]

Alongside which, Bajaj was also actively involved in encouraging, exhorting, even chiding others to contribute to the constructive programme. In 1941 for example, Bajaj chided Ramkrishna Dalmia, the leader of the Dalmia group for his ad hoc approach to philanthropy. Assuming an avuncular tone, Bajaj wrote: 'Your enthusiasm is often momentary. It is not right that your interest is not stable.' 'You must start cow protection and service work at once,' Bajaj added, 'if you devote your energy and tact and become completely successful in this work, your service will also become permanent. With service, your reputation will also become permanent.'[30]

Inspired by Gandhi, community became an important site of development for Bajaj. His philanthropy supported synthesizing elements of modernization (mostly infrastructural and institutional) with those of local (charkha and khadi, for example). It was, as should be clear by now, anti-colonial both in how it was presented to the local masses but also how it was perceived by the colonial administration. Such was the extensive scope of Bajaj's involvement that following his demise in 1942, Gandhi released an open invitation for any comrades, leaders, and other allies to take over the leadership of various causes and organizations that he and Bajaj had been involved with. These included: cow protection, Gandhi seva, *Nai taleem*, khadi, village industry, nationalist government, women's issues, promotion of national language (Hindi and Urdu), 'harijan' service, satyagraha and village service. Seeking to extricate development from politics, Gandhi concluded his invitation letter: 'Neither Bajaj nor I were ever interested in politics. He joined it because I was already involved with it. My real political interest was always in doing some constructive work. That was also his political interest.'[31]

*

---

[29]   Nanda, *In Gandhi's Footsteps*, 354–6.

[30]   Bajaj's letter to Dalmia dated 31 October 1941; from Correspondence: Dalmia, Ramkrishna, JB (1st inst.).

[31]   Invitation signed by M. K. Gandhi dated 14 February 1942; Correspondence: Gandhi, M.K., JB (1st Inst.).

Ideas of community reform such as those championed by Bajaj had a prior but less secular history, which was nonetheless intimately connection to the national question. Birlas' early philanthropy, for example, was concentrated around Pilani and Calcutta, and largely restricted to their own Marwari and/or Hindu community.

In 1904, for example, the Birlas became involved with the Vishudanand Saraswati Vidyalaya, which served as the main centre of education for the Marwari community. The Birlas also helped Bajaj raise funds in 1912 for a Marwari school in Bombay. Later in 1918, they founded the first ever high school in their hometown of Pilani. Such was the scale of their early philanthropy that by 1918, Kudaisya estimates, they had gifted over Rs. 25 lakhs in hard cash. From their early interest in education, the Birlas gradually moved on to community reform. In 1913, Ghanshyam Das Birla founded the Marwari Sahayak Samiti (literally the Marwari Welfare Organization) with his brother Jugal Kishore. In addition to the construction of a medical hospital, the Samiti outlined a social reform agenda for the Marwaris, which included: eradication of child marriage, purdah, and saving on extravagant expenditure on death ceremonies.[32] It imagined community reform as a mode of social transformation in the country. Community, therefore, emerged as an important site of social and economic change in the country in the first quarter of the twentieth century.

Part of Hindu nationalism, Birla's community development programme combined a caste-reform agenda with widening education access, and the constitution of a new public sphere which valued physical fitness, Hindi language, and literature, as well as cow protection. Guided by the revivalist impulse to restore Hinduism to its earlier—and subsequently lost—glory, it was guided by Hindu scriptures and its ancient *vedic* texts. Reflecting which, the Marwari Sahayak Samiti launched a Hindu Club. Also called the Kaligodam Vyayaym Shala (or Gymnasium), it soon became a popular public meeting-place for young Marwari men to promote physical fitness. They launched a Sahitya Sambandhini Sabha (or a Literary Association) to promote the publication of quality literature in Hindi language. They also supported the establishment of a library of Hindi books; and became patrons of a Maheshwari Vidyalaya, which also hosted leading figures of Hindi literature and journalism. The Birlas also contributed generously to cow protection programmes. Starting from the 1880s onwards, they are believed to have contributed over Rs. 100,000 in Calcutta alone for *gaushalas* and bird shelters. That

---

[32] Kudaisya, *G. D. Birla*, 33–42.

their early philanthropy was couched within a Hindu nationalism was manifest—literally so—in their support for publication of the *Tikawali Gita*. Its
cover was made out of a picture of *Bharat Mata* (Mother India) with a sword
in one hand and a *Gita*—a popular Hindu scripture—in the other.
Highlighting its willingness to battle and its choice of a guiding philosophy
made clear, the Samiti marked Birla's entry into the public realm.[33] They also
donated generously towards the restoration of Hindu temples, cremation
sites, and to ayurvedic hospitals.

Where Birlas' and Bajaj's community imaginaries and their role in India's
development, ultimately, converged was in relation to caste. Not differently
from Bajaj's assimilationist impulse, Birla's early philanthropic response—
under the influence of Lajpat Rai, also a Hindu nationalist like Malaviya—to
the caste question was twofold: development of Dalits and their assimilation
within the larger Hindu society. In a letter to Birla, Rai raised the 'problem of
Hindu unity' and the express need to '*save* our depressed classes'. Moved by
which, the Birlas started a monthly stipend of Rs. 3,000 for Rai's Servants of
the People Society and later provided him with a car and a driver for his personal use. By the mid 1920s, the Birlas had become Rai's primary benefactor,
sponsoring his trips abroad. Impressed with Birla's commitment to the cause
of Hindu nationalism, Rai wanted to promote Birla into an all-India Hindu
leader who was loved by its masses, to lead the Hindus of northern India.[34]
Later as a sign of his respect towards Rai, Birla committed himself to the task
of building a memorial to commemorate the former, following his death in
1928. Acting as the treasurer of the Lajpat Rai Memorial Fund, Birla oversaw
the collection of Rs. 2 lakhs for the fund.[35]

By the late 1920s, though, Birla was gravitating towards Gandhian developmentalism of rural communities. Along with Bajaj, he was rapidly emerging
as one of Gandhi's influential sponsors, donating actively and frequently—if
only in small amounts—to various 'constructive programmes' at Wardha.[36] In
1929, for example, Birla promised Rs. 1 lakh to various Gandhian associations. Instead of giving it away lump-sum, he promised to send monthly
instalments. This money, Bajaj suggested, could be used variously as follows:
Rs. 15,000 for Charkha Sangh and for promoting khadi in Rajputana each, Rs.
20,000 for Gandhi Seva Sangh, and the remainder would have been deposited

---

[33] Kudaisya, *G. D. Birla*, 33–42. Elsewhere, Mukul similarly notes the crucial role of Marwari charity in fostering public consciousness around Hindi-Hindu-Hindustan, as part of the making of Hindu
India; see *Gita Press*, 4–24.

[34] Cited from Kudaisya, *G. D. Birla*, 73–9.   [35] Kudaisya, *G. D. Birla*, 104.

[36] In 1928, for example, Birla made a donation of Rs. 250/- to the Wardha Education Society; from
Birla's letter to Bajaj dated 12 December 1928; from Correspondence: Birla, G. D., JB (1st Inst.).

with the latter and used as per Gandhi's wishes.[37] Even as Birla himself moved towards seemingly secular philanthropy, his family, though, continued to sponsor contemporary proponents of Hindu nationalism. Jugal Kishore, for example, provided a monthly allowance of Rs. 3,000 to Malaviya in 1932; and supported both the Banaras Hindu University and the Hindu Mahasabha. The latter financed the training of young Hindu men as part of the Burdwan branch of the Bengal Provincial Hindu Mahasbha, and was known to house the Calcutta headquarters of the Rashtriya Swayam Sevak Sangh (the Nationalist Self-Service Organization, or the RSS, which is the leading right-wing Hindutva group and the intellectual parent of India's majoritarian Bharatiya Janata Party).[38]

Birla's belated embrace of khadi and charkha were also prompted by his pragmatic commercial concerns and contemporary economic nationalism. In 1930, for example, as the Indian industry was reeling under the dual force of the economic depression and the British government's decision to impose differential duties on British and non-British cotton goods, the Indian elites were actively considering boycotting British cloth.[39] Their economic woes found a ready ally in the Indian nationalists' calls for Swadeshi. Birla believed that such a boycott offered significant benefits to the Indian mill-owners.[40] Even as he came to be actively involved, still others were more reluctant and needed further convincing. Seeking to placate Ambalal Sarabhai's (1890–1967) concerns, for example, over the boycott and his mill production, Birla wrote that the Marwari importers and distributors in Calcutta could easily purchase all the cloth produced by Sarabhai and place orders that would have kept his mills running for the next twelve months.[41] 'If they once decide to wash their

---

[37] Letter from Bajaj to Gandhi dated 8 January 1929; from Correspondence: Gandhi, M. K., JB (1st Inst.).

[38] Kudaisya, *G. D. Birla*, 105; Chatterji, *Bengal Divided*, 236.

[39] Markovits, *Indian Business and Nationalist Politics*, 70–7.   [40] Kudaisya, *G. D. Birla*, 126.

[41] The Sarabhais were a wealthy family of traders, industrialists, and philanthropists, who worked as moneylenders and traded in opium, silk, and tea between India, China, and Britain. As the largest lenders to the first mechanized cloth printing factory in Ahmedabad, called Calico, they came to own the factory when it was liquidated in 1880. The wealth from the opium trade was then used to add cotton spinning and weaving to the Calico Mills, which became the largest mill in the city.

At the age of eighteen, Ambalal took over the family business before diversifying into chemicals, oil and sugar mills, and mechanical components. They were first to recognize representative trade unions and launched a crèche and a hospital for their employees. Married to Rewa, later named Saraladevi, at the age of twenty, he was an advocate of women's personal liberties. A believer in professional management, Ambalal was widely read, and cultivated a wide range of intellectual and cultural interests. The family gradually moved from their European interests and lifestyle to adopting khadi and participating in the nationalist movement, under Gandhi's influence from 1930s. They had eight children including Vikram.

Vikram (1919–1971) expanded the family business into pharmaceuticals and market research before leaving the business to pursue his scientific interests and public duties. The business gradually

hands clean of foreign-piece goods business and devote themselves to the Swadeshi cloth business,' Birla added 'they can perform miracles.'[42] Even as Sarabhai and Birla worried over a fair purchase price for such a scheme, the former continued his efforts at convincing other mill-owners in Bombay and Ahmedabad to follow Gandhi's call. 'I have failed miserably,' Sarabhai replied to Birla. Not for want of trying but because of lack of detail in organizing such a boycott scheme, he cited, both from the Congress and the Charkha Sangh. Inviting Birla to come to Bombay to put together a scheme that could satisfy the interests of the consumers, the khadi movement, and the country (possibly even the mill-owners, although Sarabhai did not say so explicitly).[43] Meanwhile, Kasturbhai Lalbhai also launched his own efforts at forming such a scheme, which could have been acceptable to the Congress. Working with Thakurdas, they hoped to persuade Nehru to travel to Ahmedabad to discuss matters with the mill-owners.[44]

Their efforts led to the founding of Swadeshi Sabha in 1930 under the aegis of the Federation of Indian Chambers of Commerce and Industry. In addition to promoting the production of goods made in the country, the Sabha's objectives included their marketing, and protecting consumers' interests by checking prices and ensuring quality. However, mill-owners' own interest came first. Those that had already purchased cotton or had been producing only coarse-quality cotton then needed to 'make earnest and sincere efforts to substitute other sorts' provided their margin of profit per loom remained the same. Participating mills needed to pay four *annas* per loom as entrance fee. Any coarse cloth manufactured by them could not have been passed off as khadi as the use of any foreign-made yarn, thread, or silk were prohibited. The Sabha would, in turn, purchase maximum 40 per cent of their total production at current rates subject to a maximum price for onward selling.[45] This was subject to revision provided the Sabha was able to sell off its stock.[46] In order to facilitate the onward export of any British cloth that the Sabha would have purchased, Lalbhai helped organize the Foreign Piecegoods Export Co. Ltd. To help the Sabha organize itself, Lalbhai endowed it with an office, a secretary,

---

diminished as family members pursued their individual interests, before being revived again by Kartikeya, Vikram's son, with interests in chemicals, electronics, and pharmaceuticals.

[42] Letter from Birla to Ambalal Sarabhai dated 30 April 1930, file 100, PT.

[43] Letter from Sarabhai to Birla dated 4 June 1930, file 100, PT.

[44] Letter from Lalbhai to Thakurdas dated 20 June 1930, file 100, PT.

[45] The maximum price was calculated on the following basis: 8 per cent profit after deducting any depreciation, commissions, or interests; and ensuring that average profits of the last three years were maintained.

[46] Details of the Swadeshi Sabha's constitution as framed by the appointed Sub-Committee of FICCI, file 100, PT.

and a telegraphic address. He even managed to convince the Parsi industrialists and executives such as Ness Wadia, Homi Mody, and S. D. Saklatvala, who tended to maintain their distance from the nationalist movement. Lalbhai and Birla's scheme that hoped to protect the interests of traders and mill-owners proved to be wholly unfeasible and strained the former's relationship with Gandhi.[47]

Faced with discriminatory economic policies of the colonial government, therefore, India's economic elite turned their attention to crafting alternate communities—notwithstanding their limited success—of economic production and consumption. Foremost among which was Swadeshi: indigenous production and consumption, in order to fight off economic stagnation owing to colonialism, reduce dependence, counter poverty and hunger by generating income surplus, and therefore develop India. Although the elites were clear in their denunciation of colonialism and its ensuing exploitation, their embrace of Swadeshi nationalism was far from unequivocal. It was contingent, first and foremost, on protecting their own commercial interests. Less ideological and more pragmatic, therefore, the Indian elites sponsored and led voluntary associations such as the Swadeshi Sabha to collectively certify, sell, and distribute their produce.

There are two points worth noting here. Not simply against modernity or industry, national-modern development sought to constitute new communities of producers and consumers and transform their relationships with each other. They were, as might be evident by now, clearly imbricated in the national question as they sought to fight off dependence and promote self-reliance in the name of development. Secondly, unlike typical community development-type initiatives which champion the *local*, national-modern development worked at a larger scale in promoting the indigenous economy. A crucial attribute of which, in elites' imaginings, were self-reliant, responsible communities.

Self-reliant, Responsible Communities

Central to Indian economic elites' national-modern imaginaries of community in the first four decades of the twentieth century was self-reliance, with a particular emphasis on economic self-reliance. During colonialism, self-reliant communities were important in fighting off India's economic

---

[47] Piramal, *Business Legends*, 360–4.

dependence as part of nationalism's positive narrative of development. This was not only true of Bajaj and the Birlas, who have been widely recognized for their links with the promotion of khadi and the boycott of foreign goods through associations such as the Charkha Sangh, the Khaddar Board, All India Village Industries Association, and the Swadeshi Sabha, to which they actively gifted their time, money, and expertise; but also economic elites with more tentative involvement with Indian nationalism such as Purshottamdas Thakurdas. Self-reliance was soon combined with responsibility, both of which became important attributes of national-modern imaginaries of community, especially in the post-colonial period. However, the post-colonial formulations of community did not emerge anew but built on earlier, nationalist logics of self-reliance, as I go on to argue later in this section.

The Birla Education Trust, for example, launched a scheme for the construction and maintenance of village schools in 1929. The Trust ran numerous village-level schools. Starting from thirteen schools with 262 students, it rose to 395 schools by 1945 with over fifteen thousand children enrolled in them. Launched in villages around Pilani, the schools drew on voluntary contributions: from the villagers, and students and teachers from the Pilani College. Village committees collected funds for the construction of schools, organizing special days, prize distribution ceremonies, and inspections from the Rural Education Department. With a view to promoting self-help, the Department—like the Birla Education Trust itself—also encouraged village committees to collect money and subscribe for battery operated radio sets. Following Gandhi's assassination in January 1948, the Department (now part of the independent Indian state) used the radio sets to broadcast Gandhi's speeches and *bhajans*, along with serialized narrations of Hindu mythologies such as *Ramayana* and *Gita*. In some villages, the communities subscribed to newspapers and magazines, as the schools soon became important centres of social life. Under the Trust's control, the teachers began to preach *kathas* to the villagers (more on development as elites' pedagogic reflex in chapter 5). By 1952, though, the Trust had begun to prioritize its developmental role. Committing itself more extensively to the teaching and training of scientists and engineers, it handed over the control of the village schools to the government. By 1950, the Trust was supporting only 163 schools with over 8,300 students; and soon after reduced to only eight compulsory schools, six middle, three lower, and thirty-seven primary schools with over three thousand students enrolled in them.[48]

---

[48] Hennessy, *India Democracy and Education*, 146–51.

That the Trust placed self-reliance and responsibility as the cornerstones of their imaginaries of community is evident from its leader's response towards the request of an impoverished, untouchable woman named Shyami Mai of village Pipli. Having heard of the Trust's school construction and village development work, Mai requested them to build a well and a school for other people of her caste. Struggling as they did not have a well of their own as untouchables, she wanted the school to be constructed next to the well so that her caste-community no longer struggled with ostracization in the village. Mai had already collected several hundred rupees in the name of community contribution. Pande, the Trust's leader listened sympathetically but told Mai her efforts were not enough—she needed to raise over Rs. 2,000 more. Undeterred Mai travelled from town to town, she begged and starved herself before finally collecting what would have been a pittance for the Trust to provide. The Trust finally agreed, Mai pleaded for the well to be dug within the school grounds, with plants and flowers to be grown around it.[49]

*

Self-reliance was also the organizing principle of Thakurdas's educational philanthropy. His financial support for the construction of school buildings under his P. T. Cheap School Scheme—launched for the purpose of expanding primary education in the rural areas of modern-day Gujarat and on which more in the next chapter—came with certain conditions, for example. The land would have to be donated by the villagers themselves. School buildings, he directed, could only have been constructed in villages whose people were willing to contribute at least a third of the total construction costs; with priority given to those offering to contribute more than this minimum. All construction was to be overseen by a local committee, which was to include an educational inspector, a representative of the District Local Board, and two of Thakurdas's own nominees, and local residents. Once construction was completed, the buildings were to be handed over to the local Boards which would be responsible for their repairs. Finally, all buildings were to be named as per Thakurdas's wishes.[50] To demonstrate their commitment to their children's education and possibly with a view to building ownership, the villagers were permitted to contribute their third of the total cost in different ways, lending the scheme much needed flexibility. Despite their poverty, the *raniparaj* (literally people of the wild) people of the Ambachh village in Surat district, for

---

[49] Hennessy, *India Democracy and Education*, 130–2.
[50] Resolution passed at the District Local Board's meeting held on 1 March 1937, file 180 (Pt. I), PT.

example, offered to give free labour and cartage of materials. They had even managed to persuade a woman named Machi to give up her land for the construction of the school.[51] Similarly, in Kiher village whose people lived in destitution, the local community were unable to contribute any money whatsoever. They were willing, though, to gift their labour and cartage free of charge so that the school could be constructed. A local *sheth*, Nemchand Jiwanji, was entrusted with the task of constructing the school on a site donated by a Parsi from the neighbouring village.[52]

In this way, philanthropy became a development catalyst that wielded its power by roping in various development actors into its own initiative.[53] When Thakurdas extended the scheme to the Panchmahals, for example, it failed to take off as many of the tribal villagers, mainly Bhils, did not have any money to contribute. With a view to launching the programme in the district, in 1938 the District Local Board approached Thakurdas again. Citing the availability of Rs. 5,000 from the Government's Educational Department, they suggested that Thakurdas's condition of raising a third of the construction costs be met through the governmental funds in the tribal villages, which he agreed to.[54]

The focus on self-reliance and responsibility also led to the active involvement of other local elites. In 1938, for example, the N. M. Wadia Trust from Bombay donated Rs. 1,000 as part of the villagers' contribution for the construction of a school building under P. T. Cheap School Scheme in Bhagwa village in Surat district.[55] In their reply to Thakurdas's thankful letter, R. P. Masani of the Wadia Trust wrote that the Cheap School Scheme was admirable as it 'ensures the stability of the schools that are opened, teaches the people in the neighbourhood how to help themselves.'[56] Similarly, in Godsamba and Nogama villages whose peoples were very poor and could only offer their labour or cartage, if at all, other local elites came forward to bear responsibility for the construction of the school buildings.[57]

Despite their rhetoric and manifest support for developing 'community', its constitution and composition was often ambiguous. That is, it was rarely

---

[51] Letter from G. M. Desai to Thakurdas dated 4 December 1937, file 207 (Pt. I), PT.

[52] Letter from G. M. Desai to Thakurdas dated 1 December 1937, file 207 (Pt. I), PT.

[53] Elsewhere, I have argued how philanthropy has the unique capability to engineer particular institutional connections and disconnections in the development arena; see Kumar and Brooks, 'Bridges, Platforms, Satellites'.

[54] Letter from Marutisinh Thakore, vice president of the District Local Board, Panchmahals to Thakurdas dated 11 October 1938, file 180 (Pt. I), PT.

[55] Letter from Thakurdas to R. P. Masani dated 3 January 1938, file 207 (Pt. I), PT.

[56] Reply from R. P. Masani to Thakurdas dated 4 January 1938, file 207 (Pt. I), PT.

[57] Letter G. M. Desai to Thakurdas dated 18 January 1938, file 207 (Pt. I), PT.

made clear what a community was or who was, or was not, in a community. Not unexpectedly then, Thakurdas's desire to 'help the poor and most backward people to get educational facilities' in the tribal-dominated villages of the Panchmahals soon encountered geographical ambiguities.[58] In 1939, for example, the district committee met to identify the villages in greatest need of school buildings. While one member insisted that buildings should only be constructed in Dohad and Jhalod talukas where the Bhils lived, S. R. Tawde, the educational inspector also appointed chair of this committee, wanted the Kolis from the eastern parts of the district to be included; still others wanted the Naikadas Bhils of Halol taluka, who they argued were as 'primitive' as the other Bhils, to be included in the ambit of the scheme.[59] Later, Tawde wrote to Thakurdas on behalf of the Committee 'to know your idea of the Bhil area'. 'There are areas,' he went on 'where Bhils, Naiks and such other aboriginal tribes actually reside and areas, nearby, which are taken advantage of by these aboriginal tribes.' Which of the two, Tawde wished to know, served Thakurdas's mission of founding schools for 'poor and most backward people'.[60] Although I could not locate Thakurdas's clarification on the matter, such exchanges only point to the ongoing ambivalences around conceptions of different developmental sites, such as a community, that need interrogating.

*

As nationalism was translated into nation-building, post-colonialism, Indian economic elites' developmental imaginaries were no longer burdened with presenting a critique of colonial forms of modernity, as its predecessors were. Gandhi's demise and Nehru's rise to the national leadership also had a significant role to play in the elites' reconfigured imaginaries of community. Even as they continued to rely on the nationalist tropes of self-reliance, demise of kinship-based communities in favour of geographical communities, and responsibility, they now became less ambivalent in their embrace of the modern. National-modern imaginaries of community now gravitated swiftly towards Nehruvian ideals as they came to engage with science and technology, more comprehensively than before—to what we now recognize as modernization.

---

[58] S. R. Tawde's letter to Thakurdas dated 3 June 1939, file 180 (Pt. II), PT.
[59] Manilal H. Mehta's letter to Thakurdas dated 27 May 1939, file 180 (Pt. II), PT.
[60] S. R. Tawde's letter to Thakurdas dated 3 June 1939, file 180 (Pt. II), PT.

Leading the charge towards a less ambivalent embrace of modernization were the Tatas.[61] Although their earlier philanthropy (from 1892 up to 1950) was primarily orientated towards scientific development (on which more in chapters 3 and 4), this was about to change. The push for it, though, had come earlier. In 1932, S. F. Markham, a British politician and member of parliament from the Labour Party, was invited to suggest possible areas of work for the trusts. On the geographic focus of the Trust's work, Markham suggested that given that there was much that needed to be done in India alone, and there was no need for the Trusts to go beyond it. Markham suggested that the Trust should focus its resources on the eastern and the western regions of the country where, given the magnitude of its resources, it had 'great power for good'. Instead of treating the symptoms of poverty, Markham suggested that the Trust identify the root causes of poverty through a scientific investigation using available census records, tables etc. before going on to identifying remedies.[62] In his later correspondence with Navajbai Ratan Tata in 1933, Markham further emphasized that the Trust consolidate its work in India—given that the United States and the United Kingdom already had a

---

[61] Until recently, what are now collectively known as Tata Trusts were organized into two main trusts with numerous allied trusts. The two main trusts include: Sir Ratan Tata Trust (henceforth, SRTT) and Sir Dorabji Tata Trust (henceforth, SDTT). SRTT, the smaller of the two trusts, was established in 1919 and is allied with Navajbai Ratan Tata Trust established in 1974. SDTT, established in 1932 is was allied with nine other trusts. These include: JN Tata Endowment Fund for Higher Education (1892; the year in which the various trusts were founded are indicated in brackets) which sponsors the higher education of Indians abroad; JRD Tata Trust (1944) whose objectives are similar to SDTT but additionally supports higher education of Indians in India; Jamsetji Tata Trust (1974) whose objectives are identical to SDTT; JRD and Thelma J Tata Trust (1991) established specially for oppressed women and children; Tata Education Trust (1990); Tata Social Welfare Trust (1990); RD Tata Trust (1990); Lady Tata Memorial Trust which provides scholarships for leukaemia research and also funds fundamental research in science; and Lady Meherbai Dorabji Tata Memorial Trust (1932) whose objective is to support Indian women to pursue higher studies abroad. Each of these trusts has a separate board of trustees, comprising of members from within the Tata Group of companies, or experts from the related fields of development, higher education, and agriculture, among others.

The Trusts' grant-making is organized through the following: (a) programme grants to non-governmental organizations including small grants; (b) individual grants for education, medical treatment, and travel; and (c) endowment grants to large institutions. Although in their earlier years, the Trusts favoured endowments over recurring grants, this changed in 1990s when programme grants became the dominant mode of making gifts.

In the early 1990s, there was also a significant increase in the wealth of the various Tata Trusts. This prompted the increasing professionalization within the Trusts. As a result of the increasing wealth, the Trusts, separately, started to commission five-year strategic planning documents, starting from 1995, which were to provide thematic directions to the programmes. It is also worth noting that until recently, there was no singular philosophy, or strategic convergence between the functioning of the various Trusts, with each operating as per its own mandate.

Also see Lala's *Heartbeat of Trust* for a sympathetic insider's account of the Tatas' philanthropy.

[62] From the Memorandum dated 22 December 1932 on Muzumdar's interview with S. F. Markham, file no. SDTT BO Meetings, 1932–2005, TCA.

large number of philanthropic organizations—and in partnership with Indians in other parts of the world.[63]

Markham's suggestion to focus on India's poverty in the 1930s took some time to be adopted into the Tata Trusts' official policy. Rustum Choksi (1902–1986), long associated with the Tata industries and philanthropy, indicated the change of plans in a letter to the director-general of Health Services, Government of India in 1951.[64] Trustees of the Sir Dorabji Tata Trust (henceforth SDTT), he wrote, were planning to turn their 'attention to other nation-building activities'. They had been considering, he added, 'the idea of village development and would like to be free to apply a substantial measure of the Trust's resources to a workable scheme that would both establish a model group of villages, through self-help methods aided by Trust funds, and at the same time ensure continuity for constructive work of this kind on a wider scale'.[65] Turning its attention to rural poverty and community development for the first time in over half a century, the Tata Trusts launched a range of subsidiary organizations to focus on specific facets of rural poverty.

The Rural Welfare Board (henceforth RWB or Board), for example, was founded in 1953 to initiate work for 'comprehensive rural welfare and development' in Devapur in Satara, Mithapur in Saurashtra, and Mulshi near Pune city; the latter two being sites of Tatas' chemical and energy companies although this was not necessarily a characteristic feature of the Tatas' philanthropy.[66] These were designed, primarily, as demonstration projects, which could be replicated in other parts of the country. Similarly acknowledging that 'most of the blind in India come from villages', SDTT's annual report from 1959 outlined the need for working in rural villages, which led to the founding of the Tata Agricultural and Rural Training Centre for the Blind (popularly known as TACEB).[67]

---

[63] Letter from S. F. Markham dated 12 July 1933. From Correspondence with Markham on the possible directions of work of SDTT (1933–1935). File no. 178/DTT/DJT/PERS/PROP/LEG/WILLS/BO/OPT/1, TCA.

[64] Choksi served as SDTT's director and managing trustee for nearly forty-five years. He also served as a director of Tata Sons and Tata Industries; chairman of Tata Services and Marg Publication; and director and vice-chairman of Indian Hotels.

[65] Letter from Choksi to K. C. K. E. Raja dated 25 September 1951; from file no. 207/DTT/PHIL/TMH/FP/2, TCA.

[66] In the current scholarship, especially in management studies, there is a case made for businesses to synchronize their philanthropy, strategically, to serve their own commercial interests. With Mark Kramer, Michael Porter has written extensively about the challenges of creating value through philanthropy. See Porter and Kramer, 'Corporate Philanthropy', 56–68; 'Philanthropy's New Agenda', 121–30. While one might be tempted to read the location of RWB's demonstration sites as a move towards such strategic philanthropy, there is overwhelming evidence to the contrary from their wider philanthropic history.

[67] From SDTT's report of the year ending 1959; from file no. 180/DTT/PHIL/FIN/2, TCA.

Development was conceived here, primarily, as modernization. At Devapur, for example, RWB focused on enhancing agricultural productivity through soil conservation, soil moisture retention, tree plantation; extension of irrigation and water supply through conservation and piped supply; launching multi-purpose cooperatives for generating and trading economic surplus; etc. Measures of development included availability of tapped water supply at household level, road connectivity, banking, public transport, electrification, postal services, telephones, schools, and health centres.[68] A subsequent evaluation of RWB's programme at Devapur from 1986 found that households where the primary occupation was agriculture had come to enjoy self-sufficiency in food supply, per capita income had risen significantly, as had the community's resilience to droughts. Development had enhanced their purchasing power, and improvement in their lifestyle was evident from consumption of durable goods, such as, transistors, electric lights, and sewing machines, which made for 'a cheerful development for a rural area in the famine zone'. In comparison to its surrounding villages, Devapur was 'way ahead on the road to progress'; it had become an 'oasis in the famine tract of Maharashtra'.[69]

The Tatas' turn to more familiar forms of development from the 1950s to the 1970s relied on expected formulations of the poor who were described as 'these unfortunate simple folks'. 'Normally they live[d] in dire poverty, clothed in rags, and were doubtful of having even two meals a day. At the best of times life was a grim struggle against the forces of man and nature in a not too friendly environment.'[70] Such grim portrayals were not necessarily restricted to the poor but extended to their environs as well. Jehangir Ratanji Dadabhoy Tata (1904–1993; henceforth shortened to J. R. D. Tata)[71] wrote that

---

[68] From a report titled, 'Devapur Project: Achievements of a Quiet, Persistent Effort by Tatas for the Development of a Drought Prone Area (1952–1984)'. File no. 185/DTT/PHIL/RWB/BO/1963/1, TCA.

[69] Y. S. Pandit, *A Survey of Devapur*, 1986. Tata Rural Welfare Board. File no. 185A/DTT/RWB/1986, TCA.

[70] Report on work undertaken by Tata Relief Committee after earthquake in Koyna in 1967. File no. 184/DTT/PHIL/TRC/KOYNA/1967/4–7, TCA.

[71] Born to Ratanji Dadabhoy Tata, Jamsetji N. Tata's first cousin, and his French wife Sooni Tata (née Suzanne Briere) in Paris in 1904, Jehangir attended school in France, Japan, and England before being drafted into the French military service. Jeh, or J. R. D. as he was popularly called, began work as an unpaid apprentice with the Tatas in 1925. Having led the group as its chairman from 1938–1991, he is credited for the expansion of the Tata group, developing businesses in chemicals, aviation, automobiles, tea, and information technology. He is known for his love of flying, and supported the cause of scientific research, population control, and education in the country. He passed away in Geneva in Switzerland in 1993. J. R. D. Tata was awarded various civilian honours by the governments of India, France, and Germany, including the *Bharat Ratna*, and four honorary doctorates. See Lala's *Blue Mountain* and *Conversations*.

communities such as Auroville, were situated on a 'dry rocky plateau where soil erosion had played havoc with the land. Nothing but rocks, ravines and gullies met the eye; the land was literally torn asunder; the regeneration of the land was the most urgent task on hand.'[72] Their societies were bound by 'tradition' and 'custom' which had led to the destitution of people.[73] Such places and peoples were, according to J. R. D. Tata, in dire need for development which needed to be conducted 'in a systematic, business-like manner.'[74] In this way, the pre-development state was characterized by an underdeveloped subjectivity: where society was bound by 'custom' and 'tradition', where men were hungry and engaged in a 'grim struggle' against nature that was itself 'barren' and 'torn asunder'. The challenge before development and its founding logic, then, was about un-doing this state.[75]

The Tatas' post-independence philanthropy relied on economic and physical transformation of village-based communities to lead—somehow—to social modernization of communities. At Devapur, for example, the Tatas never pursued a distinct programme for dealing with the caste question. Their programme for the 'harijans'[76] was limited to the provision of additional housing subsidies, given the generally poor state of their neighbourhoods and their relative inability to contribute towards their housing construction. Where they did intervene, it was primarily by way of a technological intervention but never a social one. In order to address the stigma associated with their Dalits' work of extracting fibre by drying plant leaves under the sun—it resulted in a horrible stench and polluted water-streams nearby—the Board's response was to introduce mechanization. Arguing that 'only the lowest class of harijans would avail themselves of this work', the Board launched mechanized extraction which it believed would, somehow, 'remove the social stigma attached to this work and to a group of people who earn their living by it'.[77]

In all this, RWB was guided by self-help. 'Self-help', it was noted, was 'the essence of all work sponsored by the Board. It believes in a scientific approach; in striking at the root of poverty rather than treating the symptoms. The

[72] From the Memorandum for appeal, written by D. K. Malegamvala, Director, SDTT dated March 13, 1984 to request SDTT to make a further three-year grant to Auromitra –Friends of Auroville Research Foundation; from file no. 180/DTT/PHIL/DON/11, TCA.

[73] TACEB's founding premise was that 'custom and tradition spel[t] destitution for the rural blind'; from SDTT, Annual Report, 2005–06, file no. 210/SDTT/2005–06, TCA.

[74] From J. R. D. Tata's notes and the memorandum for appeal written by D. K. Malegamvala (director, SDTT) dated 13 March 1984 to request SDTT to make a further three-year grant to Auromitra— Friends of Auroville Research Foundation; from file no. 180/DTT/PHIL/DON/11, TCA.

[75] Escobar, *Encountering Development*, 8.

[76] While the term was made popular by M. K. Gandhi, its use was considered to be an offensive term by Dalit organizations. Its use was prohibited in 1982 by the Indian government.

[77] 'The Rural Welfare Board (1953)'; file no. 185/DTT/PHIL/RWB/BO/1963/1, TCA.

Board is not wedded to any "isms", an approach uninhibited by any dogma is preferred'. The Board was mostly successful in its efforts. An evaluation report of RWB's activities at Devapur from 1984 noted that self-help had gradually become embedded within the community. Citing people's readiness to pay for the consultation with the doctor, and pay even more for the doctor's presence for an additional day at the clinic, the report concluded that the people had come to assume responsibility for their development. More than any enhancement in local productivity, development—the report concluded—meant that the local community was able and willing to 'utilise their new resources both for public welfare and as investment for further development'.[78]

Examples where self-help, self-reliance, and responsibility had become the defining characteristics of modern Indian communities can also be found in the relief and rehabilitation work sponsored by the Tata Relief Committee (henceforth TRC). Founded in 1967, the TRC was actively engaged in relief and rehabilitation work throughout the 1960s and 1970s across India. The following example relates to TRC's work in Ahmednagar district in Maharashtra from 1973, following a drought. It is instructive both from the standpoint of imaginaries of community as the site of development, but also their imaginings of agency. It involved a dispute within the TRC over the role of local community in the plantation of trees in what its personnel referred to as 'our six villages'.

Suratwala, one of the personnel involved in the exchange, expected the villagers to dig the pits for planting trees by way of community contribution. This, his colleague V. S. Kulkarni argued, was 'an improper attitude which will kill a good proposal'. Given that TRC had been providing the villagers with employment opportunities as part of its relief and rehabilitation programmes, it was illogical—Kulkarni added—to expect the villagers to contribute free labour when they were already being paid for other manual work.

In response to which, Suratwala wrote to Leela S. Moolgaokar who led the initiative at TRC that he was not against tree-plantation but he felt that 'if everything is given to them [the poor villagers] free of cost and readily cooked, it would not have any value for them and they would not even care to look after the planted trees (…) They must feel a sense of belongingness otherwise the programme has no lasting effect'. Suratwala added: 'I feel that they do have that much of leisure time to dig pits but they are trying to be lazy. We are therefore trying our best to pursuade them to put in atleast some

---

[78] 'The Rural Welfare Board (1953)'; file no. 185/DTT/PHIL/RWB/BO/1963/1, TCA.

free labour in their own interest (*sic*)'. 'Even if we succeed to a very small extent', he argued, 'it would inculcate in them a spirit of self-reliance, which would be a great achievement instead of paying them (...) it has been a policy of Tata Relief Committee to develop the finer qualities like the spirit of self-reliance amongst the community'. Calling it a difference of opinion, Suratwala pleaded to be kept out of the intervention if any payments were made to the villagers for digging pits.[79]

Development, according to Suratwala, required the poor to fight off their laziness so that communities could become self-reliant. Even in the face of a debilitating drought and destitution, development involved inculcating 'the finer qualities...amongst the community'. Sponsored by economic elites' philanthropy, development institutions such as the RWB, TRC, etc., thus became important agents of modernization in the rural countryside; and which encouraged self-reliance, responsibility, and self-help.

*

As elites' philanthropy embraced modernization, their development organizations such as RWB and TRC were quick to denounce all political and economic ideology (not just colonialism) altogether. Development, therefore, came to be characterized by a 'de-ideologisation and technisation of decision-making'.[80] As part of which, communities were now imagined through their defining qualities of self-help and responsibility, where economic change (or its inverse, income poverty) dominated and was expected to somehow lead to social change, especially in the rural areas. The role of elites' sponsored development organizations was to support demonstration or model communities, on which subsequent development could be modelled. Making the Tata Trusts' contemporary priority in tackling poverty clear, J. R. D. Tata wrote in 1978: 'there is so much poverty, distress and lack of the basic requirements of life in our country, especially in the countryside, that we have felt it necessary to give priority to meeting such needs'.[81] In which, structural causes of poverty and inequality such as colonialism, caste, capitalism and its dispossessions, etc. were set aside completely in favour of a de-ideologized, post-political imaginary of development, which has unexpectedly so only intensified since.[82]

---

[79] Work undertaken by the Tata Relief Committee after drought in Ahmednagar, Maharashtra; file no. 185A/DTT/PHIL/TRC/MAHARASHTRA/1972/3, TCA.

[80] Murphy, *Global Managerialism*, 150.

[81] From JRD's letter to Dharma Vira, Sri Aurobindo Centre, dated 10 July 1978; from file no. 180/DTT/PHIL/DON/12, TCA.

[82] For example the following quote from *Gulliver's Travels* was published on the inside cover of SRTT's Annual Report (1998–99), which is emblematic of such post-political conception of

Like the Tatas, the Birlas also favoured such a technocratic, apolitical approach of demonstration or model communities, post-colonialism. Even though the Birlas did not engage in large-scale community development programmes, their imaginings of community development were no different. They echoed similar themes and formulations of the poor and their passivity, with de-ideologized modernization presented as the only available route to development on the model communities.

Following his travels through Egypt and Switzerland in 1954, for example, Birla outlined the significance of community development work in key demonstration sites. India, he believed, could reach its development goal quicker 'if we did intensive work in pockets rather than work extensively'. Without discounting the need for large-scale, extensive projects, Birla argued, 'the country is so big, task so gigantic, people so uneducated and frustrated that extensive work will perhaps take a much longer time to move towards our goal'. Like Devapur, Birla proposed concentrated development in model or demonstration sites: '20/30 pockets of prosperity, each pocket, say, of 1000 sq. miles or more, these in themselves will become models for others to emulate and thus attract people towards hard work and a realistic approach'. Referring to the Ford Foundation-funded community development programmes, Birla added, it was 'to some extent, are on the pattern that I am talking about. But what I mean is that we may strive to create pockets a kind of models in respect of education, sanitation, hard work, prosperity, cleanliness and so on and so forth. The importance of intensive work and its efficacy is worth our consideration'.[83]

*

Here, it is worth pointing out that much like Birla and Bajaj's earlier patronage of Gandhi and other Hindu nationalist leaders during colonialism, the Tatas' modernization of community development was similarly imbricated in a patronage-based politics. Starting from 1955 onwards, J. R. D. Tata and the Tata Trusts actively supported Jayaprakash Narayan's—politician and leader of the Sampoorna Kranti (or Total Revolution Movement) in the 1970s, which later grew into the Janata Party and culminated in the formation of the first

---

development that has animated the Tatas' philanthropy since the 1950s: 'And he gave it for his opinion, that whoever could make two ears of corn or two blades of grass to grow upon a spot of ground where only one grew before would deserve better of mankind and do more essential service to his country than the whole race of politicians put together'; from file no. 213/SRTT/1998–1999, TCA.

[83] Birla's letter to M. O. Mathai dated 22 June 1954; from file 3, 1043.

non-Congress government at the Centre—rural development work.[84] The Tatas, otherwise careful and compliant in their grant-making, were even willing to make grants in instances where Narayan's organizations were yet to be registered. In 1959, for example, Rustum Choksi, then SDTT's leader, wrote to Narayan indicating the Trusts' willingness to support the Sarva Seva Sangh (Organization in the Service of Everybody) and suggesting that the Sangh be appropriately registered as the Trusts had been running into difficulties with the income tax authorities over grant-making to unregistered bodies. He also suggested an exchange of experiences between RWB at Devapur and the Sangh.[85] In 1970, the Tatas donated a further Rs. 50,000 towards Narayan's Gramswaraj Fund (or Fund for Village Self-Rule).[86]

Such a patronage, it is suggested, was driven by J. R. D. Tata's personal admiration of Narayan. For J. R. D. Tata, Narayan was 'in many ways, the least representative of the breed, but one for whom I developed an unbounded liking and admiration (…) I was impressed by his transparent sincerity and gentle reasonableness, unexpected in an ex-revolutionary activist'.[87] As in the case of Bajaj and Birla, Tata's patronage of Narayan might have been driven by their personal proximity, but it served other purposes too. On his part, Narayan was forthcoming with an outright endorsement which helped the Tatas acquire further reputational capital in an age when private capital and capitalists were often subject to suspicion. In 1967, for example, Narayan paid 'eloquent tributes to Tatas, who not only contributed in ample measure to the industrial progress of the country, but also rendered outstanding service to society, motivated always by an enlightened and progressive outlook'.[88]

*

Echoing the philanthropic turn to partnerships with NGOs from early 1970s onwards globally, the Tata Trusts turned to funding NGOs on a far wider scale than before instead of founding and funding its own institutions from the 1990s onwards.[89] By 2017–18, for example, SRTT devoted US$123.59

---

[84] According to the records, J. R. D. Tata Trust donated Rs. 7,500 per annum from 1955–59; SRTT gave Rs. 5,000 to the Sarva Seva Sangh while SDTT gave Rs. 6,000 to it; SDTT gave Rs. 45,000 to the Gram Nirmal Mandal; and Rs. 8,500 to Mahila Charkha Samiti. Additionally, Rs. 212,500 were donated to various causes between 1953 and 1959 by the Tatas' Steel Company. Further correspondence suggests Rs. 5,000 were donated by SDTT and SRTT from 1962 onwards for a three-year period; from file no. 179/DTT/PHIL/DON/7, TCA.

[85] Choksi's letter to Narayan dated 22 May 1959; file no. 179/DTT/PHIL/DON/7, TCA.

[86] From a letter dated 30 September 1970 written by Choksi to Narayan; file no. 179/DTT/PHIL/DON/7, TCA.

[87] Lala, *Blue Mountain*, 315.

[88] From *Tata Review's* vol. II, no. 2, 1967; from file no. 183/DTT/PHIL/TRC/Bihar/1967/1, TCA.

[89] Charnovitz, 'Participation', 261–8.

millions towards such partnerships. This amounted to nearly 90 per cent of its total disbursement of the year, while the remainder was dedicated to individual grants and institutional endowments.[90] This is comparable to the 93 per cent committed towards programme grants at SDTT, where an even smaller percentage was dedicated to other types of grant-making.[91] Such programme grants, its earlier annual report from 1999–2000 noted, were earmarked for emerging organizations willing to innovate, which had close links with rural communities, and focused on women and children's issues. Moreover, they were expected to develop cost-effectiveness in their programme delivery while building long-term sustainability in their operational plans, outlined clear monitoring milestones and reporting parameters, and made effective use of their human resources (although not explicit, the latter would have referred to both within and outwith the organization).[92]

Contrary to expectations that the national question would have been rendered irrelevant or obsolete in the age of neoliberal, globalizing capitalism and managerial developmentalism, the national question remained central to the pursuit of development, post-1990s. Re-committing the Tata Trusts to India's development, Ratan N. Tata (*b.* 1937),[93] who until recently held the chair of the Tata Group and continues to lead the Tata Trusts following his retirement in 2012, noted India's unfinished development challenge of 'ending of poverty, and ignorance and disease and inequality of opportunity', despite five decades of state-led effort.[94] Elsewhere, he outlined ongoing and continuous relevance of national development to Tata's philanthropy; which was committed to supporting models of community-led sustainable development that delivered 'social justice for all'.[95]

More sharply than before, community in the post-1990s period constituted the primary mode of *doing* development: community-banking, community

---

[90]   Tata Trusts, 'Annual Report, SRTT, 2017–18, accessed 11 June 2021, https://www.tatatrusts.org/about-tatatrusts/annualreports.

[91]   Tata Trusts, 'Annual Report, SDTT, 2017–18', accessed 11 June 2021, https://www.tatatrusts.org/about-tatatrusts/annualreports.

[92]   SRTT, 'Annual Report, 1999–2000', accessed 10 April 2014, http://srtt.org/downloads/annual/annrep9900.pdf.

[93]   The chairman of the Tata group since 1991, Ratan Naval Tata is widely credited with the growth and expansion of the group's businesses overseas and his leadership of the Tata Trusts. Son of Naval Tata and his first wife, Sonoo, Ratan N. Tata was raised by Ratan J. Tata's wife, Navajbai. Trained as an architect at Cornell, he returned to India to start work with the Tatas in 1962, and later completed the Advanced Masters Programme at Harvard in 1975. Awarded widely with a number of honorary doctorates, Ratan N. Tata serves or has served on the boards of various companies, academic institutions, and philanthropic foundations, including as chairman of SRTT and SDTT. He retired as group chairman in 2012, but continued to chair the Tata Trusts. See Piramal, *Business Maharajas*, 363–407.

[94]   Annual Report, SRTT, 1996–97; from file no. 213/RTT/AR/1996–97/1, TCA.

[95]   Annual Report, SDTT, 2005–06; from file no. 210/DTT/AR/2005–06, TCA.

centres, community conservation, organizing community for management of commons, community-based media, community-based rehabilitation, etc. In this, communities were increasingly being called upon to participate, even lead, their own development (without always being allowed to determine what development meant, though). SRTT's educational funding for example, provided a separate component for community involvement within project outlays. Similarly, its health-related work supported community-based reproductive and child health care. From lift irrigation schemes, to land water resources management, pastoral and common forest management, new community-based committees, organizations, and groups were actively sponsored all over the country. In such cases, communities became 'the locus of responsibility'.[96] The commons, for example, recognized as 'a traditional feature in rural India' were in a state of decline as 'common pasturelands [had] become overgrazed and poorly maintained'. The collapse of 'traditional' socio-economic systems meant that communities needed to be equipped with new institutions to manage and govern them. Instead of revitalizing earlier structures, though, the emphasis was on replacing them with new, modern, village-level management committees to protect and regulate common property resources in the country.[97]

*

India's economic elites' post-colonial embrace of modernization, however, was also beginning to be called into question. By the turn of the twenty-first century, even the elites were beginning to recognize the irresolutions of modernization. The poor, according to SDTT's first annual report from the twenty-first century, were now affected both by traditional diseases such as malaria, diarrhoea, and tuberculosis, and 'modern' diseases such as HIV/AIDS. They suffered, therefore, 'disproportionately because of this "double burden" of traditional diseases as well as modern disease that are caused by rapid industrialization and rapid resource depletion'.[98] Elsewhere, Ratan N. Tata wrote in one of the Annual Reports of SDTT that despite the benefits of neoliberal globalization, which had made India into the fourth biggest economy in the world according to purchasing power, large number of people, who lived without access to basic services, 'cannot be empowered to claim their share in the benefits of growth'.[99]

[96] Annual Report, SRTT, 1999–2000, accessed 10 April 2014, http://srtt.org/downloads/annual/annrep9900.pdf.

[97] Annual Report, SDTT, 2003–04; file no. 210/SDTT/2003–04, TCA.

[98] Biennial Report, SDTT, 2000–02; file no. 182/SDTT/2000–02, TCA.

[99] Annual Report, SDTT, 2005–06; file no. 210/DTT/AR/2005–06, TCA.

Economic elites' increasingly uncomfortable, *fin de siècle* relationship with modernity and modernization is, however, hardly a recent phenomenon. In the following section, I argue how elites' ambivalent relationship with modernity in the postcolonial context has long been circumscribed, especially when it came to questions of caste and religion.

Circumscribed Modernity

On 25 February 1925, Leslie Wilson, then governor of the Bombay Presidency, convened a meeting at which N. H. Choksy rose to speak about the challenges in eradicating leprosy from the country. Given the debilitating effects of leprosy on the minds and bodies of those afflicted with the disease, he sought generous donations in order to aggregate a large fund for research, treatment, and early detection of leprosy. The treatment centres ought to have been run, Choksy added, on non-denominational lines. At the same time, he wanted the centres to afford 'full liberty of conscience, and allowing the Hindu, the Mahomendan, or the Christian leper to devote himself to his own religious practices'.[100] The simultaneous move in Choksy's remarks towards the secularization of treatment centres while ensuring arrangements for religious practices reflected not only an Indian formulation of secularism (not absence, but tolerance of diverse faiths); but also pointed to what I have chosen to characterize as elites' *circumscribed* formulations of modernity, which is characteristic of national-modern imaginaries in postcolonial locations such as ours. It can be found not just in the kinds of public health infrastructure funded by India's economic elites but also their imaginaries of development, more broadly.

Here, I suggest it might be analytically useful to conceive of such specific formations of modernity as *circumscribed*, and not simply as deviations or unfinished nature of the project of modernity in India. The specific ways in which it is circumscribed, though, differs not only among the Indian elites but possibly from other postcolonial locations too.

India's economic elites prioritized giving within their own communities despite the wider calls for secularization and modernization of their philanthropy. They were particularly mindful of the interests of their own caste and religious communities over that of others, including when they engaged in supposedly secular gift-making. Such philanthropic behaviour was true

---

[100] From published extracts of Choksy's speech at the Secretariat, Bombay; from file no. 50, PT.

both of caste-Hindu elites such as Bajaj and Birla, as well as the Anglophile, more 'modern' Parsis, I argue. Not only were their imaginaries of development circumscribed in terms of its exclusions and inclusions, but more importantly they were limited in their conception of what constituted reform. Thus, notwithstanding their embrace of modern forms of organizing, faith in science and technology, and pursuit of development (on which more in the following three chapters), their philanthropy continued to bear remnants of the supposedly pre-modern (caste, religion, etc.). Moreover, I argue, that their philanthropy often eschewed more radical or structural causes and approaches, and so did little to dismantle the various social vectors that divide us.

*

One of the foremost examples of what I mean by circumscribed modernity can be found in upper-caste Hindu elites' work with caste-based associations. Many of whom were frequently invited to serve on their caste-based associations. Birla, for example, was actively involved with the founding of the Maheshwari Sabha (1914) and Marwari Sahayak Samiti (1913). Bajaj, similarly, served variously as the chairman of the reception committee (1919), as general secretary, and as president (1926) of the Aggarwal Mahasabha. Endowing them with reputational capital beyond their economic and political standing, such associations provided them with a ready-made platform, from which they were quick to call for modernizing—or reforming to be more precise—their own caste-based communities in the regions they came from and its 'traditions'.

Birlas' early community development work from the 1910s to the 1930s, discussed previously in the chapter, was narrowly restricted to their own Marwari community in Pilani and Calcutta only. They focused, inter alia, on addressing the cultural and social practices of purity and taboo, inter-dining, inter-marriage across sub-castes (never across castes, note), and conventions governing education and travel overseas, within their castes. Like his early philanthropy, G. D. Birla's participation in Bengal's Legislative Council was similarly circumscribed, bounded as it were by his narrow concerns for his community and its beliefs. Nominated in 1921, Birla voted against extending suffrage rights to women, for example, and worked mostly to protect the commercial interests of the Marwaris.[101] Similarly, in his address to the Aggarwal Mahasabha from 1926, for example, Bajaj challenged the Maheshwari *baniāns'* narrowness and invited them to initiate community-reform. In

---

[101] Kudaisya, *G. D. Birla*, 163, 60.

particular, he spoke of the scourge of *ghoonghat*, child marriage, untouchability, and the need to avoid unnecessary extravagance in religious rituals, as far as possible.[102]

Bajaj and Birlas' philanthropy was modelled, in many ways, along the severely restricted Gandhian agenda of self-reform. Mainly directed at upper-caste communities such as their own, these 'welfare' programmes—Ambedkar noted in his seminal *Annihilation of Caste*—had less to do with the reform of Hindu society but more at reforming the *savrana* Hindu family. Led by 'enlightened' caste-Hindus, they were directed at getting rid of evils such as enforced widowhood, child marriage, *purdah* and *ghoonghat*, rituals around birth and deaths, etc. They were inspired, Ambedkar noted, by elites' own personal experiences and directed at reforming families and communities such as their own. Although conducted in the name of reforming the wider Hindu society, such programmes of 'modernizing' society were never serious about reform or abolishing caste altogether.[103] Not unsurprisingly, then, upper-caste Hindu elites' imaginaries of community were further circum-scribed by their reluctance to denounce the *chaturvrna* system and its evils. It never presented a systematic, leave alone radical, agenda for undoing caste.

Instead, it strived for Dalits' assimilation within the fold of the wider Hindu society while demonstrating—*performatively*—upper-castes Hindus' willing-ness to reform themselves. This stratagem was exemplified in the founding of the All-India Anti-Untouchability League. Founded in November 1932 in Bombay, the League emerged as a result of the collaboration between Bajaj, Birla, Thakurdas, and others. It is important, here, to recount the political cir-cumstances that preceded its founding. Following the British government's decision to establish separate electorates in 1932, a row broke out between Ambedkar and Gandhi, which the latter saw as an attempt at dividing the Hindu society. Various caste-Hindu economic elites participated in a Hindu Leaders' Conference at Bombay, seeking an amicable resolution to avoid the division of the Hindus at any cost.[104] Following what came to be known as the Poona Pact—where Ambedkar withdrew his demand for separate electorates and Gandhi withdrew his fast—the elites re-invigorated their efforts at reforming the Hindu caste system.[105]

---

[102] Nanda, *In Gandhi's Footsteps*, 143–6.
[103] Ambedkar, *Annihilation of Caste*, AWS vol. 1, 41–2.
[104] Nanda, *In Gandhi's Footsteps*, 198.
[105] For an overview of the Poona Pact, see Ravinder Kumar, 'Poona Pact, 1932', 87–101.

The League's central aim was to 'free the Hindu community…from all the evils springing from the institution of untouchability by all peaceful means'— note, not the eradication of caste or even untouchability itself but only their evils. It hoped to bring a 'radical change in the very mentality of caste Hindus that they will as a matter of course treat the Harijans…as equals'.[106] While Birla served as the League's president, others such as Thakurdas, Lalubhai Samladas, Ambalal Sarabhai, and Lala Shri Ram served as members on the League's central board. Not only did they make gifts of their time and money, they were also involved in fund-raising across the country, especially in the major commercial centres such as Bombay and Calcutta where they were based. Thakurdas, for example, donated Rs. 5,000 to the League on 8 November 1932. In addition to which, he promised to raise further donations worth Rs. 75,000. Birla hoped to raise a further Rs. 100,000 from Calcutta and Rs. 150,000 from Bombay. Although not all the promises were met, they kept up their pressure.[107] Shortly after its founding, the League's name was changed to 'The Servants of Untouchables Society'—denoting its patrons' seeming desire to work as the *servants* of the untouchables, an inversion of traditional caste-Hindu order. To this, C. Rajagopalachari, a Congress leader and later founder of the liberal Swatantra Party, objected, arguing that it purportedly made untouchability into a permanent feature of the Hindu society in the country. Inspired by the Gandhian service, the League ultimately came to be known as the Harijan Sevak Sangh (or Organization for the Service of Harijans). As Gandhi decided to launch a new journal to promote the Sangh's activities, Birla suggested naming it *Prayaschit*, or penance for the sins of caste Hindus; although Gandhi ultimately settled on his favoured *Harijan*.[108]

With caste Hindus, the League restricted its work to a small range of issues to change the 'very mentality of caste Hindus'. Reasonable '*sanatanis*'—if such a formulation were at all possible, a concept note on the League noted—were less resistant to the removal of untouchability but had far greater reluctance about inter-caste marriages or dinners. And that since the League was committed to working within its remit of constructive work, the *santanis* would have had no problems with the League's objectives whatsoever.[109] The withdrawal

[106] From a booklet titled 'The All-India Anti-Untouchability League: Aims and Objects, Scheme of Propaganda and Uplift Work, Budget and Constitution', dated November 1932, file no. 121/1932, PT.

[107] Birla's letter to Thakurdas dated 29 October 1932, file no. 121/1932, PT.

[108] Nanda, *In Gandhi's Footsteps*, 203–4.

[109] *Sanatanis* refers to followers of orthodox stream of Hinduism, the *Sanatan Dharma* (or Eternal Truth). In the early twentieth century, the *Sanatanis* opposed the reform-minded *Arya Samajists* as the latter challenged idol worship, Brahmin priesthood, and the caste system; from Jaffrelot, *Hindu Nationalism*, 11–12. From a booklet titled 'The All-India Anti-Untouchability League: Aims and

of intermarriage across castes from the reform agenda championed by the League came, and rightly so, for a particularly telling attack from Ambedkar in his *Annihilation of Caste*. 'Fusion of blood can alone,' he argued, 'create the feeling of being kith and kin and unless this feeling of kinship...becomes paramount the separatist feeling...created by Caste will not vanish'.[110]

In its work with Dalits, the League promised to 'give attention to *their* [Dalit] industries'.[111] Such a formulation was symptomatic of caste-Hindus' (and even the Tatas', as discussed earlier in the chapter) distancing itself from Dalits' economic activities. This distancing, Ambedkar noted elsewhere, was tantamount to separation of Dalits from the caste-Hindus and amounted to 'the surest way of perpetuating untouchability'.[112] Thus, while elites' philanthropy focused on economic and educational upliftment of Dalits, it left the more insidious and dangerous notion of caste-based purity and pollution, and even its institutional structures and rituals, intact. Circumscribed within a Gandhian, reformist paradigm, India's economic elites' engagement with caste was limited in imagination. Instead, they concentrated their efforts around a wide range of symbolic initiatives, foremost among which was securing entry for Dalits to Hindu temples. For which, elites contributed, both financially and otherwise. Their efforts were part of the Hindu nationalists' assimilative approach to strengthen the Hindu society numerically. Bajaj, for example, led the way in this by ensuring the entry of Dalits in the Lakshmi Narayan temple at Wardha, the construction of which was sponsored by his grandfather Seth Bachhraj, in 1928. Bajaj recorded in his diary, probably pleased with his effort, 'my faith in divine power has grown'.[113] The Birlas were similarly supportive in the opening of Hindu temples for Dalits' entry. In 1929, Rameshwar Das Birla expressed his support to Bajaj's leadership for this programme. Although not convinced that the temple trustees would have agreed to such moves right away, the former promised more money for such initiatives, especially for the Laxminarayan and Ambadevi temples.[114]

Objects, Scheme of Propaganda and Uplift Work, Budget and Constitution', dated November 1932, file no. 121/1932, PT.

[110] Ambedkar, *Annihilation of Caste*, AWS, vol. 1, 67.

[111] From a booklet titled 'The All-India Anti-Untouchability League: Aims and Objects, Scheme of Propaganda and Uplift Work, Budget and Constitution', dated November 1932, file no. 121/1932, PT; emphasis added.

[112] Ambedkar, 'Gandhi and his Fast', AWS 05: 373.   [113] Nanda, *In Gandhi's Footsteps*, 143–6.

[114] From R. D. Birla's letter to Bajaj dated 2 November 1929; from Correspondence: Birla, Rameshwar Das, JB (1st Inst.).

Thakurdas also supported the temple entry of the backward classes in Dakor. Disapproving the use of force if required to enforce Dalits' entry, Thakurdas was convinced 'that it is to the interests of Hinduism and of Hindu temples that depressed classes should be allowed *darshan* in the same way as high-caste Hindus'. With a view to smoothing over the agitation within the temple management committee, he suggested presenting a 'good elephant' to the temple.[115] In 1935, following Gandhi's efforts in Godhra, Gujarat, members of the *bhangi* (an 'untouchable' caste who were made to do manual scavenging work; they refer to themselves as Valmiki or Balmiki) community had mobilized money for the construction of a temple. They needed an additional Rs. 1,000 to complete it, which the Indian political leader Vallabhbhai Patel requested Bajaj to provide.[116] Similarly, Jugal Kishore Birla made a number of donations in 1941 following his wife's demise, which included Rs. 20,000 towards Dalits' temple entry and accessing water wells.[117]

The elites' support for even such largely symbolic, gestural, reform programmes was limited. They were acceptable when carried out of beneficence, but not when Dalits' themselves demanded entry as a matter of right. In 1929, for example, when Periyar E. V. Ramasamy and his followers of the Self-Respect movement demanded entry into a temple in Erode, Bajaj and his allies from the Congress were quick to distance themselves from such actions. Blaming Periyar, C. Rajagopalachari wrote an angry letter to Bajaj (who was both a personal benefactor and financial supporter of institutions led by Rajagopalachari) that the temple entry programme had fallen into 'the hands of people who are conducting a virulent anti-Congress, anti-Gandhi, anti-Hindu and anti-God propaganda'. Distancing himself, Rajagopalachari wrote, 'much as I may like the removal of untouchability, I do not like mixing up with these people. Their activities in the directions...are too aggressive and persistent for us to make distinctions as regards the present case'.[118] Thus, secularization of temples was never to be demanded as a right, nor should it

---

[115] Letter from secretary to honorary manager, Dakor Temple Committee dated 26 September 1932, file no. 128(I), PT.

[116] Letter from Patel to Bajaj dated 22 April 1935; From Correspondence: Patel, Vallahbhai, JB (1st inst.).

[117] From Jugal Kishore Birla's letter to Bajaj dated 4 December 1941; from Correspondence: Birla, Jugal Kishore, JB (1st inst.).

[118] Letter from Rajagopalachari to Bajaj dated 9 July 1929; from Correspondence, C. Rajagopalachari, JB (1st inst.); also see Ashik Kumar, 'Origin Stories: Reading Periyar Today'. *The Caravan*, 13(4), April 2021, 89-93 for an extended discussion on Periyar's exchanges with Rajagopalachari around Dalits' temple entry, imposition of Hindi language, and Gandhian vocational education programmes—all causes to which Bajaj and other Marwari elites gave generously.

involve any use of force; however, it was only acceptable if it were granted as a gift by the upper-caste Hindus.

Such symbolic interventions, Ambedkar pointed out, were not particularly useful; instead, efforts at improving the economic, educational, and social circumstances of Dalits in the country were needed, which the caste-Hindu elites were unwilling to provide in the first place.[119] In 1940, for example, Bajaj was invited to make a donation for the upliftment of Dalits. However, Birla was convinced that there was no need for such work and that Bajaj had no way of spending such money. Birla, therefore, suggested that Bajaj's money be used for educational work instead. It was decided, then, that Bajaj's donation be given to the Birla's educational programmes at Vanasthali.[120]

*

Other elites were no different. Their engagement with the caste question remained limited, occasionally, to making provisions or reporting about benefits accruing to the lower castes. In the early 1930s, for example, Thakurdas presided over the Bombay Presidency branch of the British Empire Leprosy Relief Association. Working closely with the Bombay government, local leper asylum, and the Haffkine Institute, Bombay, the Bombay branch reported overseeing the treatment of nearly fifteen hundred patients, nearly half of whom belonged to the backward or untouchable castes.[121] While the upper-caste Hindu elites' assimilationist response was hardly surprising, the anglophile Parsi Tatas were no more forthcoming or even more radical in their approach towards the caste question in India's development. In June 1917, Dorabji Tata (1859–1932),[122] the elder son of Jamsetji Tata and widely credited with the growth of the Tata Group, expressed his desire to

---

[119] Ambedkar, 'Pay More Attention', AWS 17(1): 229.
[120] From Birla's letter to Bajaj dated 8 March 1940; from Correspondence: Birla, G. D., Jamnalal Bajaj Papers (1st instalment), NMML.
[121] From the branch's annual report for 1931; file no. 50, PT. The prominent mill-owner, Ness Wadia of the Wadia family from Bombay, also donated Rs. 3,500 for five years starting from 1929 onwards.
[122] Dorabji J. Tata, the elder son of Jamsetji, was born on 27 August 1859. After attending his high school in Bombay, Dorabji went to Gonville and Caius College at Cambridge, before returning to St. Xavier's College in Bombay, from where he graduated in 1882. Working as a journalist first, he joined his father's businesses soon after. He was married to Meherbai Bhabha (1879–1931) at the age of thirty-eight. He is widely acknowledged to have established his father's businesses, particularly in iron and steel and power, for which he was knighted in 1910 in recognition of his contribution to the industrial advancement of India. Dorabji also led the Tatas' businesses in insurance, cement, and aviation in the later years. He did not have any children. He passed away in Germany in 1932, on his way to England to visit his wife's grave. He is known to have loved sports.

fund a scheme for medical research in India.[123] A scheme prepared by Colonel R. McCarrison, which envisioned a Rockefeller-like, privately funded, medical institution conducting cutting-edge medical research, with modern, up-to-date facilities 'appealed to him [Tata] most'. Tata endorsed the scheme in 1920.[124] Notwithstanding the aspiration for modernity, caste-based segregation of hospital wards and kitchens remained. All in-coming patients, following their preliminary examination by the chief physician, were to be transferred to the part of the hospital 'set apart for persons of their caste'. The five wards, it was suggested, should be suitably divided using concrete partitions. The central kitchen was to be equipped with arrangements for 'caste cooking under European supervision'.[125]

Similarly, in all the archival material relating to the Tatas' philanthropy that I have found there are no more than a handful of isolated instances where it acted to ensure access or made additional provisions specifically for Dalits. In 1968, for example, the Tatas agreed to sponsor the construction of a community centre or a library hall in Navsari city as part of its relief work following the floods in the district. Their support, though, was conditional—that 'Harijans' would not be debarred from using it.[126] Elsewhere, their response to dealing with the stigmatization attached to certain work such as nursing was to point to the economic opportunities it offered. Responding to a request from the Charotar Argoya Mandal for establishing an out-patients' department in 1978, for example, SDTT suggested that they include a nurses' training programme. Given the 'social resistance against this noble profession', they suggested recruitment 'not only from the scheduled castes but as a part of social education, candidates should be drawn from higher castes as well'. The Mandal, SDTT personnel suggested, must point that nursing was 'a very remmunerative (sic) profession which should be brought to the notice of the prospective candidates', in order to attract higher-caste Hindus to the

---

[123] From the Inquiry regarding the Institution of a Fund for Endowment of Medical Research in Bombay, file no. Department of Education, Sanitary B, Proceedings nos. 58, February 1919, National Archives of India, New Delhi (henceforth NAI).

[124] Notes on a Conference organized to select the Tata professors for the proposed school of medical research in Bombay on 16 June 1920; from FD 01/4197, The National Archives, Kew Gardens (henceforth TNA).

[125] 'A Proposal for the Foundation of "An Indian Institute of Medical Research"' by R. McCarrison, dated 28 May 1918. File no. Home Department, Medical A, Proceedings nos. 86–88, January 1919, NAI. It was not an uncommon practice for other hospitals in India and even in hospitals established in England during the World War I to follow segregation of wards and kitchens along caste lines.

[126] Work undertaken by Tata Relief Committee after floods in Navsari, Gujarat. File no. 183/DTT/PHIL/TRC/GUJARAT/1968/1–3, TCA.

profession.[127] As with RWB, the Tatas' response to questions of caste were simplistic in their assumption that the prospect of economic mobility would somehow have helped dismantle the pre-existing social order, the evidence for the failure of which abounds in the country.

That these were the only instances where the Tata Trusts engaged with the question of caste is telling in and of itself. It has remained, by and large, unresponsive even to the long-expressed although unrealized, Dalit belief in the promise of modernity.[128] Thus, even as the Tatas hoped to *prepare* Indian society for modernity, ensuring Dalits' access to it or dismantling caste was never part of their imagination of the national-modern.

*

Notwithstanding the moves towards the secularization of philanthropy towards the end of the nineteenth century in the name of modernization, gift-making to preserve religious ties within elites' own communities has persisted well into the twentieth century. Not only was such religion-inflected philanthropy justified in the name of the national question (Hindu nationalism, for example), it was also modern in the ways in which it imagined new publics and public spaces.

More than others, the Birlas have been actively involved with funding various groups and organizations on the Hindutva spectrum (from those which propagated linguistic nationalism to the more virulent right-wing Hindu Mahasabha). Launched in December 1939 in Calcutta, the Mahasabha emerged in the context of growing worries among the Hindu *bhadralok* that the Congress was no longer capable of preserving or fighting for the earlier social and economic order of Brahminism and *zamindars*. Channelling the growing communalization of the contemporary Bengali public and press, the Mahasabha secured early support from the Marwari elites. Jugal Kishore Birla, for example, led the financing of the Mahasabha's Calcutta conference.[129] Building on their earlier philanthropy for physical training and wrestling clubs (on which, more in the following chapter), he also financed the physical training of Hindus from Burdwan. The Birlas also supported the Bengal branch of the RSS and hosted the Calcutta headquarters at their Shilpa Vidyalaya.[130] He, along with his father Baldeo Das and Bajaj, was an enthusi-

---

[127] Correspondence regarding support to Charotar Arogya Mandal. File no. 181/DTT/PHIL/MIS/6, TCA.

[128] Guru, 'Dalits', 123–36.

[129] Chatterji, *Bengal Divided*, 134–6.   [130] Chatterji, *Bengal Divided*, 236.

astic supporter of Hindu nationalists' efforts to establish a Hindu university in the country. The Birlas were prominent patrons of the Banaras Hindu University (BHU). Plans for the university were designed and developed by the Hindu nationalist leader, Madan Mohan Malaviya, by the 1910s. Malaviya's objectives for BHU were to build 'an all-India movement for the resurgence of Hindu nationalism'. In search of large patrons, Malaviya turned to rulers of the Hindu princely states and Hindu mercantile groups, including Bajaj who donated Rs. 50,000 in 1920.[131] More than Bajaj, though, Malaviya was supported by the Birlas.

As a champion of indigenous business and industry and an expert of Sanskrit classics, Malaviya was very popular among the Marwaris of Bara Bazaar, Calcutta. Birla, and his brother Jugal Kishore and father Baldeo Das, were all drawn to Malaviya's Hindu nationalism. Together, the Birlas soon became the largest donor to the University. They gave, it is estimated, in excess of Rs. 30 lakhs in total. At BHU, they supported the training of Hindu preachers for propaganda (Rs. 75,000). They founded a department of Indian Religion and Philosophy in the Central Hindu College and a separate Sanskrit Mahavidyalaya. The Birlas also helped in the founding of a hostel for 400 students, a separate Rajaputana hostel in 1926, and a wing of a women's hostel. Jugal Kishore instituted a hundred scholarships at Rs. 15 each month as well as the propagation of *Gita*.[132]

That the Birlas were ideologically committed to Malviya's Hindu nationalism and therefore more forthcoming in their support to BHU over other institutes of higher education can be gauged from the secrecy surrounding Birla's donations to the Aligarh Muslim University. Although Birla also donated Rs. 25,000 to the latter on Gandhi's insistence, he was careful to keep his donation anonymous. He was worried that such a large donation to a Muslim institution would have been opposed both by Malaviya and within his own family. Although Birla later confided in Malalviya that he had made the donation under Gandhi's influence, he kept it hidden from his own family.[133]

They also collaborated with other economic elites to protect and safeguard the lives and rights of Hindus to the exclusion of other affected communities. In 1940, for example, Janakidevi, Jamnalal Bajaj's wife, wrote a letter to Jugal Kishore Birla to provide immediate support to Hindu groups amidst growing communal tensions in the princely state of Bhopal in central India. Following

---

[131] Bajaj's letter dated 15 December 1925; Correspondence: Gandhi, M. K., JB (1st inst.).
[132] Kudaisya, *G. D. Birla*, 73–9.   [133] Cited from Kudaisya, *G. D. Birla*, 91.

her travels to the state, she wrote that the lives of Hindu women were in grave danger. Although local Hindu youth had organized themselves, their work needed urgent support.[134] In his reply, Jugal Kishore noted that he had been making regular gifts to workers from various Hindu groups, including the Hindu Sabha in Bhopal and elsewhere. In addition to his monthly donations, he also made further gifts for special occasions or to fight court cases on behalf of Hindu youth and groups involved. He went on to express his surprise at the absence of a more 'organized' response from Hindus in the face of Muslim atrocities in places like Hyderabad and Bahawalpur. Outside the Muslim princely states, too, Jugal Kishore wrote that wherever there was a substantial Muslim population, such incidents were common. Jugal Kishore hoped Janakidevi's experiences would have influenced both Bajaj and others close to Gandhi. Undermining Gandhi's formulaic use of *ahimsa*, Birla wrote: 'if Gandhi has any other remedy to offer to counter such atrocities, then we [Hindus] might benefit from it. Or if Mahatamaji could pressurise the Nawab of Bhopal or if he were to write something for the newspapers, then I might think differently.'[135]

The Birlas were also enthusiastic supporters of the reconstruction of the Somnath Temple in Verawal, Gujarat. Following Patel's controversial visit to the site in 1948, a mere four days after having annexed Junagadh, a Muslim princely state on the western littoral of India, Birla and his brother Braj Mohan led the efforts to raise funds for the reconstruction of the temple. The temple has since become emblematic of Hindutva's narrative of Muslim invasion and destruction and the country's right-wing leaders' attempts at retrieving and returning to Hinduism's lost glory by reconstructing temples. Constructed at a total cost in excess of Rs. 3 crores, the temple was re-opened in 1951.[136] That Birla was seen as a supporter of Congress's Hindu right-wing under Patel was amply demonstrated by Nehru's appointment of Birla to lead the efforts at constructing a scheme for rural uplift in Patel's memory.[137] These were hardly isolated instances of support towards Hindu nationalism and

[134] From Janakidevi Bajaj letter to Jugal Kishore Birla; from Correspondence: Birla, Jugal Kishore, JB (1st Inst.).

[135] Jugal Kishore Birla's letter to Janakidevi Bajaj dated 20 July 1940; from Correspondence: Birla, Jugal Kishore, JB (1st Inst.).

[136] Kudaisya, *G. D. Birla*, 284.

[137] It involved raising Rs. 50 lakhs for a rural uplift scheme involving constructing wells, school buildings, and approach roads to villages, etc. Although Birla managed to raise the targeted sum amongst industrialists, the collections among Congress workers were far lower. While Nehru suggested rural reconstruction and digging wells as a tribute to Patel's agricultural roots, Patel's followers within the party were outraged. Following much jostling, it was finally agreed to build a statue in New Delhi at what is now known as Patel Chowk; see Kudaisya, *G. D. Birla*, 289.

crafting a Hindu *rāshtra* (nation). More recently, Basant Kumar Birla (1921–2019; son of G. D. Birla) unequivocally supported India's right-wing, Hindu nationalist Bharatiya Janata Party's leaders such as previous and current prime ministers Atal Behari Vajpayee and Narendra Modi. The latter, Basant Birla believed, 'has succeeded in creating an environment which is supportive of business houses and is, therefore, a worthy candidate for the country's leadership'.[138]

*

Despite the well-recognized Parsi Anglophilia and their claims to modernity, the Tatas' philanthropy was similarly circumscribed by their religious belief.[139] The J. N. Tata Endowment Fund, for example, was initially available to Parsis only. Similarly, Dorabji Tata's scheme for the modernization of vernacular education for girls in Bombay city and Presidency from 1913, on which more in the next chapter, was similarly restricted to the Parsi community only.[140] Elsewhere, even though the Tata Trusts viewed themselves as secular institutions, they have continued to fund Parsi denominational institutions on several occasions, in line with the directions in the wills on the basis of which the various trusts are founded. In 1935, for example, SDTT was approached by the Parsi Panchayat to provide funds so that the latter could offer scholarships to Parsi students for their higher education abroad. Reviewing the request, the Trustees argued that theirs was a 'cosmopolitan trust'. Nevertheless, the Trustees decided to award an annual grant of Rs. 10,000 from 1936 onwards on the condition that the Trust will receive the applications directly from the students, make selection autonomously, and exercise 'control over them in foreign countries'.[141]

The Tata Trusts have since provided support on an ongoing basis to various Parsi community organizations and members of the Parsi community. The Industrial Institute supported by the Tatas, for example, was known to have taught two-hundred and fifty Parsi women cooking, laundering, embroidery and other domestic arts while giving them 'livelihood with dignity and

---

[138] Sehgal, *Basant and Sarala Birla*, 175–6.

[139] For an extended discussion on Parsi Anglophilia and relationship with modernity, see Tanya Luhrmann's *The Good Parsi*, 99–109.

[140] Note and Memorandum titled 'On the Views of Sir Dorabji Tata with Reference to the Education of Girls in Bombay City and Presidency'. File no. L/PJ/6/1224, 768, IOR.

[141] From the Minutes, 22nd Meeting of the Board of Trustees, SDTT, dated 20 September 1935; and related correspondence with C. Manshardt. File no. 178/DTT/DJT/PERS/PROP/LEG/WILLS/BO/OPT/1, TCA.

self-respect.'[142] More recently, SDTT has made numerous small, educational grants for the benefit of Parsi students in technical and engineering studies (2006–07) and to the Vocational and Technical Committee of the Parsi Panchayat (2008–09). Similarly, SRTT has funded the World Zoroastrian Organization Trust for the care of elderly Parsis (2001–02); the Higher Education Committee to support scholarships for Parsi students to pursue their higher education (2001–02); endowment grants to JN Tata Parsi Girls' High School and Bai Navajbai Tata Zoroastrian Girls' High School (2002–03); Zoroastrian Trust Funds of India and the Dhobi Talao Parsee Association (2011–12), among others. To a number of the above organizations, grants of various amounts are made each year. The Parsi, not-Parsi distinction continues to be retained even in the present-day reporting of the J. N. Tata Endowment Fund. While the minutes of the Fund's Trustees' meetings do not record the community or caste profile of the applicants or selected scholars from non-Parsi backgrounds, this is not the case for those from the Parsi community.[143] Although non-denominational, in keeping with its founders' wishes, if and when it makes a grant to a denominational organization or institution, it is one within its own Parsi community only.

The above, however, is a far from exhaustive list of the Tatas' religious charity for the development of its own community as my primary purpose is less to chronicle philanthropy but more to highlight how the Tatas' religious charity is not seen as a contravention of its secular conception of philanthropy. In short, the pursuit of development under national-modern has allowed a wide range of circumscribed formations of modernity to exist alongside each other—making space for their donors' religious and caste beliefs.

*

In addition to religion and caste, elites' imaginaries of community were circumscribed, although to a much lesser extent, by geography. The ways in which their developmental philanthropy was guided by geography, though, varied widely. Birlas' philanthropy was, for example, by and large concentrated around Pilani and Calcutta, their ancestral and commercial homes. Their earlier educational philanthropy, from 1901 onwards, and later gifts directed at social reform among Marwaris in Calcutta in the 1920s, followed this pattern. In response to the famine in 1942–43 in Bengal, they became the

---

[142] From the entry pertaining to SRTT's philanthropy; from file no. 181/DTT/PHIL/MIS/3, TCA.
[143] See, for example, 122nd Meeting of the Board of Trustees, 2013, file no. 176/JN Tata Endowment for the Higher Education of Indians, TCA.

single largest private benefactor. By 1943, they were responsible for running six cheap canteens, which served nearly twelve thousand people daily. They also opened various centres for the distribution of food grains, cloth, and even free education of children from Calcutta at their schools in Pilani.[144] Even when they made donations for nationalist causes: such as khadi, charkha, or even education, these tended to be concentrated in either of the above two only. In 1941, for example, Jugal Kishore Birla gifted Rs. 50,000 to the Charkha Sangh, among other donations. Of this, nearly half, he directed, was to be spent in his native Pilani only.[145] Having discussed with both Gandhi and regional functionaries of the Charkha Sangh, Bajaj wrote that it was hardly ideal that money was earmarked to regions in this way. He reasoned that although they would follow Birla's ultimate wishes, it was important that decisions about spending the monies were left to the Sangh itself so that it could use it for the poor from other parts of the country.[146]

Similarly, Thakurdas's philanthropy was, to a large extent, restricted to the Bombay Presidency only—from the Cheap School Scheme to his work on leprosy and temperance. Still others, though, tended to be more 'national' and less community-centric (geographically) in their outlook when making gifts. The Tatas, for example, have tended to be least tied down, adopting a pan-Indian view.

*

Indian elites, therefore, sought to imagine new kinds of communities throughout the twentieth century: secular though not quite; reformed and modern but in peculiarly circumscribed ways, where affinities and interests of caste and religion superseded the pursuit of social justice or development for all.

One way of conceptualizing these differences, translations, or how modernity is received in the Third World, would be to view them as a deficit or an indication of the unfinished nature of modernity (which became the premise of development in the first place in mid-twentieth century). Such a formulation, though, is both reductive, essentialist (in its misattribution of modernity to Europe), and leads to a conceptual impasse.[147] We need, therefore, to

---

[144] Kudaisya, *G. D. Birla*, 212.

[145] From Jugal Kishore Birla's letter to Bajaj dated 4 December 1941; from Correspondence: Birla, Jugal Kishore, JB (1st inst.).

[146] From Bajaj's letter to Jugal Kishore Birla dated 10 December 1941; from Correspondence: Birla, Jugal Kishore, JB (1st inst.).

[147] In *Asia as Method*, Chen recognizes it as an impasse; others such as Pankaj Mishra, 'History's Waiting Room' have noted how the attribution of modernity to the West condemns us to the

accept and recognize these circumscribed formations of modernity as *our own*.[148] One possible way, as I have suggested, would be to think of these imaginaries of community as a particular formation arising out of modernity's entanglements with the national question, or national-modern for short.

waiting room of history. Such an attribution of modernity to Europe, more importantly, is historically inaccurate, see Kaviraj, 'Revisionist Theory', 497–526.

[148] Chatterjee, *Empire and Nation*, 150–2.

3

Self

Meritorious Few, Masses, and Citizens

In 1926, Turkey's Mustafa Kemal Atatürk decreed the adoption of the Gregorian calendar and Western time across the republic. So, clock towers were erected everywhere in preparation of on-coming modern time, soon becoming part of the urban fabric of the city in which Turkish 'citizens', the essayist Pankaj Mishra notes, 'could pretend to be modern, and anyone still adhering to Islamic time, or time-keeper's houses, was severely punished'. The sounds of *muezzin*'s prayer call or following the sun's journey to follow time became obsolete. The imposition of modern time and the tyranny of having citizens' lives organized around it became part of the story of development of the people living outside or without modernity in the Third World. Uprooted from their familiar ways of being and their pasts, they are condemned, then, to 'languish eternally in the waiting room of history'.[1]

Notwithstanding the condemnation of those living outside modernity in Atatürk's Turkey, India's economic elites have also engaged extensively in a similar programme of imagining, constituting, and disciplining modern individual selves—citizens of a post-colonial nation-state whose imaginings preceded the arrival of India's independence. Influenced variously by modernity's transformative promise, its critique and rejection, and ambivalence towards it, the 'modern self' became a crucial trope and cause to which the elites made generous donations throughout the twentieth century. As before, whose 'self'—from the meritorious modern scientist, engineer, administrator, etc. to the unnamed poor—was being reimagined and in what ways differed considerably across elites' gift-making. What was common, though, was how these imaginings of 'self' were conducted in the name of and legitimated by invoking different formations of the national-modern.

[1] Mishra, 'History's Waiting Room.' *The Guardian*, 28 February 2015.

Philanthropy and the Development of Modern India: In the Name of Nation. Arun Kumar, Oxford University Press.

'Best and Most Gifted'

As the twentieth century beckoned, Jamsetji Tata summarized his founding vision of 'constructive philanthropy'. In an interview from 1899, Tata committed constitutive philanthropy to educating and developing 'the faculties of the *best of our young men*'. 'What advances a nation,' he reasoned, was 'not so much to prop up its weakest and most helpless members, as to lift up the best and most gifted so as to make them of the greatest service to the country'.[2] Instead of charity directed at the poverty-stricken 'masses' within their own communities, elites' constructive philanthropy was directed at the 'best and most gifted'. It constituted a significant milestone in the modernization of Indian philanthropy at the turn of the twentieth century. In its focus, constructive philanthropy echoed Carnegie's more familiar philanthropic philosophy of the 'exceptional man', which followed later. Outlined in the trustees' deed of Carnegie's endowment for an Institute of Washington—a scientific research centre to which Carnegie made a gift of US$10 million in 1902—it endeavoured to 'discover the exceptional man in every department of study whenever and wherever found, inside or outside of schools, and enable him to make the work for which he seems specially designed his life work'.[3] Convinced that investing in those with potential—the meritorious few—was the best way forward, Jamsetji Tata launched the J. N. Tata Endowment Fund in 1892. Although initially launched for the higher education of Parsis only, the Fund was later extended to all 'capable natives' of the country, whose higher education abroad was supported by the Fund.[4] Elsewhere, Tata's new approach to philanthropy found its most substantive expression in the establishment of what later became the Indian Institute of Science, Bangalore, on which more in the next chapter.

Jamsetji's initial push to focus on the meritorious individual was further embedded within the Tatas' philanthropy by his younger son, Ratan's (1871–1918) philanthropic imaginary.[5] In his will, which led to the establishment of Sir Ratan Tata Trust, he provided that: 'If any research institute is

---

[2] Jamesetji N. Tata's interview published in the *West Coast Spectator* on 9 February 1899; cited from Lala, *Love of India*, 112, italicized for emphasis.

[3] Cited from Kohler, *Partners in Science*, 8.   [4] Subbarayappa, *Pursuit of Excellence*, 319–30.

[5] Ratan J. Tata, the younger son of Jamsetji, was born in 1871 and educated at St. Xavier's College, Bombay. He joined the trading business in 1896 as a partner and looked after the fire insurance and trading businesses. Ratan was married to Navajbai Sett in 1892 but did not have any children. He was known for his philanthropy and arts collection. Having supported G. K. Gokhale and M. K. Gandhi in their work, Ratan sponsored the archaeological excavation of Pataliputra and poverty research and administration at the LSE. He was knighted in 1916 for his services to humanity. Ratan died in Cornwall, England, in 1918, and was buried by his father's side.

established it is my desire that the Trustees shall establish fellowships and keep up and maintain in the work of research persons best qualified in that behalf'. The provision for scientific research on various social and developmental problems was to be led by 'competent men...brought from Europe, America and elsewhere'. In order to devise schemes of 'a practical nature calculated to promote the welfare of the said community care being taken that such work is not undertaken from a stereotyped point of view but from the point of view of fresh light', he made provisions to 'engage qualified and competent persons'.[6] Jamsetji Tata's elder son, Dorabji Tata also went on to make similar provisions for supporting 'professorships or lecturerships or giving scholarships or travelling fellowships in any branch of science or art in studying abroad'.[7] 'If any research institute is established', Dorabji Tata laid out in his will, 'it is my desire that the trustees shall establish scholarships and keep up and maintain for research work such person as are best qualified in that behalf preference to be given to pure Indians if equally suitable (sic).[8]

Investing in the meritorious few soon became the foundation of the Tatas' philanthropy. Even when financing institutes of research and teaching abroad, they hoped meritorious Indians would readily benefit from cutting-edge research infrastructure. For example, in 1920 Dorabji Tata made a generous gift of £25,000 to the Engineering School at University of Cambridge for its re-construction. In a letter to the vice chancellor of the university in 1920, Tata wrote: 'I consider it my privilege to give to my old University such assistance as I am able to give for I share the hope that the enlarged school may be the means of imparting a fuller and more thorough training in the subject to the thousands of students who will flock to it from the Empire in future years'. 'I recognise that the University in the past', he added, 'has given a most cordial welcome to young students from India, and given them also of its best. In making the gift', Tata hoped that 'in the furtherance of human knowledge, Cambridge will extend to my countrymen a yet warmer welcome; and with the growing demand for higher training in my country, bestow on it the response and the favour of increased facilities for the purpose'.[9] Dorabji's gift is particularly instructive both in the place it accords to the nation—within

---

[6] Ratan Tata's will dated 20 March 1913, with a codicil dated 29 February 1916; file no. 178/RJT/PERS/LEG/WILL/1, TCA.

[7] Deed of SDTT dated 11 March 1932; file no. 177/DTT/DEED/AGR/1932, TCA.

[8] Dorabji Tata's will dated 29 April 1927; file no. 178/DJT/PROP/WILL/1, TCA.

[9] From a letter dated 27 August 1920 from Dorabji Tata published in the *Cambridge University Reporter*, 5 October 1920; from file no. 175/Donations made by Sir Dorabji Tata to Cambridge University–1920, TCA.

the empire—and its needs as well as the emphasis on the meritorious, tasked with developing the country.

The emphasis on the 'best and most gifted' was part of the wider Indianization of different realms of the country during colonialism: administrative, scientific, economic, engineering, etc. In its submission to the Royal Commission on the Superior Civil Services in India, Delhi in 1923, for example, Ratan D. Tata, one of Jamsetji N. Tata's first cousins and J. R. D. Tata's father, wrote: 'We look forward to a state within 10 to 15 years when all the superior services in this country will be Indianised'. 'By this', he clarified, 'we do not mean that entry to the service should be confined to any particular race or community. We consider that at that time recruitment should be by examination as in the past, that such examination should be held in India and should be open to any subject of His Majesty provided the rest of the Empire reciprocates in this'.[10]

Part of national-modern development, elites' emphasis on Indianization of personnel leading different realms of the country was not necessarily a counter to colonialism (as anti-colonial nationalism might have been) but an attempt at accessing positions hitherto denied to Indians and justified in the name of India's national development. It also sought to place merit at the forefront of all development imaginaries. The Tatas' somewhat anachronistic philanthropy of supporting the meritorious few, that I have elsewhere argued was both pragmatic and paradoxical in the choice of influences that shaped it, was justified—once again—in the name of development and the nation.[11] Summarizing the origin of its philanthropic philosophy of supporting the meritorious, Burjorji Padshah, a trusted Tatas' insider, noted that Jamsetji Tata 'was of the opinion (...) that service to the needy could no more be made without brains, without investigation, without the selection of the right men, and without concentration on particular aspects, than the production of any other species of goods'.[12] The focus (one might even call it excessive reliance) on the meritorious came under challenge time and time again. For

[10]   From Ratan D. Tata's response dated 26 November 1923; from file no. IOR/Q/11/14, IOR.
[11]   Kumar, 'Pragmatic and Paradoxical Philanthropy', 1438–42.
[12]   Cited from Harris, *Tata: A Chronicle*, 120.
    Burjorji Jamaspji Padshah (1864–1941) was the son of one of Jamsetji's close friends. Following his father's death, Padshah became Tata's ward and was later engaged to one of Jamsetji's daughter, who passed away at the age of ten. Although having attended college at Bombay and Cambridge, Padshah never graduated, despite being known for his academic brilliance. He later served as a professor and then, vice principal, at a college in Sindh. In 1894, he joined the Tatas, and was entrusted with the development of a proposal that led to the establishment of the Indian Institute of Science, Bangalore.

example, in 1944 when SDTT was considering financing the Tata Institute of Fundamental Research, Bombay (TIFR; and on which more in the following chapter) questions were raised about the prudence of conceiving an entire institution around the individual scientist, Homi J. Bhabha (1909–1966). Internal correspondence suggests that questions were raised if such a philanthropic strategy was, after all, appropriate as the proposed institute was a 'one-man affair'. In response, the considered opinion of the noted British physiologist Archibald V. Hill was cited. Scientific research in England, it was noted, had similarly been 'built up around an individual', and that Bhabha's TIFR scheme was no different. Equally, the Tata Institute of Social Sciences (founded in 1936, and on which more in chapter 5; henceforth TISS) had been similarly built up around Clifford Manshardt, the American sociologist who had previously led the Nagpada Neighbourhood House, and subsequently SDTT.[13] Thus, the emphasis on the best and most gifted, so they reasoned, was merely a response to the hard realities of Indian science and development, its state, stage, and ambition—as investing in the 'right men' became the central pivot around which national-modern came to be organized.

*

As part of the national duty to 'lead' India's development in the twentieth century, the 'right men' were also expected to embody modernity. In addition to acquiring a modern education, they were expected to embody modernity in their behaviours, personality, sartorial choices, and their bodies. With a view to encouraging responsibility among the recipients of scholarships under the J. N. Tata Endowment Fund, for example, Tata offered money, in part, as a loan. This, a subsequent brochure noted, was done to 'instill (*sic*) the spirit of self-help'. He insisted, we are told, 'from the beginning that the scholarships should be in the form of loans. He could afford to give but he preferred to lend, for he knew well that self-help alone could give self-reliance and self-respect.'[14] This modern logic of self-care, initially directed at the meritorious 'right men', was later extended to the poor, on which more later in this chapter.

---

[13] Note 2 to the Trustees, SDTT, dated 10 April 1944; from file no. FP22-B, TCA.

An American sociologist with a doctorate from the University of Chicago, United States, Manshardt served as the director of the Nagpada Neighborhood House, Bombay, and from 1932 with Sir Dorabji Tata Trust. He was the founding director of TISS and later went on to serve the US Foreign Services as an officer in Karachi and New Delhi.

[14] Brochure titled 'The JN Tata Endowment for the Higher Education of Indians', from 1977; file no. 175, TCA.

Alongside the cultivation of a modern ethos of self-care, the meritorious were also expected to adopt modern mores and display familiarity with international, or Western to be more precise, cultures. Under Bhabha's leadership, the Indian scientists at TIFR, for example, were expected to abandon their regionalism and provincialism and cultivate a modern, global ethos—not only in terms of their access to modern machinery and laboratories but also through architecture, food and dining, sartorial preferences of the scientists, in their use of lavatories, and so forth, as part of the scientific temper and comportment. Each of these, the historian Indira Chowdhury notes, 'became part of the scientific institution's civilising process in which local practices and ways of being were put aside and temporarily forgotten'. Social mores at TIFR, she suggests, 'should be viewed as part of a cultural pedagogy that prepared its members for participation in global networks that the scientific work demanded'. 'They would not be found lacking', Bhabha believed, 'in adopting what came to [be] seen as "international" cultural mores'.[15] The national-modern imagined, here, was both superior and distinct from Indian scientists' local, provincial, or regional cultural mores (which were cast aside as deficient or inferior and in need of cultural modernization), but also crucial to upholding India's place on an international, again Western to be precise, stage.

As part of their cultural modernization, the 'best and most gifted' were expected not only to master their scientific and technological knowledge but also possess a modern outlook, for which they were expected to be trained in the social sciences, including management, as well as in humanities.

In his presidential address at IISc, Bangalore in 1954, John Matthai called for including social science in the science and technology programmes taught at the institute. A training in the sciences, he argued, prepared students 'for the occupations and professions that are necessary for a modern society but they do not create an awareness of the many human problems for which their own growth and development are responsible'. However, given that 'every great step in technological advance has brought with it new human problems of adjustment and reconciliation', there was an urgent need to integrate the social sciences with training in the sciences as the former was key to their understanding of emergent human problems. Not unexpectedly, training in management studies was seen as a good gateway to the social sciences. 'The young scientist and the young engineer', Matthai said, 'need to be aware of the economic aspects of technological problems and of human factor in industry

---

[15] Chowdhury, 'Laboratory', 60–1.

(...) Our Section of Economics and Industrial Psychology and the new Management Courses supply a kind of corrective to an exclusively scientific or technological education'. The modernization of Indian industry and society, therefore, required that its students and researchers were equipped with 'a new outlook and a new sense of values'.[16]

Matthai's suggestions were repeated by J. R. D. Tata in his presidential address the following year. Differently from Matthai, though, Tata's calls for the teaching of social sciences at IISc were important not just *for* their role in the modernization of Indian industry and society but because they helped mitigate against the ills of modernity. Modern science and development, Tata argued, had brought with it 'a multiplicity of ailments, both physical and spiritual — the neuroses, the maladjustments, the loneliness, the fear, the insecurity'. India's scientists, therefore, needed to be 'men not merely competent in their respective branches of science and technology, but imbued with knowledge and understanding of the broad human problems that will face them and their compatriots and equipped with a mental outlook which keeps step with the fast changing world'. The primary purpose of a training in the social sciences, J. R. D. Tata concluded, was not to simply provide more information, but 'awaken interest'.[17]

Matthai and Tata's collective efforts led to a proposal for a new section on Industrial Engineering and Administration at IISc, Bangalore in 1956. It constituted, J. R. D. Tata noted, a 'fresh approach to human problems'.[18] Plans were made for research in industrial organization and management, particularly on measurement of industrial efficiency, security, wages, structure, cooperation between labour and management, incentives, measurement of productivity, job analysis and selection methods, including testing of psychosocial metrics on personality, values, and aptitude.[19] Thus, the social sciences,

---

[16] Presidential address by J. Matthai, 17th Meeting of the Court, IISc, 20 March 1954. File no. 189/DTT/PHIL/IISC/MIS/1, TCA.

John Matthai (1886–1959) was educated at Madras, Oxford, and LSE, and worked as an officer with the Madras government before becoming a professor of economics at the Presidency College and later the Madras University. He held various offices, including that of the chairman, Indian Tariff Board (1931–34); and director-general of commercial intelligence and statistics at Calcutta from 1935. He joined Tata Sons in 1940 and became a director in 1944, later holding directorial positions in different Tata companies. He was the minister of railways and transport in 1947, and finance minister (1948–50) in the Indian government. Matthai also served as the SDTT's chairman and president of the Court of IISc, Bangalore.

[17] From the Presidential Address to the 18th Meeting of the Court, IISc by J. R. D. Tata on 26 March 1955. File no. 190/DTT/PHIL/IISC/MIS/5, TCA.

[18] From the Presidential Address to the 19th Meeting of the Court, IISc by J. R. D. Tata on 24 March 1956. File no. 190/DTT/PHIL/IISC/MIS/7, TCA.

[19] From a brochure of the IISc, from 1957; from file no. 190/DTT/PHIL/IISC/MIS/8, TCA.

and more particularly management, were seen as the gateway to acquiring new or 'modern' social values, about the industry and also society beyond it.

The growing popularity of management and its perceived significance for the economic and cultural modernization of the country meant that elites were more interested than before in founding specialized institutes of management.[20] Efforts were initially led by Kasturbhai Lalbhai and Vikram Sarabhai, as leading industrialists, philanthropists, part of the techno-managerial elites in the country and known for their proximity to Congress leadership.[21] Even as the Ford Foundation promoted Bombay city as its preferred location of the new management institute in the country, Lalbhai and Sarabhai continued to make the case for Ahmedabad vehemently. They were finally successful not only in convincing the Ford Foundation about the institute's location but also that its collaborating partner should be the Harvard Business School and not UCLA's Graduate School of Business Administration. The Indian Institute of Management (IIM) at Ahmedabad was thus founded as a collaboration between Indian elites who donated money for the construction of buildings (approximately 30 lakhs); the Ford Foundation which sponsored faculty exchange, library, and other academic infrastructure; and the governments of Gujarat and India which donated land and made an annual block grant respectively.

That these new, emergent communities of the meritorious were different from the rest of the society was reinforced by elites serving at the helm of these institutions. Lalbhai, who served on the governing board of the IIM, Ahmedabad and refused to accept the chair's position, resisted adopting rigid structures and rules at the institute. Ravi J. Mathai, the first director of the institute, recalled that Lalbhai was one of the few people convinced that the institute's 'main efforts should be to work with the community in building its own culture and norms of creative self-discipline'. Such a new self-governing culture for the meritorious, we are told, helped the institute attract the best talent at lower salaries than they would have commanded elsewhere.[22]

*

[20] Srinivas, 'Mimicry and Revival', 47–8.
[21] Widely known as the father of the Indian space programme, Vikram Sarabhai was educated at Gujarat College and Cambridge, from where he earned a doctorate for his research on cosmic rays. He was instrumental in founding a number of science and cultural institutions in Ahmedabad city, among which I discuss the Ahmedabad Textile Industries' Research Association, Indian Institute of Management, Ahmedabad, and the Physical Research Laboratory in chapters 3 and 4. Sarabhai also helped found the Indian Space Research Organization and was awarded Padma Bhushan and Padma Vibhushan, civilian honours awarded by the Indian government; also see footnote 41, chapter 2.
[22] From a brochure of the IISc, from 1957; from file no. 190/DTT/PHIL/IISC/MIS/8, TCA.

The Birlas were similarly committed to training a new generation of leaders. Training at the Birla College of Engineering in Pilani, for example, focused on building the students' behaviour and character so that they could become 'leaders and organizers' in the near future. In addition to their academic performance, they were marked on their general professional fitness. This included areas such as: physical fitness; attendance, punctuality, and earnestness; conduct and character; and their personality, leadership, and organization. The teachers kept charts and marked the students each term, with the mark confirmed at an interview conducted at the end of each academic year. The College's principal, Lakshmi Narayanan, recalled that students were imparted 'a knowledge of how to handle themselves, how to speak and behave'. Soon its graduates held positions in the armed forces, government departments, and public and private sector companies.[23]

*

Elites' strategic focus on the meritorious few had begun to fall out of favour, post-colonialism. Reflecting the post-independence nation-state's priorities of development which necessitated renewed attention on India's poor (if not only on the latter, at least partly), elites also turned their attention elsewhere. In 1952, for example, Birla was busy raising and contributing money to the Vallabhbhai Memorial Fund. In a letter to Nehru, Birla raised a point about potential uses of the funds. One possible use of the funds, he suggested, would have been to finance the higher education of Indians abroad. In response to which, Nehru wrote a rather curt reply: 'I am not very much in favour of spending the money on foreign scholarships. Personally I am getting a little tired of the number of people who are going abroad for study'. Utilizing funds in this way, Nehru concluded, was far from the original proposals for the Memorial Fund.[24] For the first time, then, India's economic elites were beginning to move away, resolutely, from the meritorious.

Notwithstanding the mid-century turn away from merit, on which more in the following section, it has remained obstinately moored to the Indian economic elites' philanthropy in neoliberal India. It now combines twentieth-century conceptions of acquiring necessary modern education and mores with those of twenty-first-century formulations of leadership, agency, and excellence for change. The Shiv Nadar Foundation, for example, has founded a range of educational institutions: in engineering, management, software

---

[23] Hennessy, *India Democracy and Education*, 233-4.
[24] From Nehru's letter to Birla dated 16 May 1952; from file 2, 1043.

development, etc.[25] Seeking to widen its funding of merit, the Foundation's Vidyagyan Academy offers free residential scholarships to over two hundred students from poor households from across seventy-five districts in the state of Uttar Pradesh. Hoping to bridge the rural-urban divide in the country, it sees itself as a 'leadership academy' for 'change agents' who will ultimately serve 'their families, communities, nation, and society at large'. In 2011, it founded the Shiv Nadar University with a vision to 'nurture the leaders of tomorrow,' by giving equal weightage to the infusion of leadership values, social responsibility and by cultivating a commitment to serve the community to create efficient professionals and responsible citizens'.[26] Not dissimilar to Jamsetji Tata's vision for IISc, the Shiv Nadar University also hopes to 'serve the higher education needs of India and the world beyond'.[27] It seeks to combine values such as social justice and public service from the twentieth century with twenty-first-century concerns over environmental sustainability and social inclusion. Emphasizing merit from primary to tertiary education levels and in rural and urban areas, the Shiv Nadar Foundation is guided by what it calls 'creative philanthropy'. Instead of filling gaps through time-bound projects, 'creative philanthropy' mimics contemporary philanthrocapitalism in its emphasis on high-impact, large-scale ('multiplier', 'lasting force'), sustainable (at least financially) giving.[28]

Like the J. N. Tata Endowment Fund, the Bharti Foundation, led by Sunil Mittal (b. 1957),[29] also sponsors the higher education of Indians at the

---

[25] Shiv Nadar (b. 1945) is the son of a district judge in Tamil Nadu. After completing his electrical engineering degree from the PSG College of Technology, Coimbatore, Nadar joined Cooper Engineering in 1967. Starting as a management trainee at DCM Data Products, Nadar quit in 1975 to start Microcomp. A year later, Nadar launched Hindustan Computers Limited (HCL). Today, HCL is a global company with US$9.7 billion revenue, with operations in over forty countries, and employs over 149,000 workers. He is married to Kiran Nadar, an art collector and founder of Kiran Nadar Museum of Art, New Delhi. Shiv Nadar was awarded the Padma Bhushan in 2008. In 2020, he retired as HCL's chairperson with an estimated wealth of US$17.8 billion (as of 2020).

As of 2019, Nadar has invested nearly US$800 million in the Shiv Nadar Foundation.

[26] Shiv Nadar Foundation, 'Institutions and initiatives', accessed 6 September 2019, https://www.shivnadarfoundation.org/what-we-do/institutions-and-initiatives/ssn-institutions.

[27] Shiv Nadar University, 'About us', accessed 6 September 2019, https://snu.edu.in/about.

[28] Shiv Nadar Foundation, 'Our philosophy', accessed 6 September 2019, https://www.shivnadarfoundation.org/why-we-do-it/our-philosophy; for a criticism of philanthrocapitalism's obsession with metrics, managerialism, and inability to fund structural change, see, for example, Ramdas, 'Philanthrocapitalism', 394–5.

[29] Born to a Congress politician, Sunil Mittal started his first business venture making bicycle parts. After launching various trading companies, he entered the telecommunication manufacturing business; before launching Bharti Cellular Limited in 1995, which offered mobile service in Delhi under the brand name of Airtel. It now operates in eighteen African and Asian countries. The Bharti Group has since diversified into food, banking and insurance, and real estate industries. Mittal was awarded the Padma Bhushan in 2007 by the Government of India.

Mittal's wealth is estimated at US$10.2 billion (as of 2002). In 2017, the Mittal family agreed to donate 10 per cent of their wealth to educational philanthropy.

University of Cambridge in the United Kingdom. Between 2010 and 2017, it has provided scholarships to fifteen students under its Manmohan Singh Bursary scheme, which covers their fee and a means-tested maintenance fund for undergraduate studies in any field apart from medicine and veterinary sciences.[30] As does the Keshub C. Mahindra Trust, which has since expanded more extensively into higher education in the country, including through the Mahindra École Centrale, Hyderabad, which offers an interdisciplinary education in science, technology, and liberal arts for 'excellence in engineering education'; and the UWC Mahindra College in Pune which trains its students to become 'agents of change'.[31]

In addition to funding the meritorious, elites have also turned their attention to those living at the other end of the class spectrum: the country's poor impoverished masses, on which more next.

Making Masses into Citizens

As part of his membership of the executive committee of the Indian Council of the British Empire Leprosy Relief Association, Purshottamdas Thakurdas was frequently approached with requests for conducting surveys in order to understand the specificities of leprosy across the country. Spelling out these differences, a letter from 1925 suggested interrogating 'their mode of living even among those not paupers, their promiscuous intercourse with their family members even in cases of infectious diseases and reluctance to avail themselves of special treatment even if offered free'.[32] Similarly in 1930, the executive committee including Thakurdas was asked to support efforts by Dr. Ernest Muir, the renowned British leprologist who served as the director of the School of Tropical Medicine and Hygiene in Calcutta, to gather detailed statistics about leprosy in the country. Although the committee ultimately resolved not to conduct such a survey as it was not feasible given the Association's limited resources, it asked to prepare notes that could be

---

[30] The Manmohan Singh Bursary Fund, 'Report, October 2017', accessed 20 August 2019, https://www.bhartifoundation.org/uploads/bhartifoundation/files/1512377147-manmohan-singh-fund-report-2017.pdf.

[31] Sundar, *Giving with Thousand Hands*, 149. Also see Mahindra École Centrale, 'About us', accessed 11 June 2021, https://www.mahindraecolecentrale.edu.in/about-us; and UWC Mahindra College, 'Educational Vision', accessed 11 June 2021, https://uwcmahindracollege.org/about-us/educational-vision.

[32] Letter from N. H. Choksy to Thakurdas dated 11 September 1925, file no. 50, PT.

included in the all-India and provincial censuses instead.[33] Leprosy, in such a formulation, was framed less as a medical problem, but more an administrative problem that required control and supervision of those afflicted with leprosy by the ruling regime.

It was part of elites' wider efforts, I argue in this section, at governing the masses—in which counting the specific categories of various populations merely constituted the crucial first step in labelling, categorizing, and disciplining them. Differently from their funding directed at the best and most gifted—where the emphasis was on self-care, discussed previously, the mode of dealing with the masses, I argue in this section, was built around ideas of persuasion and control. It involved the use of a wide range of 'technics' of research, training, adult education, consciousness raising, etc. It constituted, ultimately, a move towards their governmentalization: where the native bodies and lives were brought under the expert gaze of the scientists (including the doctor, public health and sanitation experts) and the social scientists (including the statistician, the social worker, and the sociologist).[34]

Such efforts at moulding the masses into worthy citizens began early in their lives—in schools. In 1910, Bajaj founded a students' hostel at Wardha, followed by a boys' high school two years later. A girls' school was established in 1914. He also supported the opening of a new school at Sikar in his elder brother's memory. In each of these schools, free food, clothes, and books were provided to all school children. Apart from supervising the schools' operations actively, Bajaj kept in touch with the teachers and students and even arranged picnics for them. His early efforts at education earned him the Coronation Medal in 1912 at Wardha.[35] Like Bajaj, Dorabji Tata was also an early supporter of education to rid India of social ills through reform of individual selves. However, their imaginaries of reform were based not in the annihilation of 'tradition' (as much of development tends to); but in its incorporation of 'tradition' within modernity to craft new national-modern citizen subjects from its masses. As with community, in doing so they re-inscribed particular formations of gender, caste, religion, and class into modern education.

---

[33] Minutes of the Executive Committee's meeting on 21 March 1930; file no. 50, PT.

[34] In *Another Reason*, the historian Gyan Prakash has argued that such 'technics' of science were crucial to the imagination and organization of India (pp. 10–11). Elsewhere, in *Politics of Governed*, 34–41, Partha Chatterjee makes a related point where he argues, following Foucault, that the production of a knowable 'population' in need of development was part of the organizing premise and a crucial source of legitimacy of the post-independence nation-state.

[35] Nanda, *In Gandhi's Footsteps*, 20–1.

In February 1913, Dorabji Tata approached the Board of Education, Government of India, with the proposal of a scheme for 'improving the education of Indian (especially Parsi) girls in the Bombay Presidency' which was also shared with the governor of Bombay, Lord Willingdon, among others. Classified confidential, the note and attached memorandum began by outlining the Tatas' dissatisfaction with the present education for girls, particularly for those from the 'upper and more progressive classes of society in the City and Presidency of Bombay'. The chief defect of the present system was identified as follows: 'it does very little for the formation of character, that the object of education should be to imbue girls with a sense of responsibility for duties which as wives, mothers and members of Society, they will have to perform'. The proposed reform of the contemporary 'mere elementary vernacular instruction' in place was expected to 'encourage the all-round development on the best lines of the girls themselves, and through them, of the communities from which they came'. Any proposed reform was also expected to play close attention to the part 'that should be played in the general educational system by the training of girls in the management of their homes etc'.

Before any such effort towards reforming the education system could be initiated, there was a need, Tata suggested, for conducting a survey of the educational needs of girls from various 'upper and more progressive classes' who would benefit from this. The memorandum outlined the detailed questions that the survey ought to answer, including among others, the communities considered by the survey and their characteristics, the number of girls likely to benefit from the reformed education, as well as the results of the effects produced by the present educational system on the 'minds and characters of those women who have come under their influence'. It went on to say that while Dorabji Tata had not any financial commitment thus far, he remained interested in definite and detailed proposals for 'reforming' vernacular education for girls, and that he was open to the possibility of recruitment of suitable persons that might lead the survey, both in England and in India, as well as the necessary terms for this.[36]

Even as the vernacular education system in the country was deemed deficient, and so in need of modernization, the formulation of modern, reformed education remained circumscribed (similar to the discussion on community in chapter 2). Not differently from examples discussed in the previous chapter,

---

[36] Note and memorandum titled 'On the Views of Sir Dorabji Tata with Reference to the Education of Girls in Bombay City and Presidency'. File no. L/PJ/6/1224, 768, IOR.

proposals for education reform were both gendered and restricted to girls from specific classes of society only. Directed at overcoming the vernacular education system's primary failure in the development of young girls when it came to the discharge of their duties as 'wives, mothers, and members of Society', reformed education was restricted to girls from the 'upper and progressive classes' only. Primarily disciplining, reformed education hoped to train the girls to become better wives and mothers, and lastly members of society. It sought therefore to engender citizenship for girls by restricting their functioning, primarily, to the private sphere of the family, and only lastly, to the 'public' through the community. This containment of modernity—to girls from the upper classes—sought to discipline their roles within the private sphere of the family and constituted a departure from modernity's universally transformative promise.

*

Unlike Tata, Purshottamdas Thakurdas directed his attention to children from impoverished families in rural villages of the country, starting from the mid-1920s onwards. It was, however, similarly circumscribed in the caste-communities it targeted—his philanthropy focused on brahmin and *baniān* communities only, at least to begin with—and geographically. More instructively, though, it remained disciplining in its ambition to produce nation-modern selfhood in particular ways.

In 1924, Thakurdas paid Rs. 21,000 for the purchase of the building of the Sansthan High School in Dakor, Guajarat. On top of which, he paid an additional Rs. 13,000 for the repair and alteration of the school building. Having recently placed an order of 'modern' textbooks, the school was able to apply for registration as a high school, which was awarded shortly after. Unlike other contemporary schools, it placed an emphasis on physical education and sports (for which Sheth Mangaldas Girdhardas of Ahmedabad promised to donate his adjacent lands), English language, and music.[37] By 1926, the school's pupils were performing well and the school itself was in sound financial shape as it received annual grants of Rs. 1,200/- from the Dakor Sansthan, Rs. 2,400/- from Girdhardas, and additional grants from the government and the Dakor municipality.[38] Inspection reports recognized the efforts of the school's headmaster, who—Thakurdas also commended in a letter—had

---

[37] Report of the educational inspector, Northern Division dated 17 September 1925, file 5, PT.
[38] Report of the Inspection Committee dated 4 December 1926, file 5, PT.

'worked heroically for the uplift of the Brahmin population of Dakor'.[39] In 1928, a retired educational inspector of the Baroda state visited the school and complimented the premises, library, museum, laboratory, and its apparatus. Commending Thakurdas and Girdhardas' philanthropy, he urged other 'liberal-minded gentlemen' to come forward to make arrangements 'as is quite necessary in these times, industrial and commercial sides in addition to the side of liberal education so carefully imparted here'.[40] Such moves to impart modern education instead of the earlier and contemporary 'vernacular' education was animated by the pragmatic need to secure their future contribution to the industrial and economic development of the country.

Thakurdas also made numerous smaller, ad hoc donations for widening access to education in the Bombay Presidency. In 1924, for example, he made a generous donation of Rs. 30,000 for the construction of a building for the Modh [the *baniān*—merchants, traders, moneylenders, etc.—caste, mainly from Modhera region] boarding school in Bhavnagar, present day Gujarat.[41] In 1936, he donated over Rs. 5,000 to the Parvatibai Leper Hospital in Surat for the construction of a school. His donations were used, among others, to construct the school building and purchase of desks and blackboards.[42]

Building on his ongoing, ad hoc donations to a small number of schools, Thakurdas expanded his philanthropy to launch the P. T. Cheap School Building Scheme to finance the construction of primary and secondary school buildings in selected rural areas of the Bombay Presidency, now part of modern-day Gujarat. From the early 1920s up to the 1940s, Thakurdas made numerous grants to district-level school buildings' funds. By 1937, he had helped the construction of over 110 schools in Surat district alone.[43] In 1939, he agreed to provide a further sum of Rs. 10,000 for the construction of twenty additional school buildings in villages inhabited by the Raniparaj and Koli communities in the Surat district.[44] He launched an identical scheme in the Panchmahals, which also had a large Bhil population. Thakurdas offered

[39] Letter from Thakurdas to G. M. Bhatt, headmaster, Dakor Sansthan School dated 28 April 1927, file 5, PT.
[40] Notes of Chhaganlal Thakurdas Modi dated 16 April 1928, file 5, PT.
[41] Letter to Thakurdas dated 3 November 1924, file 33/1923–27, PT.
[42] Letter from A. G. Shah to Thakurdas dated 2 May 1936, file 155, PT.
[43] Resolution passed at the District Local Board's meeting held on 1 March 1937, file 180 (Pt. I), PT.
[44] The adivasis of modern-day Gujarat mainly comprise of the Bhils and Kolis. While the Bhils reside in the hilly regions of the state, Kolis are known as adivasis of the plains. In some parts of the state, such as in Kutch, the Kolis are considered to be adivasis although in some other sub-regions of the state they claim to be kshatriyas. For a brief overview of the Bhils and Kolis and their later-communalization starting from the 1980s, see Lobo, 'Adivasis, Hindutva and Riots', 4844–5.
From the minutes of a meeting of the Sir P. T. Village School Buildings Fund Committee on 30 December 1939, file 207 (Pt. II), PT.

an initial sum of Rs. 10,000 on an experimental basis,[45] which supported the construction of school buildings in six villages.[46]

Alongside financing the construction of school buildings, Thakurdas also launched schemes for children's intellectual development, the latter of which was perceived as an area in which Gujarat was seen to be particularly backward. Following trials at Pardi taluka of Surat district, Thakurdas launched a Circulating Library Scheme for each of the other talukas in the district. Each taluka-level library was expected to cost a maximum of Rs. 1,000. He suggested that each circulating library have a different set of books so that they could be exchanged and children could have more opportunities to read.[47] Three-quarters of the sanctioned amount was to be spent on the purchase of books, with the rest spent on purchase of tin boxes to store books, remuneration paid to senior school boys involved in the distribution and circulation of books, and for awarding prizes to children for extra reading.[48] A report on the outcomes of the scheme in Surat district found that most of the schools had been making good use of it. The students had read a number of books and their descriptions of their favourite books were 'very beautifully given in some cases'. Overall, the scheme was more popular in girls' schools than it was in boys' schools.[49]

In 1931, Surat's District School Board drafted a further proposal to extend the scheme to other talukas as well as raise funds for the repair of boxes and books. They argued that the allotted forty minutes for students to read were insufficient to 'keep up their interest sustained'. Instead, it suggested permitting the students to borrow the books to take home.[50] Responding to the suggestion that he bear an annual recurring charge of Rs. 600 for this, Thakurdas made it clear that he did not wish to undertake any continuous payments. 'It will be at my discretion', he added, 'I may say that I will watch the progress and the utility of the scheme closely and decide'.[51] By 1933, a total of Rs. 11,496 had been received in total. As his support became uncertain, the District Board began to scale down the library scheme. In 1934, it was pro-

[45] Letter from Marutisinh Thakore, vice president of the District Local Board, Panchmahals to Thakurdas dated 11 October 1938, file 180 (Pt. I), PT.

[46] From S. R. Tawde's letter to Thakurdas dated 3 June 1939, file 180 (Pt. II), PT.

[47] Letter from Thakurdas to K. M. Vakil, educational inspector, Northern Division, Ahmedabad dated 18 October 1926, file 51/1925–51 (Pt. I), PT.

[48] Resolution No. 3834 dated 26 January 1926, Educational Department, Government of Bombay, file 51/1925–51 (Pt. I), PT.

[49] Report by M. H. Chokshi, headmaster, P. R. Training College for Men, dated 26 November 1929, file 51/1925–51 (Pt. I), PT.

[50] Letter from G. R. Desai to educational inspector, Northern Division dated 27 March 1931, file 51/1925–51 (Pt. I), PT.

[51] Letter from Thakurdas to Bhimbhai R. Naik dated 12 October 9133, file 51/1925–51 (Pt. I), PT.

posed that fifty-five of the biggest schools in the district would receive copies of three children's magazines (*Balmitra, Baljiwan,* and *Balodayn*), which they could then circulate amongst themselves, at an annual cost of Rs. 160.[52] Thakurdas was to contribute Rs. 600 towards maintenance charges of the scheme and Rs. 500 for the initial purchase and repair of existing books. He was also responsible for supplying a cupboard and a half of the books in the library, with the villagers expected to contribute for the costs of the other half of the books.[53] By July 1934, the scheme was ready to be launched in 150 schools of the district at a total cost of Rs. 6,875 to Thakurdas.[54] The scheme was later revised downwards and was to run in a hundred schools, initially, with a focus on ensuring that the libraries ran effectively and efficiently.[55] By 1937, the scheme covered 350 schools with a further one hundred libraries sanctioned by Thakurdas and twenty furthermore through other private donations.[56]

*

Like Thakurdas, the Birlas were also committed to educating the rural masses. They started in 1900 with the establishment of the Birla *pathshala* (school) in Pilani for the education of the younger children of the family, including Ghanshyam Das and his brother Rameshwar Das. Over the next two decades, the lower primary school was raised to an upper primary, later a middle school, finally, becoming a high school in 1925. As more and more children came to study at Pilani, new school buildings and hostels were constructed. With a view to systematizing the income and expenditure, the Birla Education Trust was founded in 1929 (with immovable assets then worth £18,750; and income from securities estimated to be £52,500). The Trust's activities were impelled by, according to Jossleyn Hennessy who wrote its earliest and most detailed chronicle, Birla's desire to provide 'a first class modern education' for boys and young men from the Shekhawati region at a cheap cost to them. Birla wanted an education, Hennessy adds, that 'combine[d] Western learning with respect for Hindu ideals. He [Birla] was interested in character building; he wanted to turn out good citizens rather than passers of education'.

Distinguishing Birla's educational philanthropy from the impulses of colonial educational infrastructure, Hennessy notes that Birla sought to combine

[52] Letter from G. M. Desai to Thakurdas dated 4 March 1934, file 51/1925–51 (Pt. I), PT.
[53] Letter from G. M. Desai to Thakurdas dated 3 April 1934, file 51/1925–51 (Pt. I), PT.
[54] Letter from Bhimbhai R. Naik to Thakurdas dated 9 July 1934, File 51/1925–51 (Pt. I), PT.
[55] Letter from Bhimbhai R. Naik to Thakurdas dated 8 August 1934, file 51/1925–51 (Pt. I), PT.
[56] Letter from G. M. Desai to Thakurdas dated 23 October 1937, file 51/1925–51 (Pt. II), PT.

education with handicraft to 'improve the productive capacity of the cultiva-
tor and the artisan, and this enable[d] them to fit into their native surround-
ings'. [57] On Madan Mohan Malaviya's recommendation, Birla tasked Shukdev
Pande with conducting this experiment. Recruited as the principal of an
intermediate college started in 1929 with twelve boys and eight teachers on its
rolls, Pande was experienced in combining higher education with rural upliftment schemes at Malaviya's Banaras Hindu University. Such was the growth
in Birla Education Trust's activities that by 1952, 5,442 students were studying
at various Birla institutions. This included over 4,300 children studying at
fifty-seven Birla schools at primary, middle, and high school levels. Nearly
1,660 young men and women read at various Birla Colleges, many of whom
studied science and engineering. By the end of the year in 1952, the various
institutions had incurred a total expenditure of Rs. 15,670,000, of which more
than a third was funded by the Trust (or £11.9 million in current value), with
the remainder raised in fees.[58]

That the purpose of education was linked to constructing 'citizen' selves
can be gauged from the tasks assigned to the students from time to time. The
students of the Birla College, for example, travelled to the village schools
every evening with lanterns and drums. They were expected to teach not only
the children but also the adults living in the villages. Drumming up support,
the students would then teach the adults alphabets by drawing in the sand;
ultimately encouraging them to write postcards and read the replies sent to
them. Similarly, the Birla High School sought to create 'citizen-students' by
admitting boys from different class backgrounds. In addition to boys from
middle-class Marwari families, the school admitted homeless refugee boys
following the Partition of the sub-continent, sons of peasants and artisans in
Pilani, and others whose education was financed as part of the Birla Mills'
scheme for educating its employees' children.[59]

In organizing activities inside and outside the classrooms, Birlas' educational institutions hoped to iron out the weaknesses they saw within its society: inadequate social cooperation, preserving what it deemed best in
Hindu-Indian society, while imparting applied scientific education that would
ultimately contribute to the country's industry and therefore, to its economic
growth. It hoped to correct the malaise of 'resistance to authority' inculcated
during India's nationalism struggle during colonialism, and discipline the

[57] Hennessy, *India Democracy and Education*, 53–9.
[58] Hennessy, *India Democracy and Education*, 74–5.
[59] Hennessy, *India Democracy and Education*, 125–32.

masses into prospective model citizens with a respect for order, 'merit', and authority.

Examples of such a disciplining gaze can also be found elsewhere at the Banasthali Vidyapith. Founded by Hiralal Shastri (later the first chief minister of Rajasthan state) and his wife Ratan Shastri in the memory of their daughter, Shanta, the school conducted both school and higher education for girls in Jaipur, Rajasthan. Given that the school was modelled, by and large, along Gandhian philosophy, it was hardly a surprise then that Bajaj and Birlas extended their support to the Vidyapith. Aimed at educating girls as young as eight, the school hoped to impart conventional education but also prepare the girl students—much like Dorabji Tata's school scheme for girls, discussed earlier—for their future roles in running the household and at least one livelihood skill. In a letter from 1935, Shastri invited Bajaj to send any girls whom he believed might benefit from such an education to their school.[60]

Officially launched in October, 1935, the Vidyapith included the Shri Rajasthan Balika Vidyalaya and a girls' hostel named Shri Shantabai Shiksha Kutir. Hoping to train girls to be independent yet proficient in playing their conventional gendered roles, the school also provided physical training to improve girls' health. There was a particular emphasis on maintaining a 'pure' personality. By adopting khadi compulsorily for all students and teachers, upholding caste-Hindu notions of purity, and training girls to be proficient in their 'traditional' roles as well as making them economically independent by learning a livelihood, the school saw itself and its work as part of 'national development'.[61] However, the school and the hostel both struggled to raise money to run the school and hostel from time to time, for which they received various gifts—of money and references—from Bajaj and Birlas. In 1938, for example, Bajaj advanced a loan of Rs. 2,500 from the Mahila Seva Mandal.[62] Similarly in 1940, Jugal Kishore Birla donated Rs. 10,000 to the school.[63]

Building on its earlier work, the Birla Education Trust continues to run a large number of Birla schools across the country, including the Ashok Hall Girls' Higher Secondary School, Mahadevi Birla Shishu Vihar, and G. D. Birla Centre for Education in Calcutta; the G. D. Birla Memorial School for Boys in Ranikhet; and the Aryaman Vikram Birla Institute of Learning in Haldwani. The schools and centres are now run under the leadership of Manjushree

[60] Letter from Hiralal Shastri to Bajaj from 1935, Subject File 1, JB (2nd Inst.).

[61] From a pamphlet titled 'Vanasthali's Shri Rajasthan Balika Vidyalaya and Shri Shantabai Shiksha Kutir' from 1938, Subject File 4, JB (2nd Inst.).

[62] Letter from Bajaj to Ratan Shastri from 30 August 1938, Subject File 4, JB (2nd Inst.).

[63] Letter from Hiralal Shastri to Bajaj from 10 January 1940, Subject File 1, JB (2nd Inst.).

Khaitan (the daughter of Basant Kumar Birla and G. D. Birla's granddaughter). Some of the other schools founded by the Birlas are now under the leadership of her sister, Jayashree Mohta.[64]

*

In addition to educating the masses, the bodies of India's prospective citizenry were similarly subject to elites' disciplinary gaze in the name of the country's development. Part of caste-Hindu elites' support and subscription to Hindu nationalist ideology and programme, was the emphasis on 'fit' bodies, especially among adolescents and youth. The focus on the body as a site of the national-modern took various forms: from regulating diet and nutrition, to promoting hygiene and self-care, as well as a culture of sports, training in martial arts, and exercise. Both Birla and Thakurdas, for example, championed programmes for fit and healthy bodies in their educational institutions.

In 1910, and possibly in response to communal clashes between the Hindus and Muslims in Calcutta, Birla launched the Marwari Sporting Club in 1911 in the city. A popular meeting place for young men, the Club provided instruction in self-defence while promoting a culture of physical fitness. Along with bodybuilding, wrestling, and shooting, the club also provided lessons in the use of *lathi*, and Hindi language. Five years later, Birla supported the Bara Bazaar Yuwak Sangh (Youth Association of the Bara Bazaar) in Calcutta, which provided instruction in wrestling and physical fitness. Bearing most of the Sangh's expenses himself, Birla earmarked Rs. 2,000 annually for its recurring expenses, along with the gift of a house for full-time members. By 1920s, Birla and his brother Jugalkishore, had sponsored numerous *akharas* all over the country. In 1928, for example, they founded the Birla Mill Vyayamshala in Delhi, which was led by the later legendary Indian wrestler, Guru Hanuman.[65] Relatedly, they also supported the construction of a gymnasium in Lahore and at the Dayanand Anglo-Vedic high school in Delhi; whose instructors, Birla believed, were 'messengers of the old *rishis*' of India.[66] A physical education programme was also launched at the Birla Intermediate College in Pilani in 1933. It involved compulsory instruction in gymnastics, athletics, 'traditional' Indian self-defence (such as *lathi*––using a wooden stick as a weapon, *patta*––a sword-like weapon, and mud-wrestling), swimming, and team sports such as cricket and hockey. Instruction in physical education was soon extended to diet and nutrition control at the College.

---

[64] Sehgal, *Basant and Sarala Birla*, 132–3.
[65] Kudaisya, *G. D. Birla*, 31–2.   [66] Kudaisya, *G. D. Birla*, 74–5.

Under Pande's leadership, the diets of all the girls and boys living in Pilani were planned carefully at 3,000–3,200 calories each day, to be consumed over three meals instead of the usual two. All the children also received a bowl of milk every day, procured from Birla's model dairy farm.[67]

The diet of the girls and boys studying at Birla schools was also carefully monitored. Wheat was introduced to the daily diet of the girls at Balika Vidyapeeth, who were also instructed in practical hygiene, first aid, and home nursing. Girls received lessons in cooking and nutrition as part of their domestic science class, with lessons in knitting and embroidery to follow later in the day. Such 'handwork' was deemed important in women's education: both for financial and utilitarian reasons, but also for its aesthetic and 'psychological satisfactions'.[68] Eating together was an important social activity and one that was aimed at breaking down social barriers among students irrespective of their caste and religion. The students' diet, though, was—in keeping with Birlas' own religious belief—wholly vegetarian to the exclusion of even eggs.

*

Like the Birlas, Thakurdas also promoted physical education in schools sponsored through his donations. By 1938, a physical education programme was running in twenty schools as part of the Gujarat Vyayam Mandal, with a further twenty to be added in that year.[69] B. G. Kher, then prime minister of the Bombay Presidency visited the schools to inspect the three schemes launched by Thakurdas—the Cheap School, the library, and the *vyayam* schemes. Kher, according to those accompanying him, was satisfied with what he saw and readily appreciated their worth.[70] Following his successful inspection of Thakurdas's schemes, it was proposed that a district-level school for physical training should be launched. Such a school could be founded through a non-recurring grant of Rs. 60,000, and an annual recurring grant from the government of Rs. 5,000. The non-recurring grant included costs of purchasing the land, construction, equipment, and a further Rs. 20,000 to supply materials to primary schools with sufficient space for playgrounds. The objective of such a school would have been the 'train[ing] and retrain[ing of] primary school teachers…in batches'.[71]

[67] Hennessy, *India Democracy and Education*, 69.
[68] Hennessy, *India Democracy and Education*, 210–4.
[69] Letter from G. M. Desai to Thakurdas dated 23 October 1937, file 51/1925–51 (Pt. II), PT.
[70] Letter from G. M. Desai to Thakurdas dated 16 February 1938, file 207 (Pt. I), PT.
[71] Letter from G. M. Desai to Thakurdas dated 9 July 1938, file 207 (Pt. I), PT.

Elites' legitimized their disciplinary gaze by invoking the indifference of the colonial administration towards the health and fitness of the Indian masses. Recognizing the slow progress when it came to medical inspections and in the introduction and rollout of physical education, Thakurdas began considering launching a new scheme in rural schools built as part of the Cheap School Scheme in 1941. It involved maintaining detailed medical records (taking measurements of height, weight, chest, eyesight, and arm and leg muscles) of school children, and rewarding schools which showed periodic development as a start. It was designed as a useful first step in developing data and standards; but hardly solved the problem of poor physique amongst such students. The proposal recognized the need for more serious steps to address the main causes of the poor physical condition of children, including malnutrition, an indifference to questions of the physical development of children owing to ill-conceived notions of prestige, dignity, and manners. The scheme proposed further propaganda to change parents' views. At the same time, it proposed the training of students for citizenship.[72] It was aimed, therefore, at creating 'a sort of healthy consciousness' among India's citizens-to-be. The total expenditure in a district was estimated to be Rs. 2,300; from which some help was likely to be sourced from the government's funds for children's medical inspection.[73] Thakurdas's interest in promoting physical fitness among the Indian youth was hardly unique. It could be seen, one might argue, as part of a particular Hindu nationalism to counter the stereotypes, especially among Hindus and more so among the Marwaris, that they were weak, unfit, or effeminate.

*

Following the Poona Pact, elites' disciplinary gaze fell on to Dalits and backward classes across the country, albeit in narrow, reformist ways only. The All-India Anti-Untouchability League championed by G. D. Birla, Thakurdas, Ambalal Sarabhai, and Lala Shri Ram, for example, urgently began work on reforming the Dalit self, while maintaining its distance. The League's programme was designed around sponsoring their education, covering their hostel expenses, improving their economic conditions by establishing cooperative in 'their industries', ensuring their access to public services, etc.[74]

---

[72] Letter from L. R. Desai to Thakurdas dated 6 October 1941, file 207 (Pt. II), PT.

[73] Letter from Durlabhji Desai to Thakurdas dated 24 October 1941, file 207 (Pt. II), PT.

[74] From a booklet titled 'The All-India Anti-Untouchability League: Aims and Objects, Scheme of Propaganda and Uplift Work, Budget and Constitution', dated November 1932, file no. 121/1932, PT.

Disregarding the economic and social structures and practices and the historical denial of civic services to their localities, the League's proponents demanded that their bodies and neighbourhoods be cleaned first. Lest there be any doubt about elites' gaze on Dalits, the League mandated its workers to personally scrutinize and supervise Dalits' personal hygiene and cleanliness from time to time as part of its upliftment work. Thus, even as elites' philanthropy sought to enable access to particular forms and infrastructures of modernity, such as education, economic production, drinking water, etc., it left the caste system fully intact.

The cause of temperance was also folded into the national-modern development. Consumption was widely seen as a significant source of revenue for the provincial governments, and thus maintaining India's colonization.[75] To fight consumption, therefore, became part of Indian nationalism and its fight against colonialism. Such a move required first and foremost, though, the recasting of consumption as an alien problem, imposed from the outside. In a paper read at the 20th International Congress on Alcoholism at London, it was argued that 'all traditions and religions and social sentiment favour in India the abstention from all intoxicating drinks and drugs. Manu, Apastamba, Buddha and the Quran', it went on, were all unanimous in their condemnation of alcohol as evil. Marking India's difference from the West, it noted that 'while in the western countries, the ignorance of the masses with regard to the moral aspect of the problem, the interweaving of the drinking habit into the social life of the people, and the influence which the trade has in municipal and national politics and in the press combine to make prohibition impracticable, the conditions in India are very different, and favourable'. In India, though, alcoholism was widely seen to be evil; even where it was consumed, the paper argued, it was consumed in private or in segregated places. The paper blamed the imperial government for the existence of the liquor trade in the country as it was a crucial source of tax revenue for them—through manufacturing and import duties, and the sale of licenses to run liquor shops—and ultimately sustained its own costly administration. It noted that the government's *mala fide* intentions became clear when it rolled back its own temperance propaganda in the Madras Presidency.[76] According to

---

[75] According to *Abkari*, the quarterly journal of the Anglo-Indian Temperance Association, consumption accounted for nearly a quarter to a third of the revenue of the various provincial governments in India in 1927–28; from *Abkari*, no. 153, July 1928; file 64 (pt. I), PT.

[76] From a paper titled 'Survey of the Position in India Regarding Alcoholism', for the 20th International Congress on Alcoholism, London, 1934; from file 108/1931, PT.

Mukhtar Ahmed Ansari, the president of the Indian National Congress, for example, 'the evil of drink would not have spread so rapidly and extensively had the Government taken a sympathetic attitude towards those who were endeavouring to stop it'.[77]

Realizing its ruinous effects on 'home life and the race', women too had begun to call on the government to reduce the number of licensed shops and enforce rules about their early closing. Workers, both in urban and rural areas, were also being organized to fight for prohibition. Public health experts, too, voiced their concerns about consumption and disease. Prohibition, Dr. C. Muthu, chief physician of the Mendip Hills Sanatorium in England, submitted 'will be a great boon to India…bring[ing] about sobriety, health, and happiness to the many millions of India'.

Leading the fight for prohibition among Indian economic elites was Thakurdas.[78] In July 1927, he was approached by the Anglo-Indian Temperance Association in England to donate some money for its activities. In response to which, Thakurdas donated £10 and also persuaded his friend Ambalal Sarabhai of Ahmedabad to make a similar donation. The former was also invited to the all-India delegate conference of the Prohibition League of India.[79] Later, in December 1927, Thakurdas was invited to recommend names for a future president, possibly M. A. Jinnah (later Quaid-i-Azam of Pakistan). In a letter to Thakurdas, Herbert Anderson, then serving as honorary general secretary of the Prohibition League, wrote, 'I do not know him [Jinnah], and I do not think it is necessary to let any communal consideration come into the matter'.[80] Shortly after which Thakurdas received a further letter from Anderson suggesting that the officers wished that the former be elected its next president, and not Jinnah.[81]

Speaking before the Indian legislative assembly at the debate about the finance bill in 1928, Thakurdas argued, 'it is a disgrace to any Government that their budgets should depend upon such tainted money as money coming out of the degradation and deterioration of their people'. Contrasting the case for prohibition of alcohol with the imperial government's earlier decision to forego its revenue from the sale of opium to China, he added that it had been done 'not for the benefit of the sons of the soil, but for the benefit, sir, of the

---

[77] From *Abkari*, no. 153, July 1928; file 64 (pt. I), PT.
[78] Alongside Thakurdas, B. M. Birla served as the honorary treasurer of the League, while others like Walchand Hirachand made infrequent gifts; from correspondence sent to Thakurdas; file 108/1931, PT.
[79] Letters from Frederick Gruff to Thakurdas dated 27 July and 25 October 1927; file 64 (pt. III), PT.
[80] Letter from Anderson to Thakurdas dated 12 December 1927; file 64 (pt. II), PT.
[81] Letter from Anderson to Thakurdas dated 17 December 1927; file 64 (pt. II), PT.

Chinese, and even that benefit the Chinese did not get...I do not grudge, sir, any benefit which China may have got from this self-denial policy of the Government of India'. He invited the Government of India to work with other provincial governments to deal with the loss of revenue.[82]

That the prohibition movement was framed, clearly, as a development question can be gauged from Thakurdas's presidential remarks at the second biennial session of the Prohibition League. A summary of his remarks was published in the League's quarterly *Abkari*. Those who drink, Thakurdas said, were 'largely composed of those he preferred to call, not the depressed, but the oppressed classes and the Bhils and other aboriginal tribes. Hindus and Moslems do not follow their religious tenets if they drink'. Prohibition required, therefore, preventing the 'illiterate masses from having the temptation to drink thrust upon them as it is at present'.[83] Elsewhere, it was argued that prohibition was part of the Gandhian fight against poverty, which was seen to be India's greatest affliction. The promotion of charkha and khadi, boycott of foreign cloth, and abolition of drugs and drinks were part of the same battle: which involved reforming the masses. Prohibition, therefore, was 'being baked in the moral furnace of the Swaraj fight in India...The struggle against alcoholic drinks has became (*sic*) part and parcel of the fight for national freedom'.[84]

*

Post-colonialism, population control became an important area of elites' philanthropy from the 1950s to the 1970s, which was similarly subject to elites' disciplining gaze. The Tatas became one of its leading proponents in the country. According to Lala, then chairperson of the Tata Group and Tata Trusts, J. R. D. Tata had been interested in the problem of population control from as early as 1951. The problems of India's population, according to Tata, had hitherto been framed only in relation to food production. Instead, he exhorted India's post-colonial government to appoint a 'high-powered commission consisting of eminent scientists, economists and sociologists to investigate the problem in all its aspects'.[85] Characteristic of their philanthropic approach to invest in scientific research and training, the Tatas' initiated plans to fund a demographic research centre. In 1954, Tata and John

---

[82] From *Abkari*, no. 153, July 1928; file 64 (pt. I), PT.
[83] From the summary of Thakurdas's address on 19 February 1928; from file 64 (pt. I), PT.
[84] 'Survey of the Position in India Regarding Alcoholism', paper for the 20th International Congress on Alcoholism, London, 1934; from file 108/1931, PT.
[85] Lala, *Blue Mountain*, 309.

Matthai suggested that the central government and TISS collaborate to establish a School of Population Studies. It ultimately led to the formation of the Demographic Centre for Training and Research (henceforth DCTR) in July 1956 through a collaboration between the central government, SDTT, and the United Nations, and which later came to be known as the International Institute of Population Studies (IIPS).

I discuss it in detail here for two main reasons: firstly, it is emblematic of elites' efforts at governmentalization India's poor masses into post-colonial citizenry—an initial step of which was defining 'populations' that would subsequently become the subjects of social welfare and other anti-poverty interventions, in the name of its development. Unlike the abstract, normative conceptualization of citizenship, populations, according to Chatterjee, are 'identifiable, classifiable, and describable by empirical or behavioral criteria and are amenable to statistical techniques such as censuses and statistical surveys'. It makes available to governments—and even business elites, I would argue—'a set of rationally manipulable instruments for reaching large sections of inhabitants of the country as the targets of their "policies"'.[86] Unlike some of the government-mandated policies for controlling India's population that involved coercion, though, elites' efforts at governmentalization were designed around research and education. Secondly, elites' interest in population control relied both on the transformative promise of science and their pedagogic ambition—themes that I go on to develop further in the following two chapters.

The establishment of DCTR began with demographer Frank W. Notestein's letter along with a three-page note sent to the then health minister in the Government of India, Rajkumari Amrit Kaur in 1955. Casting population as a development problem, Notestein argued that 'the slower rate of population growth would assist the program of economic development in achieving its ultimate goals, i.e., relief from crushing poverty and sustained additional gains in the health of our populations'. He outlined a 'program of instruction in the simplest kind of physiology of reproduction' to educate the people on the means of birth control, before making the case for scientific research and training on the subject.

Premised on the deficiencies of scientific research and training institutions in the country as a primary cause of India's development, Notestein cited the lack of 'well-trained and experienced demographers' in the country, lack of detailed study particularly for the purposes of social and economic planning,

---

[86] Chatterjee, *Politics of Governed*, 34.

and the need for evidence-based research on the effectiveness of various methods of family planning, and suggested the establishment of a leading research and training centre in Bombay. He proposed founding a semi-autonomous institute affiliated to a university thus providing flexibility while allowing DCTR to benefit from the pre-existing facilities at the affiliated university. It was proposed as a multi-disciplinary institution with expertise drawn from public health, economics, sociology and social psychology, statistics and could also draw on the affiliated university for ancillary subjects such as mathematics and biology.[87]

An undated and modified proposal from the same period suggested that DCTR partner institutionally with the School of Economics and Sociology at University of Bombay, TISS, and the Human Variation Unit at the Indian Cancer Research Centre (ICRC). It was also proposed that DCTR establish a cooperative exchange with an American university, with scientific research focused on factors which affected population trends, and the social and economic consequences of population change.[88] It was expected to be financed using funds from the central government in India, the Tata Trusts, and the United Nations. While SRTT was expected to make a gift of more than two acres of its land, SDTT promised to contribute Rs. 125,000 over five years. The central government was asked to provide Rs. 570,000 towards capital expenditure, and Rs. 572,000 towards recurring expenditure. UNDP was expected to bear costs involved in bringing non-Indian experts, fellows, students, consultants, and overseas travel facilities for staff members.[89]

Plans for the centre were further developed by Dr. K. C. K. E. Raja who later served as its founding director. His eight-page note with additional appendices is instructive in its constitution of demography as an episteme, which he argued was crucial to the country's modernization. Breaking away from existing higher education institutes and their practices, Raja proposed establishing an independent centre with affiliation to a selected university, since 'a considerable measure of freedom is desirable, and which may not be available under the rules and regulations of a university'. Further challenging

---

[87] Letter from Frank W. Notestein to Rajkumari Amrit Kaur dated 5 August 1955; file no. 187/DTT/PHIL/IIPS/MIS/1, TCA.

[88] From a note titled 'Suggested Modifications in the "Proposal for a Co-operative Unit for Demographic Studies in Bombay"'; file no. 187/DTT/PHIL/IIPS/MIS/1, TCA.

[89] From an internal note of SDTT dated 23 May 1956 by R. Choksi. However, a letter dated 4 February 1957 from John Matthai to Amrit Kaur, minister of health, Government of India reveals that the expenses had been under-estimated, and the central government was asked to cover the shortfall in estimates, while keeping the contribution of SDTT the same; file no. 187/DTT/PHIL/IIPS/MIS/1, TCA.

'The tendency of modern education in India and elsewhere is to pour so much factual knowledge into the student as to make him (…) a passive agent for the assimilation of such information', Raja proposed that the Centre develop the powers of 'observation, initiative, independent thought, and curiosity' among its students and staff. The curriculum was expected to be a combination of economics, sociology, statistics, demographic analysis, genetics, and the physiology of reproduction; along with field work in rural and urban areas, and instruction in the use of the library and the development of 'powers of observation and of critical thinking'. Further distinguishing itself from India's existing institutes of modern education and training, the centre proposed using the 'group discussion method' pioneered in the case of medical teaching in London, and doing away with formal assessments, terminal or ongoing, and focus instead on thoroughgoing, non-intrusive assessment by instructors.[90]

Raja also proposed a comparative research programme involving studying demography in Bombay City, a rural area which was 'essentially rural in character and mainly uninfluenced by urbanization tendencies', and a further rural area, which 'although rural in character [was] subject to urban influences'. He proposed researching 'fertility, mortality, migration, employment and socio-economic conditions' in all three locations for comparative insights. Setting out demography as a development issue, Raja's proposal argued that:

> A planned programme of utilization of land, urban and rural, should form, it is considered, part of the social objective of the community towards creating improved conditions of life. Can smaller townships dispersed over the countryside facilitate a more satisfactory spatial distribution of the population and can these townships be linked, in their economy, with those of the larger towns and of the rural areas in a manner designed to promote a rise in employment and improved industrial and agricultural production, eliminating at the same time the squalor and dreadful living conditions which uncontrolled urbanisation and growth of industry tend to produce?

Worryingly, Raja's proposal also planned to 'take steps to measure the distribution of intelligence among the people, particularly the children, as well as of certain defects and disorders known to be heritable'. 'Unless a picture of

---

[90] From a note written by K. C. K. E. Raja with the subject line: 'Certain Suggestions for the Preparation of Teaching and Research Programmes for the Demographic Centre'; from file no. 187/ DTT/PHIL/IIPS/MIS/1, TCA.

existing conditions is built up', he added, 'it will be difficult to ascertain, through later investigation, in what direction the country is tending to develop in these matters of vital importance'.[91] Palimpsestic in its imaginings of the modern, as much as the Centre eschewed India's pre-existing institutions of modern education such as the University of Bombay and the Gokhale Institute and their methods of teaching, certification, and research, it also sought to imagine modernity, development, and its spatializations anew. Hoping to collect data on a whole range of subjects from fertility to marriages and maladjustments, distribution of intelligence, to migration and the socio-economic conditions of India's masses—both rural and urban—the Centre constituted a significant first step in elite imaginings' of 'population'.

The Tatas' interest in the problem of population, however, was not limited to establishment of DCTR. At a board meeting of SDTT in 1965, J. R. D. Tata, in his capacity as the Trust's chairperson, raised the problem of population control and its centrality to India's development. He urged the trustees to launch a medical research programme on fertility-inhibiting drugs, starting with a systematic analysis of the present state of knowledge on the subject in the country. Tata raised the problem of population again in the next meeting, suggesting that the Trust actively seek collaboration on the subject with interested institutions.[92]

Tata's efforts at population control, thus, constituted a significant intermediate step in the translation of India's masses into its citizenry. Knowing population—through detailed demographic, and comparative, surveys such as those proposed for DCTR above—and naming and labelling them, together became key to establishing a modern mode of governing which was not based on questions of politics, but of administrative policy, and was constitutive of the political society in the postcolonial world.[93] Although Chatterjee attributes political society to the realm of politics—where the relationship between post-independence nation-state and its poor citizens are mediated—I would argue that elites' and their philanthropy were similarly involved in the making of India's 'population'.

*

---

[91] From a note written by K. C. K. E. Raja with the subject line: 'Certain Suggestions for the Preparation of Teaching and Research Programmes for the Demographic Centre'; from file no. 187/ DTT/PHIL/IIPS/MIS/1, TCA.

[92] Minutes, 120th Meeting of the Board of Trustees, SDTT, dated 21 January 1965. File no. 637/ SDTT BO Meetings, 1932–2005, TCA.

[93] Chatterjee, *Politics of Governed*, 34–41.

In addition to disciplining the minds, bodies including reproduction, and habits of India's poor masses, elites' imagining of prospective citizenry was the production of new, 'modern', skilled, and scientifically trained workers and their socio-spatial relationships. What such imaginings looked like, though, depended on elites' economic visions. These visions vacillated between Gandhian rejections of mechanization and large-scale industrialization to Nehruvian 'high modernity' with its emphasis on industry, science, and technology in different sectors of the Indian economy. Instead of casting them as for and against modernity, one useful way of characterizing different economic visions for twentieth-century India would be through the interplay of modernizing and localizing forces. By modernization of the economy, here, I do not imply simply the movement from subsistence to primitive accumulation and further on to industrialization but the turn to modern technology, forms of economic organization, management control and supervision, and production processes. Conversely, localization should not be understood as the opposite of modernization as it was not simply a rejection of modern technology or processes but similarly crafted around thoroughly modern tropes and characteristics including, inter alia, the emergence of the individual producer, the decline of collective production, as well as modern notions of self-reliance. It also drew, but at a very different scale, from modern technology, processes, and production and organizing.

Notwithstanding their markedly different relationship with and scale of modernity, both forces of modernization and localization were animated by the impulse to counter economic dependency and build self-sufficiency, post-colonialism. This indigenization of industry has almost always been folded into the national-modern in particular ways: on the one hand was the revivalist logic of recovering India's rightful place in the global order; on the other, indigenization was also impelled by the modernist logic of disjuncture and departure from the stagnant, tradition-bound, inefficient industry in the country. Either version of indigenization required, however, new kinds of skilled and disciplined workers and managers; in the making and training of whom the Indian economic elite gave generously to found such institutions across the country.

Jamsetji N. Tata's industry and philanthropy, for example, were committed to—using the all too familiar developmental trope—*catch-up* with the West.[94]

---

[94] The West, Dube contends, is both bloated and reified, against which the state of modernity in the so-called Third World is 'assiduously plotted', including one might argue in development; see Dube, 'Enchantments of Modernity', 731–2.

India, he believed, was almost a century behind the West, at least on the linear, modern, temporal path of development. Its economic system was 'medieval, machinery scarce, labour suspicious, ignorant and poor in quality, the methods of transport were primitive and the [colonial] Government had scant interest in encouraging Indian industries.'[95] Founding the Empress Mills in 1877 in Nagpur, Tata also laid out his vision for their industrial workers—to 'house their employees in decent quarters, and leased a plot of land for the purpose'. Their attempts, though, did not bear fruit as the 'men preferred to reside in their own huts and to choose their own localities. *They reverted to a primitive social order* (sic), joining their companions of the same caste, or living with their relatives and friends'. Undeterred, Tata continued with his efforts to 'teach his men the value of regular labour and improve the conditions of factory life'.[96] If not outside, Tata turned his attention to the factory floor where the mill was equipped with the necessary ventilation, regulating humidity on the shop floor, launching provident fund and pension schemes for the workers, and setting up crèches for the children of women workers, and primary education for boys.

Tata's modernizing vision of industrial workers came together, in detail and at scale, in the industrial township of Jamshedpur, named in his honour. He instructed his son Dorabji in 1902: 'Be sure to lay wide streets planted with shady trees, every other of a quick-growing variety'. 'Be sure that there is plenty of space for lawns and gardens,' he added, and 'reserve large areas for football, hockey and parks. Earmark areas for Hindu temples, Mohammedan mosques, and Christian churches'.[97] In 1916, the Tatas invited L. T. Hobhouse, E. J. Urwick, Sidney J. Webb and his wife Beatrice Webb of the Fabian Society, then working at the London School of Economics, to constitute a committee to 'benchmark the development of the town and conditions for work against the highest possible standards'. Asked to develop a 'programme on scientific lines', Hobhouse et al.'s suggestions were perceived important to realizing the Tatas' visions of an industrial township and its society, including in dismantling the prevalent social order through the inter-mingling of races, castes, and religions, instead of segregation.[98]

---

[95] From file no. 181/DTT/PHIL/MIS/3, TCA.

[96] Harris, *Tata: A Chronicle*, 34; italicized for emphasis.

[97] 'The Quotable Jamsetji Tata', Tata Group, accessed 12 November 2014, http://www.tata.com/aboutus/articlesinside/The-quotable-Jamsetji-Tata.

[98] Mukherjee, *Century of Trust*, 62.

It resulted in order—both in society and the township's infrastructure where dwellings, roads, water supply, drainage, lighting, schools, hospitals, burial-grounds, etc. were all 'done upon the most modern lines'. Even though the workers initially lived in *chawls*, they were soon moved into better housing facilities.[99] To still others, the town 'seemed a model for all great industrial enterprises, not only in India, but in any part of the world where land is easily obtained'. 'There was a bazaar containing both European and Indian shops', a visitor noted and 'institutes had been provided for both European and Indian workmen. A court-house, a post and telegraph office, and a police station were among the adjuncts of *this extremely modern town*'.[100] Noting the apparent success of the Tatas' programme of spatial and social re-organization of India's urban areas, Elwin Verrier noted that Jamshedpur was one of the few parts of India unaffected by violence during the Partition riots. The social divisions of caste and religion were, according to Elwin, no longer relevant in Jamshedpur. 'The working men and women, especially away from their homes', he reasoned, were 'no longer conscious of caste differences'. The mason-training scheme, for example, was 'thrown open to everyone and a number of boys from the so-called higher castes work side by side with the traditional masons.' And that even though 'in the Company's own canteens in the early days, there were separate kitchens for Hindus and Muslims. But many years ago it was decided (...) to abolish them'. Naively optimistic, Elwin noted that 'everyone look[ed] for a golden life of happiness and opportunity in the iron town of Jamshedpur'.[101]

*

In stark contrast to the Tatas' modernizing impulse, Bajaj focused his attention on championing the localization of Indian industry. In the 1920s, for example, he launched a nationwide training programme for the production and distribution of khadi to scale up the production of hand-spun and hand-woven cotton and wool in the country. Hoping to move Gandhi's economic programme past its leader-centricism, Bajaj suggested it was time for the ordinary Congress workers to assume leadership of the programme.[102] With a view to building grassroots leadership and widening the appeal of khadi and boosting its consumption and to address its quality, Bajaj suggested recruiting six hundred 'travelling instructors', each of whom were expected to train thirty workers each and cover two villages every month. It was expected that

---

[99]   Harris, *Tata: A Chronicle*, 210.
[100]   Cited from Mukherjee, *Century of Trust*, 61–2; italicized for emphasis.
[101]   Elwin, *Tata Steel*, 103.
[102]   Bajaj's letter dated 15 December 1925; Correspondence: Gandhi, M. K., JB (1st inst.).

the instructors would be paid a monthly salary of Rs. 30 each. Bajaj also suggested recruiting sellers, on commission, to increase their market reach and create an appropriate incentive structure for them.[103]

He was also interested in promoting trade unionism among nationalist-minded workers by combining training with Gandhian disciplining of the self. As part of which the Ahmedabad-based Textile Labour Association prepared a scheme for training workers to take up executive positions within trade unions of the country in 1929. Gulzarilal Nanda, secretary of the Textile Labour Association suggested a two-tier training programme aimed at both senior and junior positions within trade unions, with no fee charged. Submitted to Jamnalal Bajaj, the scheme proposed running a 6–12-month-long programme that would have combined studies with practical work. Prospective trainees needed to practice abstinence, regularly weave khadi, believe in *ahimsa*, and the removal of untouchability. Training would have covered studies in subjects as wide-ranging as economic and social theory, labour legislation and movement, trade unionism, and working conditions, as well as social service, personal hygiene, propaganda, alcoholism, and indebtedness. Field work, on the other hand, was expected to cover areas such as complaints and case work, data compilation, first aid, and temperance work, mobile libraries, and promoting physical exercise among communities.[104]

Bajaj's attempts at encouraging workers to adopt khadi was also supported by the Birlas, albeit on a smaller scale. Following the demise of his wife, Jugal Kishore Birla, for example, made a number of donations towards such activities. As war-time shortages loomed in 1941, he worried about the paucity of cloth in the country. In a letter to Bajaj, he called for further work to promote the charkha, both to counter shortages and to make possible the improving weavers' and spinners' earnings. He donated Rs. 10,000/- to the Charkha Sangh for promotional work in the Kulu and Kangra Valleys. Jugal Kishore Birla donated a further Rs. 50,000 to the Charkha Sangh. Of this, nearly half was to be spent in his native Pilani, while the remainder, he suggested, should be earmarked for the distribution of charkhas in the hilly villages in the Kangra. 'The Rajputs, Brahmins, and Dalits of the region', he wrote 'were extremely lazy and useless'.[105]

*

---

[103] Nanda, *In Gandhi's Footsteps*, 107–8.
[104] Scheme from Textile Labour Association submitted to Jamnalal Bajaj, cover letter dated 18 October 1929; from Correspondence: Nanda, Gulzarilal, JB (1st inst.).
[105] Jugal Kishore Birla's letter to Bajaj dated 4 December 1941; Correspondence: Birla, Jugal Kishore, JB (1st inst.).

Even as Bajaj's imaginary of a modern Indian worker remained moored to the Gandhian 'constructive programme', industrialists such as Birla and Thakurdas committed themselves to the simultaneous pursuit of localization via indigenization, and to a lesser extent modernization of economic activity. In so doing, they launched vocational training programmes for adolescents and youth studying at their educational institutions, discussed previously. Thakurdas, for example, sponsored vocational training facilities in a number of schools supported by him. At Godsamba, for example, he funded pro-grammes for the teaching of weaving, carpentry, tailoring, gardening, etc. to the children and it was developed as a model vocational training school.[106]

Similarly, at the Birla College, Pande—building on his earlier efforts at BHU—combined craft programmes with training for the physical and intellectual development of the students. Initially introduced as an optional subject in 1931, craft was soon made compulsory. By 1944, book-binding, carpentry, carpet-making, hand-spinning, leather-work, paper-making, printing and dyeing, and tailoring were taught at the Birlas' educational insti-tutions. Each student was expected to spend up to three periods each week working on a craft to develop their 'intelligence, concentration, and observa-tion, in ways untouched by books and blackboards', strengthening their brain–muscle coordination and promoting respect for manual labour among the boys. Discussing its difference from the Gandhian approach of encouraging people to take up khadi-work as a means of becoming self-reliant—both individually and collectively as a community—and generating surplus as a way out of their poverty, the teaching of craft work at Birlas' educational institutions was, Hennessy notes, impelled by a pedagogic logic. In addition to learning the craft itself, students studied markets, conditions of production and consumption, and developed their knowledge of running a commercial venture by selling their wares in local markets. Training in crafts, therefore, was seen as complementary to academic teaching. Not only did it open an avenue for future work, but it was also believed to help combat the caste-linked stigmatization of manual labour as menial or undignified. Boys of the Thakur caste, though, were reluctant to participate and sought exemption.

Craft-based training was soon extended to various village schools run by the Trust. However, the use of such instruction was soon found to be unfeas-ible. At the Basic School, which was meant to be an exemplar of such an edu-cation, students found themselves reduced to 'objects of a cranky experiment,

---

[106] Letter from G. M. Desai to Thakurdas dated 2 February 1938, file 207 (Pt. I), PT.

compelled to be "different", and many grumbled that they were being exploited rather than educated'. The school itself was closed down shortly after.[107]

Like Birlas, the Godrej group has also been running the Udayachal schools in Bombay since 1955. The schools were founded on the belief that the 'one main cause of our backwardness is ignorance' and that 'without good basic education, people cannot become self-reliant'. To make people self-reliant and overcome India's backwardness, Godrej funded education as 'one of the main pillars of nation-building'. In addition to conventional school education, the schools also helped their students 'achieve dexterity in the use of hands'. They imparted training in skills such as carpentry, smithy, embroidery, and sewing as well as teaching nature conservation and population control. All this was aimed at transforming their students from 'a Maharashtrian girl to an Indian girl'.[108]

*

With independence and the waning influence of a Gandhian formulation of modern economy and workers, the focus shifted—far more intensively than before—on the industrial worker in urban towns and cities across the country. Birla, for example, launched numerous relief operations for refugee workers from across the border in the aftermath of the Partition. In addition to making his companies' resources available for evacuation, relief, and rehabilitation—the Birla companies provided their cars for the evacuation of refugees from Western Punjab, his Bharat Airways undertook evacuation flights, and some of his staff worked in an honorary capacity for the Indian government— Birla was also involved in an advisory capacity with the newly constituted Ministry of Relief and Rehabilitation. Charged with helping the government prepare long-term plans for economic rehabilitation of incoming refugees, he focused his attention on generating opportunities for gainful employment; the lack of which, he believed, would have led to 'bitterness and excited the people to retaliate'. In order to solve the problem of their employment, Birla suggested undertaking an economic census in the country to ascertain industries facing labour scarcities and matching in-coming refugees to specific industries across the country. For unskilled workers, he recommended, launching large public works such as dams in order to create employment for them.[109]

---

[107] Hennessey, *India Democracy and Education*, 68, 133–6.
[108] Accession no. PER15-15-1-1, Godrej Archives, Mumbai (henceforth GA).
[109] Kudaisya, *G. D. Birla*, 243–4.

Not distant from the Cold War anxieties around disgruntled unemployed youth in the country and unencumbered from Gandhian ruralism, Birla intensified calls for industrialization and vocational training to help India develop. Counting India's achievements towards its self-sufficiency during his tour of the United States in 1954, he noted: 'Food production was up by 5 million tons and in 1954 it might reach the planners' target of 7 million tons. It was mostly the fruit of small and big irrigation projects, reclamation of land, fertilisers and better methods of cultivation'. Once major projects had been completed, Birla hoped 'there would be much more food and other products like cotton and jute etc'. Noting favourable moves towards self-sufficiency in the production of cotton, jute, and cement, among others, there had been significant jumps in production. India's labour, he added, 'was working hard and relations between employers and employees were fairly satisfactory'. Despite its achievements, the job was far from complete. 'Hundreds of thousands of young men', Birla argued, 'were coming out of universities. They needed employments (sic)—not jobs but occupation. Unless we could divert 25 per cent of the population from field to secondary and tertiary professions, we could have no appreciable effect on the standard of living'. Land, he concluded, could not sustain three-quarters of the country's population.[110]

Although prior efforts at training India's workforce were framed around logics of self-sufficiency and obviating the socio-spatial relations within which economic production was embedded, the attention on skilling, upskilling, and reskilling India's youth, especially those from rural and semi-urban towns and cities across the country, picked up momentum come neoliberalism, on which more next. The interest in funding programmes to train and re-train workers across the country was based, paradoxically, on the fallout of neoliberalism itself.

To Market-ready Citizens

At the turn of the twenty-first century, there was growing recognition within the Tata Trusts of the impact of neoliberal economic policies on the poor: peasants, artisans, workers, and entrepreneurs. At the turn of the twenty-first century, SDTT's biennial report noted that neoliberal globalization had 'taken

---

[110] Birla's letter to Mathai dated 11 September 1954; file 3, 1043.

its toll on farmers, artisans and small entrepreneurs in our country. One increasingly reads about incidents', it went on, about the 'farmers from Jallandhar and Sangroor having to throw away much of their produce for want of reasonable prices, suicides by farmers in Punjab and Maharashtra, and crises in the handloom sector prompting weavers to commit suicide'. Instead of resisting neoliberal globalizing capitalism given its aftermath, the Tata Trusts (and others too)—and not unexpectedly—both expanded and intensified their investment among India's poor, aimed at enabling their access and capability to participate in the neoliberal markets. They focused on building the '*competence* of the people to *manage* their assets and resources in a sustainable way and to develop *innovative* systems and structures to cope with the increasingly *competitive* world'. It focused, therefore, on programmes around credit provision, capacity building of self-help groups, conducting experiments for improving agricultural practice, promotion of non-farm activities, developing innovative marketing strategies, and vocational training.[111]

To illustrate the Tata Trusts' approach to manufacture market-ready citizens, I cite the example of their grant-making for the Sukhi Baliraja Initiative (SBI henceforth).[112] Established jointly by SDTT and SRTT in 2007–08, SBI was designed to address the increasing agrarian distress and the growing instances of farmer suicides in Vidarbha, Maharashtra.[113] It proposed:

a holistic livelihood promotion strategy for the region with the key objective of reducing distress among the farming community and enhancing livelihoods. The strategy would revolve around promoting better livelihood options for the rural communities in the region, through various thematic focus interventions (...) The overall goal of the SBI is development of sustainable and diversified livelihoods for the households/families to reduce agrarian distress and allowing households to face production and market risks without falling back into poverty.[114]

---

[111] Biennial Report. SDTT. 2000–02. File no. 182/SDTT/2000–02, TCA; italicized for emphasis.

[112] Roughly translated into a 'prosperous farmer'.

[113] For a discussion on the issue of farmers' suicide, including causes, responses of the state, and their limitations, see Government of India, 'Fact Finding Report'. For further discussion on the topic, see Mishra, 'Farmers' Suicides', 1538–45; Mohanty and Shroff, 'Maharashtra', 5599–606; Suri, 'Political Economy', 1523–9.

[114] 'Sukhi Baliraja Initiative', Sir Ratan Tata Trust, accessed 6 March 2015, http://www.srtt.org/institutional_grants/rural_livelihoods_communities/sbi.htm.

In so doing, it hoped to address the root causes of farmers' suicide, which according to SBI were caused by high input costs and reduction in farm productivity; indebtedness to money lenders; and heavy investments in social ceremonies, which further exacerbated the farmers' indebtedness. SBI designed its programmes around the deployment of technology for enhancing productivity and the reduction of input costs of farming; risk diversification at the household level by encouraging off-farm and non-farm livelihoods; and access to institutionalized microfinance. It chose to dovetail its efforts with ongoing programmes being implemented by the state government in Maharashtra and other multi-lateral aid institutions, including the International Fund for Agricultural Development. Expectedly so, SBI supports the 'promotion of non-farm enterprises such as backyard poultry, goatery, petty shop, services such as repairs, retailing, tailoring, etc. for landless or marginal farmers'. Arguing in favour of developing a comprehensive procurement supply chain as part of *business development* in agriculture, it hoped to 'ensure reduction in cost of production by nearly 30–40 per cent because of bulk procurement on favourable terms with private companies such as Arvind Mills, Noble, Tata Chemicals, etc'.[115] Its unequivocal focus, therefore, has been to support the integration of the farmers with the market—the predominant sphere of neoliberal development—where citizenship is mediated.[116]

Hoping to illustrate the success of its strategy, SRTT's annual report from 2011–12 showcases the story of a local farmer, Gianchand Shinde. 'Driving past the stark landscape of Vidarbha', it reports, 'we stop at the wayside *dhaaba* for a cuppa. A diminutive turbaned figure squatting on the charpoy looking pensively at the cloudless sky. "Hey…this man seems to have a lot on his mind; must be one of those distressed farmers that we read about the other day" exclaims the lone lady in our group'. Shinde's cotton and red gram crops, we are told, were affected by drought. The lack of warehousing facilities meant that he could not hold onto his produce in the hope of accessing a better price by selling later. As a result of SBI's intervention, the farmers' were organized into a producer company; when 'Lady Luck smiled. Tata Chemicals Limited (TCL) collaborated with ACSPCL [farmers' producer company] to market the red gram produced by the members under its "Grow More Pulse" programme'. Since TCL offered a better price than what was available in the local

---

[115] SRTT, 'Agrarian Sustainability through Action Research (AGRASAR) in Vidarbha', accessed 13 February 2013, http://srtt.org/institutional_grants/rural_livelihoods_communities/cini_indian_grameen_services_aug08.htm.

[116] For a further discussion on neoliberal development's obsession with markets and market-led change, see Brown, *Edgework*, 40–4 for a general overview.

market, the farmers 'wisely' sold to them. Titled 'Savvy Rural Market Saves the Day', Shinde's story, presented as a boxed item lest we miss it, is presented as a 'win–win situation for both' (TCL and farmers' producer companies).[117]

Instructively, though, the approach and programmes designed at SBI completely sidelined structural causes of agrarian distress in the region including farmers' vulnerability to market prices, and the failure of the state's minimum procurement price support mechanism and the monopoly cotton procurement scheme, which were even accepted in central government's own reports.[118] In Shinde's story, for example, there is little attempt at challenging the governmental policy of dismantling the procurement price; even corruption that plagued the irrigation projects in the region is disregarded. The increasing volatility within a de-regulated market is no longer deemed problematic. Instead, it is seen as an opportunity that could be exploited through better warehousing facilities and information regarding prices in various local markets. The agrarian distress in Vidarbha is framed, primarily then, in terms of the lack of access to the market, despite evidence to the contrary. Moving away from supporting any large-scale social organization of farmers—despite the rich and somewhat successful history of peasants' political mobilization to protect their interests in areas such as Vidarbha, historically that have since witnessed farmers' suicides—SBI's programmes are designed around farmers' integration with the market in the hope that it will help them draw greater returns.[119] Discounting the many failures of the market and governance that caused agrarian distress in the first place, its solution is to propagate coordination between a Tata company, a non-governmental organization supported through the Tatas' philanthropy, and a farmers' producer company.

Markets, therefore, become the foremost realm of national-modern development in the twenty-first century, with philanthropy directed at building infrastructure, informational or physical, and farmers' capabilities to access it. Even as state withdrawal goes completely unchallenged, the primary burden of elites' philanthropy, then, become pedagogic—an idea I explore in greater detail in chapter 5. Its ultimate ambition, then, I would suggest is to manufacture market-ready citizenry.

*

[117] SRTT, Annual Report, 2011–12, 20. The word *dhaaba* refers to inexpensive restaurants that dot the highways in the country.

[118] See Government of India, 'Fact Finding Report'; Mishra, 'Farmers' Suicides', 1538–45.

[119] Suri, 'Political Economy', 1526–8.

Different from earlier efforts where the focus was on building local, indigenous markets collectively, contemporary development's emphasis on market-ready citizens is organized around neoliberal globalization's characteristic individualizing tendencies. Related to Tata's meritorious individual from the early twentieth century, the individual self emerges, once more, as the central subject and site of development. The crucial difference, though, is that while Tata's efforts a century ago were directed at the 'best and most gifted', neoliberal development championed by twenty-first-century philanthropy promises opportunities to one and all, provided they are willing. In the late 1990s, SRTT launched a new public initiatives theme, following its first widely organized strategic planning exercise since the expansion of its resources from the early 1990s onwards. It offered financial grants to 'enable women and men to attempt to respond to the needs of the changing society through *individual endeavour*'.[120]

Directing attention away from community-based, community-led development, the Tata Trusts began to invest heavily in building individual—not collective—capacities to participate in the market. Skill-building for individual citizens has become an important part of the Tata Trusts' development programmes, examples of which can be found across the various development themes they support. SRTT's Arts and Culture initiative, for example, that hitherto committed itself to the promotion of art and culture in public life in the country was now re-cast into a developmental problem of livelihood and employment of individual artists, with work on promotion and institutionalization of arts in the country pushed into the background. By 2018, the initiative focused on grant-making for (a) sustaining livelihoods in the performing arts; (b) crafts-based livelihood initiatives; (c) community media and livelihood; and (d) conservation and digitization. Likewise, the Youth and Civil Society initiative (with which I was involved closely from 2008 to 2012), that primarily focused on enhancing the public participation of young people and their associations in community-development programmes, was also reorganized. It was re-orientated towards 'enhancing the quality of life of youth, particularly from marginalized socio-economic backgrounds, by

[120] Annual Report, SRTT. 1997–98. File no. 213/SRTT/1997–98, TCA; italicized for emphasis. It is also instructive to note here that 'women' precedes 'men'. This, one could argue, was more the desire to be politically correct than a substantive commitment to women's issues, of which I found little evidence during the course of my association with the Tata Trusts, and is also evidenced from the lack of any firm commitment to women's issues in any corporate communication of the Tatas' philanthropy.

investing in their capacity building to access meaningful livelihoods, thereby augmenting incomes'.[121]

While some might see such investment for its utilitarian value, such a restrictive focus on skill-building *as* development is problematic. Not only does it marginalize certain modes of development such as activism, advocacy, and research; it also prioritizes individual-centric development over investment in communities and collectives. The social, cultural, and political practices and expressions of citizenship thus become subservient to the economic contributions of individuals. Most significantly, though, such approaches do little to challenge the structural causes of poverty and inequality; instead they re-cast development and poverty into a simplistic deficit of individual capacities that must somehow be overcome, to develop links between the poor and markets. This focus is repeated in a number of different livelihood sectors, supported by the Tata Trusts.[122] It works, ultimately, to naturalize markets—making them both inevitable and irreversible to development in the country.

---

[121] SRTT, 'Annual Report, 2011–12', 10, 11; accessed 6 April 2014, http://srtt.org/downloads/annual/AnnualReport2011-12.pdf.

[122] For example, according to the SDTT's annual report from 2002–03, the 'Trust has consciously supported the creation of environment conducive for the rural poor to develop linkages with the private market for sale of products as well as for buying affordable technologies'; from file no. 182/SDTT/2002–03, TCA.

4

Making Science Indian

Jamsetji N. Tata's biographer described him as the 'man who saw tomorrow'.[1] The 'tomorrow' that Tata imagined for India, as it stood on the cusp of the twentieth century, was to be modelled on the West. It emerged, Subbarayappa wrote, from Tata's extensive travels to Canada, England, France, Germany, and the United States, where his 'alert and receptive mind perceived the social transformation that was rapidly taking place in the West' as a result of its 'multi-level industrialization, higher education and scientific research'. 'Science and its methods,' Tata found, 'were changing the human mind in the West. Alongside, machines of diverse structures and intents were becoming subservient to man for enriching his material well-being'. Tata, we are told, was increasingly convinced that the transformation sweeping the West was based on a 'solid foundation of education of the highest quality. And the West was progressing fast in this direction too'.[2]

Tata's belief in the potential and significance of science and technology, and higher education more generally, for transforming 'material well-being' echoed the growing contemporary belief in many Indians educated in the English language from the late nineteenth century. Their belief and efforts led to the production of what the historian Ross Bassett termed the 'technological Indian', who deemed mechanization necessary for 'eradicating the undesirable and establishing the desirable in society'.[3]

Extending and building on Bassett's argument, I argue that India's economic elites not only generously endowed training institutions on which India's future technological development could be built; but also contributed to the development of scientific research capabilities in the country. The gift-making was impelled, I further argue, primarily by the perceived need to overcome the historical deficiencies—institutionally and intellectually—of modern science and technology in the country. Such institutions remained, however, imbricated in particular national-modern logics of self-reliance and

---

[1] Lala, *Love of India*, xiii.   [2] Subbarayappa, *Pursuit of Excellence*, 17–18.
[3] Speech by M. M. Kunte, the headmaster of Poona High School, on 30 May 1884; cited from Bassett, *The Technological Indian*, 1–2.

Philanthropy and the Development of Modern India: In the Name of Nation. Arun Kumar, Oxford University Press.
© Arun Kumar 2021. DOI: 10.1093/oso/9780198868637.003.0004

sovereignty. Despite their nationalist—and later national—character, elites ensured that the institutes themselves remained insulated from governmental control and interference; and were, paradoxically so, international-facing, thus enabling India and Indian scientists to assume their place in the global scientific research community.

Overcoming Deficits

Jamsetji Tata's *fin de siècle* philanthropic vision sought to break away from nineteenth-century alms-giving. Recognizing the 'importance of the Western type of education and of English as the medium of instruction,'[4] he turned his attention to 'new ideas', directed 'towards higher education and the spread of education'. 'Men began to recognise', J. R. D. Tata wrote about the changing focus of Jamsetji Tata's philanthropy, 'the importance of science and engineering for answering the needs of a rapidly changing world. The new philanthropy turned in every conceivable direction to pioneer schemes of human welfare and to increase human knowledge'.[5] In addition to funding the higher education of Indians abroad as part of the J. N. Tata Endowment Fund discussed previously, Tata's most ambitious gift to scientific development came in the form of the Indian Institute of Science (IISc), later established in Bangalore.

In 1896, Tata left a third of his personal wealth for the 'foundation of an indigenous University...upon as broad as institutions of a like nature which have been founded through the munificence of private gentlemen in Europe and America to the intent that such University may become the means along with similar others of meeting the growing educational and scientific needs of this country'.[6] He recruited Burjorji Padshah to prepare an initial proposal. Padshah was 'sent all over the world--no, not Africa and South America, for I believe there could have been no institutes of science at that in those countries which J. N. Tata would have cared to investigate'. Padshah toured institutions of scientific research and teaching in 'England, Germany, France, Belgium, Switzerland (and probably Australia, Japan, Java, and the United States and other European countries)' over an eighteen-month period to prepare a detailed plan for Tata's university.[7] In an interview in 1899, Tata

[4] Subbarayappa, *Pursuit of Excellence*, 19; also see Harris, *Tata: A Chronicle*, 121.
[5] From J. R. D. Tata's 'Foreword' in Harris, *Tata: A Chronicle*, 2nd ed., xi.
[6] Tata's will dated 16 December 1896, cited from Subbarayappa, *Pursuit of Excellence*, 319–30.
[7] Sebaly, 'Tatas and University Reform', 119.

acknowledged that the Johns Hopkins University in Baltimore, United States, was a major source of inspiration for his proposed Institute. In the US press, it was hailed as 'another illustration of the quiet working of American influence and example in the Orient'.[8]

With the help of a provisional committee, Padshah finalized plans for an Institute of Research in India in 1899. It was to be built on the 'principles followed…in Europe, e.g., in the *German Seminaria*, the *French Conferences*, and the English and American Research Classes'. The proposed Institute was to conduct scientific research and teaching in the following areas: (a) scientific and technical science with physics, chemistry, and technical chemistry as the main subjects; (b) medicine, including bacteriology, hygiene, and physiological and pathological chemistry; and (c) philosophical and educational fields specializing in methods of education, ethics and psychology, Indian history and archaeology, statistics and economics, and comparative philology. Each department was expected to train graduate students in subjects that were 'mainly professional and technical and not simply liberal'. They were expected to create and maintain their own libraries, laboratories, and museums for the purpose of teaching and research. In addition to teaching faculty, the proposal outlined recruitment and salaries for laboratory staff, including demonstrators, mechanics, glass blowers, curators, and librarians.[9] Unlike other universities in the country, the Institute was envisaged as a centre of teaching and not merely examination.[10]

On Tata's behalf, the provisional committee approached George Curzon, then newly appointed viceroy of India (1809–1905), to discuss the scheme and secure the government's approval. Pointing to its supposed 'imperial' character, the committee argued that the Institute's benefits were not provincial but 'intended for all India, including Native States'. It sought a special legislation on two main counts: granting power to confer degrees and diplomas, without which, the committee argued, the Institute's 'effective working and popularity cannot be ensured' and because the endowment involved a family settlement including lands and houses.[11] Their demands for a special legislation, though, led to a protracted exchange between the two sides.

[8] From 'The Hopkins, his Model: A Parsee Millionaire Will Found a University in India along the Same Lines', *The Baltimore Sun*, 19 May 1899; cited in Subbarayappa, *Pursuit of Excellence*, 27–8.

[9] Tata's scheme for a research institute in India; file no. L/PJ/6/554, 2150, IOR.

[10] It is worth pointing out that Indian universities were only examining and degree-awarding institutions, while the teaching was limited to the colleges affiliated to the respective universities. It was only in 1904 that this was changed with the passing of the Indian Universities Act.

[11] Provisional Committee's presentation before Curzon on 2 January 1899; file no. L/PJ/6/554, 2150; IOR.

While the committee continued to make its case for approval, the colonial government continued to treat Tata's proposal with circumspection, challenging the potential and relevance of an institution such as theirs to science and technology in India and internationally.[12]

Following Jamsetji Tata's death in 1904, his sons Ratan and Dorabji continued their written correspondence with Curzon. In a letter to Dorabji Tata in 1904, Curzon made his frustration with the ongoing exchange clear. He wrote: 'why do not the representatives of the late Mr Tata themselves make up the alleged deficiency instead of perpetually appealing to the Government of India?' 'There seems (…) to have been too much scheming to get the Government into an enterprise private in its origin and character and to produce a situation in which, if the project failed at any time', he added 'it would be possible to say, "It is all fault of the Government".'[13] Countering the allegation that theirs was a private scheme, Dorabji Tata reiterated that they had all along proposed a 'National Institute for the advancement of the moral and material progress of India in trying to raise her, if possible, to the same level, scientifically and intellectually as the rest of the World'.[14] Particularly instructive here is Tata's invocation of the familiar nationalist trope of overcoming the scientific deficit in the country and *raising her* to the world's standards. Even though he makes reference to the 'rest of the World', it would not be unreasonable to decipher that he was referring really to the Western world.

Despite the sometimes-acrimonious exchange which lasted for a full decade, IISc was finally established through a vesting order of the Government of India in 1909. Through it, the Tatas sought to bring a new kind of scientific institution to the country: one that was simultaneously focused on postgraduate teaching as well as research. It was distinct from other Indian universities whose roles were largely restricted to examinations and certification, with teaching was concentrated in the affiliated colleges. Contrary to the contemporary Hindu-nationalist impulse which turned to ancient science to articulate its difference from colonial forms of modernity, the Tatas posed their faith, singularly, in modern Western science.[15]

*

[12] See Subbarayappa's *Pursuit of Excellence* for a detailed discussion of the back and forth between the two sides.

[13] Curzon's letter to Dorabji Tata dated 12 July 1904; cited from Sebaly, 'Tatas and University Reform', 129.

[14] Tata's response to Curzon on 13 July 1904; cited from Sebaly, 'Tatas and University Reform', 129.

[15] Prakash, *Another Reason*, 88.

Jamsetji N. Tatas' unbridled belief in the transformative power of modern science and education was carried further by his sons, who remained committed to his largely secular visions of science.

In their respective wills, Ratan and Dorabji committed their philanthropy to the advancement of scientific research and training. Having provided for his family and employees, Ratan J. Tata bequeathed the remainder of his properties to a trust to be applied for the 'advancement of Education Learning and Industry in all its branches including education economy sanitary (*sic*)-- science and art for the relief of human suffering or for other works of public utility'. The trust's objectives, he dictated in his will, must be of a public character and not sectional unless they were specifically directed for the Parsis; and that any research institutions endowed by it must recruit the 'best qualified' (a point I discussed in the previous chapter). Turning more pointedly to scientific research and development, Tata provided for the establishment of 'research stations' across the country to 'study social problems and problems of agriculture geology and other departments of science'. Finally, he supported engaging experts to:

> investigate into matters that pertain to the social, economic, or political welfare of the Indian community, the object being to devise [a] scheme of a practical nature calculated to promote the welfare of the said community, care being taken that such work is not undertaken from a stereotyped point of view but from the point of view of fresh light that is thrown from day to day by the advance of science and philosophy on problems of human well-being.[16]

Donating part of his wealth to endow SDTT in 1932, Dorabji Tata also supported the 'advancement of learning in all its branches especially research work in connection with medical and industrial problems or in giving further aid to IISc by providing funds for instituting professorships or lectureships or giving scholarships or travelling fellowships in any branch of science or art in studying abroad'. He directed that the trust support the 'institution, maintenance and support of schools educational institutions, hospitals, relief of any distress caused by the elements of nature'.[17] His obituary published in *The Times of India* on 4 June 1932 recognized Tata's contribution to India's scientific

---

[16] Ratan J. Tata's will dated 20 March 1913, with a codicil dated 29 February 1916; file no. 178/RJT/PERS/LEG/WILL/1, TCA.

[17] SDTT's deed dated 11 March 1932; file no. 177/DTT/DEED/AGR/1932, TCA.

development. It noted his 'singleness of purpose' and his 'use' of his wealth to 'pioneer for India the study of social sciences; of fundamental sciences; the treatment of and research in cancer; integrated rural development; and more recently, preservation of the country's rich heritage of the performing arts'.[18]

Akin to 'scientific philanthropy' from the twentieth century US that sought to attack the 'root causes' of any malaise, SDTT's formal philanthropic policy similarly called for large-scale investment in scientific research. Moving decisively away from a curative to a preventative approach as a principle of its philanthropic policy, one of SDTT's earliest memoranda noted that 'a single discovery can be of benefit to millions'. It was worth remembering 'always that though we may spend lakhs and lakhs on relief or education or economic uplift, unless the ravages of disease are, with the help of Science checked or prevented, or at least mitigated, misery must breed only faster than can be relieved'.[19] A separate note of SDTT's policy from 1944 went as far as recommending earmarking a fixed percentage to be gifted to scientific development each year. Rehearsing the deficit in scientific institutions across the country and resources available to them, it noted that 'there [was] general agreement in the country that more money should be forthcoming for scientific work, that Government should even ear-mark a certain percentage of revenue'. Promising to provide at least 10 per cent of the trust's gifts each year, the policy note supported a more national outlook. SDTT must support, it argued, 'work in other parts of India—notably in Calcutta, which has always been a centre for scientific work, and in Bangalore'.[20]

*

The Tatas' faith in the transformative power of science and technology intensified, post-colonialism, where it was deemed central to India's sovereignty and self-reliance. In his address delivered to the court of IISc as its president in 1955, J. R. D. Tata outlined his vision for the future. Worth quoting at length, Tata remarked:

With unlimited power at his disposal; with a constantly growing range of new materials, products, machines, vehicles, devices, chemicals, and drugs

---

[18] Lala, *Heartbeat of Trust*, vii.

[19] Memorandum dated 22 December 1932 on Muzumdar's interview with S. F. Markham; file no. SDTT BO Meetings, 1932–2005, TCA.

[20] From 'A Note on Sir Dorabji Tata Trust Policy', dated 10 April 1944. File no. FP-NO-022B-1944-04-10, TCA. The note is initialled as RC/SK, which would mean that it was drafted by Rustum Choksi who served as director of SDTT from 1941 to 1950, and as its managing trustee from until 1980.

to satisfy all his material needs; with machines and automatic processes doing most of the work for him; with the remaining killers which still threaten his life—cancer, polio, tuberculosis, heart disease—and other scourges consigned to oblivion; with the appalling threat of over-population banished through the use of safe drugs inhibiting fertility; with his life span substantially lengthened; with speeds and travel facilities multiplied many times over; with growing control over his climatic environment; and finally with increased leisure and opportunities to occupy and enjoy it, Man (*sic*) will have the resources, the knowledge and the skills, if he uses them wisely, to usher in an era of unbelievable abundance, material well-being and happiness.[21]

The success of Nehruvian centralized, planning-led development, according to Tata, was contingent on their ability to harness science and technology: 'It is inevitable that the success of these great plans of economic development should depend largely on the extent to which science and technology can be harnessed to them'. He then went on to list the areas in which IISc—through its cutting-edge research which would be useful both to the industry and the national government—could contribute: power and internal combustion engineering for improving industrial efficiency, atomic and solar energy and gas turbines for new sources of energy, and metallurgy and chemistry for the expansion of industrial sectors.[22] In his address the following year at the same venue, Tata repeated the 'technological Indians' optimism in scientific development. 'Farsightedness in our own policy making', he spoke, 'should take cognisance of the ever-widening horizons opening up before us, aim at knowledge for its own sake and at the same time direct the search for knowledge into the life-giving channels of an ever expanding technology' which provided 'the only modern means of leading our people to a fuller and happier life'.[23]

Science—in Tata's imaginings—offered the necessary materials, knowledge, and skills to men (*sic*) to enjoy the fruits of development: prosperity, well-being, and happiness. Moreover, technology was not one of many modern means available to us in the pursuit of development; it was the *only* one.

---

[21] Tata's presidential address to the 18th Meeting of the Court, IISc on 26 March 1955; file no. 190/DTT/PHIL/IISC/MIS/5, TCA.

[22] Tata's presidential address to the 18th Meeting of the Court, IISc on 26 March 1955; file no. 190/DTT/PHIL/IISC/MIS/5, TCA.

[23] Tata's presidential address to the 19th Meeting of the Court, IISc on 24 March 1956; file no. 190/DTT/PHIL/IISC/MIS/7, TCA.

The Tatas' enduring commitment to scientific development and higher education is evident from their gift-making in proposing and endowing scientific research and training institutions. These have included, among others, (a) proposal for a National Indian School of Research in Tropical Medicine at IISc, Bangalore in 1913; (b) schemes for a School of Tropical Medicine in Bombay and for the Imperial Institute for Medical Research in Delhi in 1917–18; (c) Tata Memorial Hospital in 1941, which was later transferred to the Government of India in 1957; (d) the Tata Institute of Fundamental Research, Bombay, established in 1945; (e) the Demographic Research and Training Centre, Bombay, in 1956 with the collaboration of Government of India and the United Nations, and which is now known as the International Institute of Population Sciences; (f) the National Institute of Advanced Studies, Bangalore, in 1988; and (g) the Tata Medical Centre, Kolkata, in 2011.

Alongside which, they also helped establish a number of institutes in social sciences and humanities, some of which hoped to replicate the methods and principles of scientific research to the social sciences. These included: (h) a research chair endowment at the London School of Economics and Political Science, London, from 1913 onwards; and (i) the Tata Institute of Social Sciences (1936, originally named as the Sir Dorabji Tata Graduate School of Social Work)—both of which I discuss in detail in chapter 5. Recognized as the only ones to found institutions in 'all fields of "science, arts, and industries"', the above list is demonstrative of the breadth and extent to which the Tatas committed themselves to overcoming the national deficit in scientific research and training in various fields and disciplines.[24]

*

Unlike the Tatas, other Indian elites adopted a more conservative approach to funding scientific and technological development. There were three main differences: first, starting from the 1920s onwards, their philanthropy focused by and large on training and education over research. Their approach to scientific and technological research was largely conservative in the first half of the twentieth century, especially when compared to the approach of building large-scale research institutions favoured by the Tatas. During his visit to Switzerland, for example, G. D. Birla travelled to the Ciba laboratories. There, he witnessed drug-testing on cats, dogs, frogs, and guinea pigs, and the recording of drug effects drawn automatically, using advanced electronics.

---

[24] The Tatas also founded the National Centre for the Performing Arts, Bombay in 1968; see Sebaly, 'Tatas and University Reform', 135 for an acknowledgement of the breadth of Tatas' philanthropy.

'These are', Birla wrote in a letter to M. O. Mathai in 1954, 'undoubtedly, big things, but a little too premature for India. We have neither resources nor men to undertake the task'. He went on to admit, though, that India needed to start somewhere and perhaps a new Medical Research Institute could be established.[25] There is little evidence of his subsequent support for this.

Second, they tended to focus more on research and training in the applied science and technology fields, especially those which had direct industrial applications. They concentrated their efforts, therefore, in areas that were deemed most closely aligned with the needs of India's economy and industry. Thakurdas, for example, was actively involved in the establishment of the Institute of Plant Industry at Indore in the 1920s. Established under the initiative of the Central Cotton Committee, on which Thakurdas served, the Institute received a capital grant of Rs. 2 lakhs with an annual recurring grant limited to Rs. 1 lakh from the Committee. It received a further recurring grant from various Central Indian princely states such as those of Indore, Datia, Dewas, Sitamau. He later served on the board of the Institute as well. In addition to researching varieties of cotton, the Institute was dedicated to the training of Indian research students in agricultural research for improving the quality of cotton grown in the country.[26]

Similarly, making the case for investing in technological development and training, and not just fundamental science institutions, Lakshmi Naraynan, the principal of the Birla College of Engineering in Pilani noted that there had been a 'needless and unreal argument in favour of pure science' in the country. Arguing for their complementary and inter-dependent roles, he added, India needed 'engineering-scientist or the scientist engineer' in areas such as electronics, atomic, and solar energy; whom they wished to train at their College.[27] His, and more widely Birlas' engineering philosophy, was exemplified in the Birlas' involvement with the Technological Institute of Textiles in Bhiwani. With a view to training textile technicians prolific in both the theoretical and practical aspects of a mill, Ghanshyam Das Birla purchased a mill in Bhiwani, Haryana in the 1940s. Its profits were turned over to the Birla Educational Trust to be re-invested in the training of textile technicians. One hundred students trained at the institute, with over 2,500 workers employed in three shifts. All students lived on campus and worked at least three hours a day in the mill in addition to their class and laboratory work. In addition to

---

[25]   Birla's letter to Mathai dated 12 July 1954; from file 3, 1043.
[26]   From the annual report of the Institute of Plant Industry, Indore, for the year ending 30 June 1927; file no. 48 (pt. I), PT.
[27]   Cited in Hennessy, *India Democracy and Development*, 232–3.

production, the students also learnt about mill management, labour relations, and welfare work.[28]

In 1948, the Birlas responded to Vallabhbhai Patel's call to extend technical education in the country, especially in his home state of Gujarat. G. D. Birla helped establish a Birla Vishwakarma Mahavidyalaya (or Birla Engineering College) at a cost of Rs. 25 lakhs in 1948.[29] Offering training in civil, mechanical, and electrical engineering, the College was part of an exemplary experiment at making a rural university in Vallabhvidya Nagar. It recognized, following Gandhi's desire to model rural education differently from industry-centric urban education, the predominance of cottage and small-scale industries in villages which warranted a different conception and application of science.[30] They also started a pharmacy school in 1949. Started in January under the leadership of M. L. Schroff trained at Cornell and the Massachusetts Institute of Technology in the United States, the school gained a reputation for its modern equipment and high training standards. It played, according to Hennessy, a crucial role in 'building up traditions of professional integrity in the Indian industry'.[31]

Similar to Birla's interest in training textile engineers, Lalbhai was also interested in researching the textile industry. On behalf of the Ahmedabad Textile Industries' Research Association (ATIRA), which was a joint collaboration between industry and academia, Lalbhai managed to secure funding from the Cotton Textile Research Fund. While the Ahmedabad Millowners' Association provided 50 lakhs collected from the city's mills, the central Indian government provided an additional 20 lakhs, and agreed to share half of the annual recurring expenditure to a maximum of Rs. 150,000. ATIRA was founded in 1947 to help build the Indian textile industry's global competitiveness. That it was imbricated in the national question can be gauged from Lalbhai's warning when he was lobbying with the Indian government to fund his proposal. Unless Indian textile industry learnt to apply research techniques, 'we will fall behind other countries'.[32]

Third, unlike the Tatas' who favoured investing in training in social sciences and humanities in order to develop more *worldly* scientists and technicians, the Birlas had little interest in the arts and social sciences. This disinterest was evident in the student enrolment at its flagship Birla College in

---

[28] Cited in Hennessy, *India Democracy and Development*, 306–9.
[29] Kudaisya, *G. D. Birla*, 283.
[30] From Mountbatten's inaugural address on 14 June 1948 at the College, cited in Hennessy, *India Democracy and Development*, 304–5.
[31] Hennessy, *India Democracy and Education*, 71–3.   [32] Piramal, *Business Legends*, 407–10.

Pilani. In 1951, for example, of the 587 enrolled students, only sixty studied the humanities and arts, with most favouring science and commerce. Not only was this a reflection of the growing influence of science in post-colonial India, but it was also telling of the Birlas' own predisposition towards technological development in the country's modernization.

Notwithstanding his conservative approach to institution-building, Birla's major contribution to technological training institutions was still to come.

*

By 1960, though, Birla was ready for more. Worried that his own Birla College of Engineering would pale in comparison to the Indian government's proposed Indian Institutes of Technology (IITs), he turned his attention to endowing a pioneering engineering institute in the country. Birla started corresponding with James Killian, former president of the Massachusetts Institute of Technology (MIT) in the United States about a potential collaboration, where MIT could 'gift' personnel to run a new Birla University and later start an Indian campus of MIT, which Birla would sponsor. Given Killian's disinterest in the proposal, Birla scaled down his plans. He asked Killian to recommend names of individuals Birla could possibly recruit for his institution. He began contacting various individuals recommended by Killian saying that he was hoping to start a new institute 'on the lines of MIT'. Thomas Drew, a professor of chemical engineering at Columbia University, replied, suggesting launching something along the lines of a practice school (which involved working for a semester on an industrial site, under the supervision of MIT's faculty).[33]

In 1962, Birla proposed establishing a new institute of technology, modelled on MIT, to celebrate a century of the establishment of their business. Outlining their plans in a short letter to Nehru, Birla wrote that he wished to establish a world-class institute. Likely to cost over a crore (or 10 million) rupees, the campus would have been located in Delhi or Dehradun. He added that he had requested MIT leadership to depute some faculty members. Interested in helping Birla, they had promised to identify one or two professors who might help the institute. In his response, Nehru expressed his full support to the institute.[34] The Indian government was launching a new IIT at Kanpur, curiously also with MIT's support, which made IIT, Kanpur, the direct competitor of Birla's proposed institute.

---

[33] Bassett, *The Technological Indian*, 233–4.
[34] Birla's letter to Nehru dated 24 February 1962; from file 5, 1043.

By 1963, Birla was successful in attracting both MIT and Ford Foundation's officials to his scheme. Drew and his colleague, Howard Bartlett of MIT's humanities department drafted a new plan for Birla's proposed institute. Not dissimilar in their autonomy of the government to the Tatas' model of development (on which more in the following section), the new institute, named the Birla Institute of Technology and Science (BITS) in 1964, mimicked the American model of privately funded institutions which 'being free of control of well-meaning government committees, have been able to quickly adjust their programs to the needs of their country and her industry and to experiment with new techniques of instruction'. Over the following decade, BITS was also supported by the Ford Foundation and MIT—the former providing $3 million in grants, and the latter providing some of its personnel. It was, according to Bassett, a 'combination of modernity and tradition. Pilani was tradition…MIT was modernity, committed to using science and technology for ceaseless innovation'.[35]

*

Speaking at TIFR's inaugural ceremony in 1945, the then governor of Bombay remarked: 'India stands in urgent need of the speedy development of her resources, both agricultural and industrial', for which it needed the 'aid of science'. 'For modern industry and agriculture rest, to an ever-increasing extent', he concluded, 'upon scientific foundations, and economic progress depends on continual advances in the field of fundamental research, which provides the material on which the applied scientist can work'.[36] Recognizing the potential *use* of science and technology for India's development, India's economic elites set out to overcome its historical deficiencies. Founding institutions of scientific research and training, they hoped to overcome its institutional and intellectual deficiencies. Led by the Tatas who were unequivocal in their embrace of Western science and modernity, they concentrated their efforts on scientific research in India and training of prospective Indian scientists in the country and abroad; others such as Thakurdas and Birlas were more interested in supporting the technological training institutions.

*

[35] Bassett, *The Technological Indian*, 238.
[36] Speech made by the governor of Bombay at the inauguration ceremony of the Tata Institute of Fundamental Research, Bombay on 19 December 1945. File no. 196/DTT/PHIL/TIFR/MIS/04, TCA.

Building 'big' scientific and technological institutions to support the meritorious, though, was not the only way in which the elites' responded to the challenges of overcoming the deficits in India's scientific development. They also turned their attention elsewhere.

Alongside their focus on the 'best and most gifted' individuals, the elites also turned towards propagating science among the 'ordinary' masses, albeit on a much smaller scale. Thakurdas led the early efforts at cultivating what has since come to be known as 'scientific temper' at the Sansthan English High School in Dakor, Gujarat. His programme involved, among other things, the widening of science education in the country. As a result of his efforts and those of the school's headmaster, the scientific teaching at the school was evaluated as satisfactory by the inspector of science teaching. In his report from 1928, he commended the school for keeping records of rainfall but suggested adding records of temperature and atmospheric pressure. More instructively, he suggested that the students cultivate a scientific temper. Their approach to experiments, he found, was largely deductive. Instead their objective, he believed, should have been driven by curiosity—that is, 'to find out etc.'[37]

Barring such early though sporadic efforts, more concerted efforts at cultivating a scientific temper came at the apogee of Nehruvian socialism, with its emphasis on the 'scientific temper' or 'spirit': that is a rationalism based on empiricism, on scientific research with its practical applications in industry, and extensive industrialization—all of which were duly inserted into the modern national question, most particularly as part of the five-year centralized planning.[38] The Birlas were at the forefront of running such mass educational programmes and creating the institutional infrastructure for this. In 1956, for example, they decided to gift their family house, 'Birla Park' in Calcutta, to the nation. It was later converted into an industrial museum. Receiving their gift, Nehru wrote to Birla that he would like to perform its opening ceremony, as it would 'serve a very useful purpose'.[39] In 1962, they launched the Birla Planetarium in Calcutta, which was formally inaugurated by Nehru the following year, with the aim of educating the public and popularizing astronomy in the country.

[37]   Report of B. B. Kamat dated 14 September 1928, file 5, PT.
[38]   Seth, 'Nehruvian Socialism', 465–8.
[39]   From Nehru's letter to Birla dated 6 February 1956; from file 3, 1043.

By the 1960s there had been increasing recognition of the need to further the extension of scientific research outside the laboratories of TIFR. In 1973, a group of scientists within TIFR suggested the consolidation and institutionalization of its pedagogic effort, particularly among children from the underprivileged city schools. They approached the Ministry of Education initially for support to design and run the programme. The promised support took longer than expected to fructify as the government officials were reluctant. One of whom questioned the relevance of the programme on the grounds that 'Municipal school children had a low IQ (*sic*)'. To this, the TIFR-group replied that 'our experience was that they were poor financially but not intellectually'.[40] However, the Institute was unable to interest the government in its programme. Later in 1974, with support from SDTT, they launched the Homi Bhabha Centre for Science Education, which was subsequently supported by the Department of Atomic Energy, Government of India in the 1980s. The Centre has since been working to promote 'equity and excellence' in the education of science and mathematics, but more importantly for us, the growth of 'scientific literacy in the country', or the 'scientific temper'. It works through the development of teachers, research on scientific teaching, and popularization of the sciences.[41] The attempt, therefore, was to sustain the nation-building project, again through the sciences, not necessarily within the laboratories, but even outside it.

*

In addition to founding large, higher education institutions of research and training—that involved institutional endowments, collaboration with governments: whether colonial or post-colonial, extensive and expensive machinery and laboratories, and involved skilled scientists, clinicians, and technicians, working in specialized fields such as atomic energy, cosmic rays, radiation therapy, tropical diseases—to overcome the deficits in Indian sciences, the elites also financed science on a much smaller scale. Related to what subsequently came to be known as 'appropriate' or 'intermediate' technology,[42] small-s science imaginaries were crafted around relatively inexpensive

[40] From 'The Birth of the Homi Bhabha Centre for Science Education: Role of Sir Dorabji Tata Trust'; from file no. 194/DTT/PHIL/TIFR/FP/1, TCA.

[41] 'Homi Bhabha Centre for Science Education', Tata Institute of Fundamental Research, accessed 8 January 2015, http://www.hbcse.tifr.res.in/.

[42] Schumacher, *Small Is Beautiful*; see McRobie, 'Intermediate Technology', 71–86 for development-specific discussion; and Chambers, Pacey, and Thrupp's *Farmer First* for the implications of such technologies on inverting the power dynamics in development.

technology, requiring smaller-scale infrastructure, and was primarily meant to be used widely by the masses on an everyday basis. It was aimed, less at industry and more at farm and farm-based economic activities such as agriculture, irrigation, animal husbandry, agro-processing, etc. Differently from the 'big S' scientific development that I have discussed until now, science worked on a much smaller scale: household- or farm-based and had a very different relationship to capital. Expectedly so, unlike the endowments involved in the financing of large-scale institutions, science involved a very different mode of philanthropy and relationship to science itself.

Bajaj was one of the earliest proponents of such science. Influenced by Gandhi's 'constructive programme', Bajaj actively financed and led activities of various subsidiary organizations, such as the Gau Seva Sangh (Organization for the Service of Cows). Founded in 1941, the Sangh's programme of activities for the 'cow' constituted an assemblage of scientific research and practice that sought to re-constitute or correct a series of economic, moral, religious, and human–animal relationships around it, with the ultimate objective of the development of the rural economy. Through scientific measurement, animal husbandry, and veterinary care, it aimed at both increasing the cow's productivity and preventing its exploitation. Scientific breeding was expected to improve the country's livestock, thus, improve household incomes. The elevation of the 'cow' to a more sacred place was a moral appeal to fight off those indulging in adulteration.[43]

Similarly, the Tatas were also actively involved in promoting science through their subsidiary organizations, especially from the mid-1950s onwards. Activities such as those of RWB, TRC, and on a far more extensive scale, via the Tata Trusts' grant-making since the 1990s, involved the financing and propagation of science in national-modern development. At Devapur (discussed previously in chapter 2), for example, they promoted: high-breed and cross-breed cattle and poultry; use of decorticators for extracting fibres, thereby enhancing agricultural production through its modernization; water mills for agriculture extension, and scientific soil moisture conservation. Alongside which, they promoted new scientific technologies and infrastructures in the areas of water supply, sanitation, health care, and family planning.[44] Such examples typically focused on a lab-to-field-type diffusion of science and technology. Although prior efforts were mostly sporadic, they

---

[43] Nanda, *In Gandhi's Footsteps*, 354–6.
[44] Report, 'Devapur Project: Achievements of a Quiet, Persistent Effort by Tatas for the Development of a Drought Prone Area (1952–1984)'; file no. 185/DTT/PHIL/RWB/BO/1963/1, TCA. Also see Lala, *Heartbeat of Trust*, 149–55 for further details of the Board's activities at Devapur.

focused on using science and technology to solve the problems of development. The leader of the Indian Green Revolution, M. S. Swaminathan noted the signal contribution of the Tatas' philanthropy in the area. In particular, he cited the J. R. D. Tata Ecotechnology Centre, the Centre for Medicinal Plants Research, and the Sir Dorabji Tata Centre for Research in Tropical Diseases, among others.[45] Such experiments belonged to the earlier generation of lab-to-field science from the 1950s to the 1990s.

*

The turn to 'small science' intensified in the post-1990s. Here, the Tatas' philanthropy adopted an approach that sought to bring together laboratories, fields, and policy. Summarizing its experiences over the previous five years' strategic planning, SDTT's annual report from 2004–05 noted that: 'discussions with partners and experts reconfirm the unique role that the Trust can play in a "lab to land" transfer of knowledge and ideas'. It outlined the Trust's support to the Gene Campaign, for example, as part of its engagement with biotechnology policy—to understand the safety of biotechnology, costs and associated risks, trade impact, policy and ethical concerns. The Trust saw its distinctive role in creating a favourable public discourse through public education and dealing with common misconceptions.[46]

This led to the founding of a number of think-tank-like 'cells' within the Tata Trusts' ecosystem. Such 'cells' sought to combine more familiar 'demonstration farms' from an earlier generation (such as those championed by RWB) with agricultural research, on the one hand, and policy research and advocacy (from US-style think tanks), on the other, thus, bringing lab-field-policy together into the same institutional space. No longer responsible for *funding* science or endowing institutions for it, philanthropy in the new reconfigured nexus of 'lab-field-policy', works to *orchestrate* it. The change in the role of philanthropy is recognized in several places within the Tata Trusts. For example, discussing its role in natural resource management, SDTT believes that: 'pure research on MNR [management of natural resources] issues will continue to be led by consortia of government and scientific institutions, the Trust in the coming years, will focus on the "livelihoods perspective"'.[47] Similarly, SRTT believes that the problems plaguing the water

---

[45] Swaminathan is widely credited for his role in India's Green Revolution in the 1970s, particularly in his role as the director general of the Indian Council of Agricultural Research; from SDTT, Annual Report, 2003–04; file no. 210/SDTT/2003–04, TCA.

[46] Annual Report, SDTT, 2004–05. File no. 182/DTT/AR/2004–05, TCA.

[47] Annual Report, SDTT, 2004–05. File no. 182/DTT/AR/2004–05, TCA.

sector in the country result from a split between science-as-knowledge and policy-making/development-as-doing. India, it notes, 'has a huge scientific competence base in water resources comprising hydrologists, hydro-geologists, water resource engineers, water quality experts, and soil scientists'. The deficit in scientific knowledge, according to SRTT, has already been over-come. 'Unfortunately, politicians or bureaucrats, who have very little under-standing of the nature of the problem', it finds, 'formulate the nation's water strategies'. The Trust's role, therefore, is to present scientific work and ideas in a policy-relevant fashion. Against this backdrop, the Trusts have supported research initiatives that seek solutions to water-related issues.[48]

Instead of endowing institutions (up to the 1960s) or setting-up subsidiary organizations (1950s to the 1990s), the Tata Trusts now operate through a number of specialized knowledge institutions that seek to *bridge* academic institutions where research resides with technical resource agencies with the know-how of doing it, and organizations with the poor communities in the field, and developing 'innovative concepts for field-level piloting'.[49] Some of these knowledge institutions promoted by the Tata Trusts include: Central India Initiative (CINI) Cell, Coastal Salinity Prevention Cell, Himmotthan Pariyojana, among others, in rural livelihoods, and Kalike Samruddhi Upakram in the field of elementary education.[50] The CINI Cell, funded by the Tata Trusts together, is one of many examples of Tata philanthropy's changed role. It works to steer: 'the activity of converting research findings into action plans, and testing the recommendations of the research in the field. It sup-ports field experiments and tests ideas through small grants and brings to the fore replicable models'.[51]

Likewise, its Sukhi Baliraja Initiative (SBI; discussed in the previous chap-ter) proposes tackling the agrarian distress in Vidarbha by building nexuses and networks between scientists (geneticists, agricultural scientists, animal husbandry experts, and veterinarians), field (farmers, now termed 'prod-ucers'), and policy (development experts, think-tanks, etc.). Relying on famil-iar tropes from the development discourse of the 1950s where Third World peasants were characterized by their ignorance, lack of access, and illiteracy,

[48] SRTT, 'Water Sector Research', accessed 4 December 2014, http://srtt.org/institutional_grants/rural_livelihoods_communities/water_sector_research.htm.

[49] 'Kharash Vistarotthan Yojana', SRTT, accessed 4 December 2014, http://srtt.org/institutional_grants/rural_livelihoods_communities/kharash_vistarotthan_yojana.htm.

[50] For further details, see Tata Trusts, 'Our Associates', accessed 11 June 2021, https://www.tatatrusts.org/our-associates.

[51] SRTT, 'Central India Initiative, accessed 28 February 2015, http://srtt.org/institutional_grants/rural_livelihoods_communities/central_india_initiative.htm

SBI imagines contemporary farmers similarly, describing them through their lack of 'necessary technical know-how',[52] or 'knowledge of basic agronomic practices in the region', etc. The job of its agricultural extension workers is to 'provide continuous hand-holding support to farmers from sowing to harvesting'.[53] Seeking to move science outside the clinics and laboratories, SBI hopes to develop villages into 'farm-based knowledge centres', where science and technology could be both demonstrated and later, diffused via regular village, cluster, and regional meetings.

In a further intensification of its lab-field-policy approach, SRTT funded a Tata-Cornell Initiative in Agriculture and Nutrition (or TACO-AN) in 2008–09. Established through an endowment, it hoped to 'equip a new generation of Indian policymakers, practitioners, researchers, and educators with the skills to address the multi-faceted problems related to the food system and rural development'.[54] With Vidarbha as its 'field', it worked on the complex and inter-related questions of agricultural production and diversification, nutrition, household-level distribution and availability, and access to drinking water and sanitation. Reflecting the growing popularity of 'partnership' mode of philanthropic intervention in development globally, TACO-AN was designed as a collaboration within a range of research, implementation, and production organizations, located both in the private and public sectors, and in various parts of the globe.[55] In this way, philanthropic organizations increasingly become *intermediaries* which broker, translate, or mediate developmental imaginaries across a range of institutions.[56] The manner in which such institutions describe their primary role makes clear their relationship with science and technology, public policy, and development practice, which include a 'knowledge bank, which would be a single source for information' and an 'idea incubator', which provides monitoring and technical support.[57]

---

[52] SRTT, 'Dissemination of Integrated Pest Management', accessed 19 February 2013, http://srtt. org/institutional_grants/rural_livelihoods_communities/sbi_six_projects.htm.

[53] SRTT, 'Annual Report, 2009–10', 20, accessed 6 April 2014, http://srtt.org/downloads/annual/SRTTAnnualReport2009-10.pdf.

[54] SRTT, 'Annual Report, 2008–09', 10. Accessed 6 April 2014, http://srtt.org/downloads/annual/SRTTAnnualReport2008-09.pdf.

[55] Tata-Cornell Agriculture and Nutrition Initiative, 'TCi Research Agenda', accessed 8 March 2015, http://tci.cals.cornell.edu/about/research-agenda.

[56] For a detailed discussion on partnership mode of philanthropy, see Kumar and Brooks, 'Bridges, Satellites, and Platforms'.

[57] SRTT, 'Central India Initiative', accessed 28 February 2015, http://srtt.org/institutional_grants/rural_livelihoods_communities/central_india_initiative.htm.

The above ideas are repeated for the Himmothan Pariyojana, or the intervention cell in the Central Himalayan region, which seeks to develop a 'database on the status and management needs of natural resources', as an 'idea incubator by exploring new innovations' and facilitating linkages. See 'Himmothan Pariyojana', SRTT, accessed 4 December 2014, http://srtt.org/institutional_grants/rural_livelihoods_communities/himmothan_pariyojana.htm.

Others claim to promote the 'appropriate use of technology, while remaining people-oriented'.[58]

*

Even as the Tatas sought to 'bridge' hitherto segregated institutions, others used a similar logic of connecting hitherto atomized individuals to build a stronger society by using twenty-first-century digital technologies. Rohini Nilekani Philanthropies, for example, suggest 'we cannot be mere consumers of good governance; we have to co-create it'.[59] Invoking hyper-individualization of responsibility, it entrusts technology with connecting our now atomized selves. Technologies, Nilekani notes, 'allow people to connect, to access knowledge and to drive action as never before. Yet, they also allow people to recede into comfort zones, to shut out ideas and people who are different'. Through her philanthropy (which she calls her 'work'), Nilekani hopes to 'enable more creative collaborations across divides and silos. Today's complex social issues demand participation from all entities that have a stake in positive change'.[60]

It supports building digital infrastructures to solve problems in areas of literacy and numeracy (through the EkStep Foundation) and sustainable development (through its Societal Platform). The former is premised in the 'digital empowerment' of 'multiple adult ecosystems', which will ultimately enhance learners' access. It funds both new digital curricular resources and learning experiences.[61] Its Societal Platform initiative hopes to identify grassroots' and dispersed pockets of solutions to complex developmental problems such as poverty, hunger, education, access to clean water, etc. and enable them to 'plug and collaborate' with others.[62] It helped develop, for example, the PuraSeva app in Andhra Pradesh, which was then implemented by the state

[58] Annual Report, SDTT, 2004–05. File no. 182/DTT/AR/2004–05, TCA.

[59] Rohini Nilekani is the wife of Indian IT entrepreneur, and later politician Nandan Nilekani. Starting with charity in 2001, she started Arghyam which funds initiatives for sustainable water and sanitation. Following a steep increase in their personal wealth in 2004, Nilekani, along with her husband, began engaging in what she calls 'strategic philanthropy'. She believes India's biggest challenges is the lack of 'intellectual infrastructure'; and that its philanthropy is not 'edgy enough'. See Nundy and Dastoor's 'Q+A with Rohini Nilekani', *Stanford Social Innovation Review*, accessed 20 August 2019, https://ssir.org/articles/entry/qa_with_rohini_nilekani.

[60] Rohini Nilekani Philanthropies, accessed 20 August 2019, https://rohininilekani.org/. Along with Premji, the Nilekanis have also signed up for *The Giving Pledge*.

[61] EkStep, 'Transforming Education', accessed 18 December 2019, https://societalplatform.org/inspiration/ekstep-transforming-education/.

[62] Societal Platform, 'Aligning Societal Platform thinking to SDGs', accessed 20 August 2019, https://societalplatform.org/inspiration/aligning-societal-platform-thinking-to-sustainable-development-goals/.

government, and helped link municipal authorities with citizens' grievances. It promised to offer transparency to citizens and training and stream-lined workflows to municipal employees, thus 'unlocking data-driven governance through performance metrics and comparative analyses'.[63] Similarly, the Shiksha initiative of the Shiv Nadar Foundation uses digital technologies to improve retention and enhance learning outcomes for school children. In Uttar Pradesh, for example, it has converted the primary school syllabus into interactive, animated, exercises.[64]

Such digital technologies hope to by-pass existing development organizations and organizational routines by creating new and alternate platforms and resources that operate, somehow, above and outside conventional spaces of development.[65] The Nilekanis, for example, view this as the new way of doing philanthropy, which they call 'extreme risk capital'. It involves, according to the Nilekanis, investment in areas where both markets and governments are reluctant to go and civil society organizations lack the scale to venture into. Thus, it is left to the philanthropists to make investments in creating models for future interventions. More troublingly, though, Nandan Nilekani views it as capital that is not necessarily accountable to anyone.[66] Sundar is more benign in her attribution of the Nilekanis' approach. Instead of making social investments which would expect a financial return of sorts, the Nilekanis invest—according to Sundar—in philanthropic capital: an investment in creating philanthropic models where none exist.[67] Sundar, however, refuses to think through the implications of such an approach towards accountability of such platforms and programmes.

Others, though, are willing to continue to invest in brick-and-mortar infrastructure, albeit in relation to information and communication technologies. The Bharti Foundation, for example, has funded schools and centre of research and training in communication technologies. In 2000, it funded the Bharti School of Telecommunication Technology and Management at the Indian Institute of Technology, Delhi. It runs postgraduate and doctoral research programmes in telecommunications and management. Through

[63] The Better India, 'Digital Andhra: Complain, Track and Resolve Your Civic Issues through One App', accessed 20 August 2019, https://www.thebetterindia.com/149828/digital-andhra-puru-seva-app/.

[64] Shiv Nadar Foundation, 'Annual Report, 2018–19', accessed 20 august 2019, http://blog.shivnadarfoundation.org/annual-reports/shiv-nadar-foundation-annual-report-2018–19.

[65] Kumar and Brooks, 'Bridges, Platforms, Satellites'.

[66] Nandan and Rohini Nilekani, 'The Art of Giving', interview with ET Now, posted 23 November 2017, https://www.youtube.com/watch?v=mGaXCrBuyCk.

[67] Sundar, Giving with Thousand Hands, 186–7.

buildings, laboratories, merit-based awards, and a lecture series, it hopes to develop 'young telecom leaders' who will ultimately make India into a 'telecom superpower'.[68] It also funds a Bharti Centre for Communication at the Indian Institute of Technology, Bombay to 'generate fundamental knowledge in telecommunication and allied systems' and become an 'internationally recognised contributor in moving the frontiers of knowledge' through its support to research and teaching at the Institute.[69] Unlike the Tatas, who often funded relatively autonomous institutions, the Bharti Foundation chose to partner with existing eminent institutions in the country and fund smaller, more focused centres of research and training in fields that are directly linked to its own parent corporation.

*

Throughout the twentieth century, India's elites funded modern science and technology—both big and small—to help the country overcome its deficit. These gifts, I argue in the following section, were always imbricated in the national question in particular ways. That the elites' imaginaries need to be read separately from the state-led national development becomes clear from the many contestations between the ruling regimes and the elites over the role and future of science and technology institutions in the country.

National, But Also International

The collocation of science and technology as part of national-modern formations of development is evident both from the elites' gift-making but also those seeking or receiving them. In 1917, for example, the renowned Indian physiologist and physicist Jagadish Chandra Bose (1858–1937) established a new institute of interdisciplinary scientific research.[70] A year later, he wrote a letter to Bajaj whom he considered to be like a son, seeking funds for his institute. Although more was promised to him (Rs. 2 lakh), Bose asked Bajaj to send whatever little had been collected thus far—approximately Rs. 47,000. In

---

[68] Bharti School of Telecommunication Technology and Management, 'About', accessed 3 January 2020, http://bhartischool.iitd.ac.in/About.php.

[69] Bharti Centre for Communication, 'Vision', accessed 3 January 2020, https://www.ee.iitb.ac.in/bharticentre/vision.html.

[70] Deepak Kumar, '"Culture" of Science', 204–5. Previously in the 1890s, Bose refused to accept his salary from the colonial government for three years in a row as the government paid Indian scientists with equivalent qualifications and designations two-thirds of the amount paid to their European counterparts.

return, Bose gifted his personal watch for Bajaj's daughter and a magnifying microscope for his son.[71] In another letter later that year, Bose asked Bajaj for further help reminding the latter that funding scientific development in order to overcome the various deficits that plagued the sector in the country was, first and foremost, a national duty. Appealing to Bajaj and the wider Marwari community, Bose wrote 'that the (...) community which made large fortunes during the wartime had not, with [Bajaj's] sole exception, done much to help this *national work*'.[72] Making his frustration clear, Bose added: 'If the people of the country did not take sufficient interest,' he lamented, 'the Government cannot be expected to do anything'.[73] Thus, the support for Indian science, scientists, and its institutions was imbricated within India's contemporary nationalism and designated crucial to its national development. Pointing this out, Bose wrote elsewhere: 'The salvation of India will not be through knowledge alone, through politics alone, through social service alone, but through all these'. 'The problem of each is very difficult', he added, but a collaborative approach could help 'find light in the darkness'. Among others, it required, according to Bose, 'keeping the mind alert and sympathy extended in all directions. Above all we have to throw ourselves as an offering to the great cause which raises the level of humanity'.[74]

Equally, the production of an 'Indian science' required, first and foremost, having more Indian scientists in influential positions in colonial India. While the initial focus had been on sponsoring their higher education and training abroad, it later turned to their recruitment. Economic elites had a crucial role to play in this. When endowing scientific research institutions, for example, they could expand opportunities for the recruitment of Indian scientists. Others used, or were urged to at least, their influence to recruit more Indians into senior positions at scientific research institutes and commissions, particularly in positions that were reserved for foreign experts only or unavailable to Indians, informally. Thakurdas, for example, was appointed as a member to the first board of the Institute of Plant Industry, Indore. In 1930 P. Parija applied for the director's post at the Institute of Plant Industry, Indore. His application was recommended to Thakurdas by a B. Das, who apart from recommending Parija for his scientific training and output, added: 'While we are on the doorstep of Swaraj we have to see foreign tutelage even

---

[71] Letter from Bose to Bajaj dated 8 April 1918; Correspondence: Bose, J. C., JB (1st inst.).

[72] Letter from Bose to Bajaj dated 14 September 1919; Correspondence: Bose, J. C., JB (1st inst.); emphasis added.

[73] Letter from Bose to Bajaj dated 14 September 1919; Correspondence: Bose, J. C., JB (1st inst.).

[74] Letter from Bose to Bajaj dated 23 July 1925; Correspondence: Bose, J. C., JB (1st inst.).

in fields of research must cease'. And that his move from Cuttack's Ravenshaw College was a loss to Orissa, it 'will be a distinct gain to India'.[75]

Similarly, Prof. N. Gangulee of the Department of Agriculture, University of Calcutta also wrote to Thakurdas applying to the same position as a test case. 'I have been fighting', Gangulee wrote 'like grim death for young Indian scientists in order to place them in authoritative positions. But it is not always easy to press their just claims', he added, unless Indian scientists such as himself knew that scientific knowledge was the only criteria for selection.[76] Assuring Gangulee, Thakurdas replied that his qualifications and application will be considered fully.[77] Elsewhere, Walchand Hirachand wrote to Thakurdas to use his position as the vice-president of the Central Cotton Committee and member of the selection committee to recruit Rajul Shah to the post of senior botanical assistant at the Institute of Plant Industry. If she were selected, Walchand wrote, 'female education in this line [will] be encouraged'. Thakurdas forwarded Shah's application to the Institute's director for their full consideration.[78]

Thus, science was not only important from the narrow point of view of indigenizing it, but also because it offered a pedagogic model for the rest of Indian society. Homi J. Bhabha, the founder of the Tata Institute of Fundamental Research (TIFR), Bombay, and credited for his leadership of India's atomic research programme, similarly placed science at the centre of India's social life. In a lecture from 1945, Bhabha said: 'Science to-day was no longer a subsidiary social activity but formed the basis of our social structure'. It had finally opened, he added, 'the possibility of freedom for all from long hours of manual drudgery and we stand to-day at the beginning of an age when every single person will have the opportunity to develop himself spiritually to his fullest stature'. Although Bhabha was unique in making a case for fundamental and not just applied research, his remarks are important as they sought the intellectual advancement of the nation, alongside its material progress and the individual well-being of its people. Progress in science, he concluded, was of 'great philosophical importance in widening our mental horizon and in showing the limitations of commonsense ideas based upon the world immediately perceived by our senses'.[79]

---

[75] From Das's letter to Thakurdas dated 8 October 1930; file no. 48 (Pt. II), PT.
[76] Gangulee's letter to Thakurdas dated 28 January 1931; file no. 48 (Pt. II), PT.
[77] Thakurdas's reply to Gangulee dated 4 February 1931; file no. 48 (Pt. II), PT.
[78] Hirachand's letter to Thakurdas dated 29 June 1934; file no. 48 (Pt. II), PT.
[79] From the Summary of Dr. Homi J. Bhabha's Lecture on 19 December 1945; from file no. 196/ DTT/PHIL/TIFR/MIS/4, TCA.

Offering the possibility of freedom of all kinds, science—according to India's leading scientists and their patrons—was fundamental to the organization of its society and its development. The opportunities were many. Science had become, therefore, 'pivotal in the imagination and institution of India'.[80] These entanglements of science and technology with the national-modern are best exemplified in TIFR—in its establishment, in the recruitment of scientists, and in the nature of scientific research it hoped to conduct, which I discuss in greater detail next.

*

In a letter to J. R. D. Tata from 1943, Bhabha noted 'the lack of proper conditions and insufficient financial support', which hampered the 'development of science in India at the pace which the talent in the country would warrant'. Progress of science, he concluded, required far greater financial support, without the expectation of immediate returns, and the large-scale visits of distinguished international scholars, the benefits of which far outweighed the costs involved.[81] In his response, Tata invited Bhabha to draft a more concrete proposal. 'There is at the moment in India no big school of research in the fundamental problems of physics, both theoretical and experimental', Bhabha began. Invoking the nation, he added, it was 'absolutely in the interest of India to have a vigorous school of research in fundamental physics, for such a school forms the spearhead of research not only in less advanced branches of physics but also in problems of immediate practical application in industry'. Seeking to move away from applied research—otherwise more appealing to economic elites across the country—to fundamental or pure research, Bhabha added: 'If much of the applied research done in India today is disappointing or of very inferior quality it is entirely due to the absence of a sufficient number of pure research workers who would set the standard of good research'.[82]

Bhabha fervently made the case for establishing an institute dedicated to fundamental or pure research. In a separate note, he cited the fundamental research conducted by Faraday and Maxwell, which was later developed for wider application, as evidence of the importance of doing

---

[80] Prakash, *Another Reason*, 3.

[81] From Bhabha's letter to J. R. D. Tata written on 19 August 1943, cited in file no. 194/DTT/PHIL/TIFR/FP/1, TCA.

[82] Bhabha's proposal dated 12 March 1944 sent to Sorab Saklatvala for the establishment of the TIFR; from file no. 194/DTT/PHIL/TIFR/FP/1, TCA; underlined in original.

fundamental research in India.[83] He proposed modelling such an Indian institute along the lines of the UK Department of Scientific and Industrial Research. Bhabha argued that once the institute was fully developed, 'India will not have to look abroad for its experts but will find them ready at hand. I do not think that any one acquainted with scientific development in other countries would deny the need in India for such a school as I propose'.[84]

Established in 1945 along the lines proposed by Bhabha, TIFR received extensive state patronage including: land from the Bombay government and later the defence ministry, financial support from the Atomic Energy Commission, Ministry of Natural Resources and Scientific Research, and Council of Scientific and Industrial Research, and finally the Tatas.[85] Its extensive support from the post-colonial Nehru government was enabled, in no small measure, by the proximity between Bhabha, J. R. D. Tata, and Nehru.[86] Not only was the national question central to the underlying logic of the institute, it was widely invoked when it came to the recruitment of scientists. That is, working at TIFR even if it meant eschewing better remuneration and laboratory facilities elsewhere was often constructed as part of one's national duty. Recalling his own decision to stay in India following his holiday in 1939 and not return to his job at Cambridge later, Bhabha wrote: 'I had the idea that after the war I would accept a job in a good university in Europe or America, because universities like Cambridge or Princeton provide an atmosphere which no place in India provides at the moment'. 'But in the last two years', Bhabha concluded, 'I have come more and more to the view that provided proper appreciation and financial support are forthcoming, it is one's duty to stay in one's own country and build up schools comparable with those that other countries are fortunate in possessing'.[87] The call of national duty was similarly repeated when Bhabha wrote to S. Chandrashekhar at the University of Chicago, and who was later awarded a Nobel Prize in 1983 as a US citizen, inviting him to work at TIFR. Citing his own example, Bhabha

---

[83] Such references to the value of 'pure' science over applied science are repeated in a number of documents available at the TCA. For example, in file no. 195/DTT/PHIL/TIFR/MIS/2, TCA.

[84] Bhabha's proposal, dated 12 March 1944 to Sir Sorab Saklatvala, for the establishment of the TIFR; from file no. 194/DTT/PHIL/TIFR/FP/1, TCA.

[85] From the speeches made by Nehru, J. R. D. Tata, and H. J. Bhabha. Foundation stone-laying ceremony of the Tata Institute of Fundamental Research, Bombay, 1 January 1954; from file no. 196/DTT/PHIL/TIFR/MIS/12, TCA. Indications of the above can also be found in Chowdhury, 'Fundamental Research'.

[86] See Chowdhury, 'Laboratory', 4; for a similar acknowledgement, also see Chowdhury and Dasgupta, *Masterful Spirit*.

[87] Bhabha's proposal, dated 12 March 1944 to Sorab Saklatvala, for the establishment of the TIFR; from file no. 194/DTT/PHIL/TIFR/FP/1, TCA; underlined in original.

urged Chandrasekhar to fulfil his national duty to help India create and develop institutions such as those in 'Cambridge and Paris'.[88]

The invocation of national duty worked as more than an appeal as it was also written into the institutional design strategy. Compared to the United States, India possessed only limited financial means. 'The best return can be obtained', the renowned British physiologist Archibald V. Hill noted, 'by concentrating on theoretical work in which India already has workers who are in the front line of advance'. Similar to Jamsetji Tata's turn-of-the-century philanthropy that sought to sponsor the 'best and most gifted' amongst the Indians, TIFR thus developed its institutional strategy around the availability of talent. 'You [Indians],' Hill cautioned, 'are not so rich in such people that you can give them away to America'.[89] This approach was adopted by Bhabha who believed in 'support[ing] ability wherever it was found'.[90]

While TIFR's national character was emphasized in several places, Bhabha was equally invested in simultaneously developing an international outlook. He was committed to ensuring free and frequent exchange between scientists from different parts of the world to build and maintain the international character of the institute. He actively lobbied for a frequent and unencumbered exchange of scientists from different parts of the world. In a letter to J. R. D. Tata from 1943, for example, he sought support for funding large-scale visits of international scholars to the institute, arguing that any costs involved will far outweigh the benefits of such an investment.[91]

*

The entanglements of national-modern and scientific development can be characterized—to borrow J. R. D. Tata's phrase—as 'Indian science'. Although Tata never fleshed out the contours of such science, they are not hard to decipher. Firstly, Indian science relied, to a large extent, on the patronage of the state. Speaking at TIFR's foundation stone-laying ceremony from 1954, Indian science—Tata noted—had been fortunate to have received Nehru's extensive and enthusiastic support, who 'appreciated so deeply and fully the

---

[88] From a letter dated 20 April 1944; cited from Chowdhury and Dasgupta, *Masterful Spirit*, 112.
    Here, it is important to note that the existing budgetary outlay was insufficient to recruit Chandrasekhar. J. R. D. Tata wrote to Ness Wadia of the Wadia family to endow a chair in order to recruit Chandrasekhar at TIFR; from file no. 195/DTT/PHIL/TIFR/MIS/2, TCA.
[89] File no. 195/DTT/PHIL/TIFR/MIS/2, TCA.
[90] Chowdhury, 'Fundamental Research', 1114.   [91] File no. 194/DTT/PHIL/TIFR/FP/1, TCA.

importance and vital role of scientific research in the development and future of our country'.[92]

Elsewhere, Tata exhorted scientific institutions such as IISc and TIFR to dedicate themselves to 'directions in which we can be of the greatest service'.[93] Such exhortations, the historian of science Indira Chowdhury notes, were constitutive of the national-modern trope of self-reliance: where the Indian ability to produce cutting-edge scientific research was indicative of having shrugged off its dependency on the West.[94] In such a formulation of Indian science, secondly, the sovereignty of the nation was tied to the sovereignty of its science in two ways: not only was India no longer dependent on any other nations of the world, but equally its scientists embodied national sovereignty as they fronted, as far as possible, the production of Indian science.

Although Tata only coined the term in 1954, the case for indigenizing the production of Indian science had also been made previously. Founded in 1932, the Lady Tata Memorial Trust (LTMT) for example, dedicated four-fifths of its annual income to international research, 'open to suitably qualified persons of any nationality' on blood-related diseases, particularly leukaemia. Only a fifth of the income was reserved for Indian workers researching any scientific problem related to relieving human suffering. However, none of the international awards were made to Indians until 1946, even though there were numerous Indian applicants between 1932 and 1945—all of whom were found inadequate by the international selection committee. In 1946, Dr J. J. Dubash was awarded a fellowship to work for six to eight months in the United States. It led S. S. Sokhey of the Indian Medical Service to suggest in 1948 that the Trust's philanthropy should have been restricted to research in India and by Indian scientists only. This, he noted, would also help enlarge the scope of medical research funded by the Trust.[95]

Thirdly, 'Indian science' had a utilitarian role to fulfil in India's development, as J. R. D. Tata noted elsewhere (discussed earlier in the chapter).[96]

Notwithstanding the nationalist—and later national—character of Indian science, the elites and the scientists they patronized remained committed to building the international character of their institutions. Despite Sokhey's

---

[92] Speeches made by Nehru, J. R. D. Tata, and Dr. Homi J Bhabha at TIFR's foundation stone-laying ceremony in Bombay on 1 January 1954; file no. 196/DTT/PHIL/TIFR/MIS/12, TCA.

[93] From J. R. D. Tata's presidential address at the 19th Meeting of the Court at IISc on 24 March 1956; file no. 190/DTT/PHIL/IISc/MIS/7, TCA.

[94] Chowdhury, 'Fundamental Research', 1108–16.

[95] File no. PP/DAG/D/2/2, Wellcome Library Archives, London (henceforth WLA). Also see, Kavadi, 'Leukaemia Research', 72.

[96] Speeches made by Nehru, J. R. D. Tata, and Dr. Homi J Bhabha at TIFR's foundation stone-laying ceremony in Bombay on 1 January 1954; file no. 196/DTT/PHIL/TIFR/MIS/12, TCA.

proposal to Indianize research funded by LTMT, for example, there was little interest in it. In 1949, H. H. Dale, chair of LTMT's scientific advisory committee, reported that over the preceding year there had been some discussion on amending the Trust's deed to restrict its entire income to activities in India and to be led by Indians only. The advisory committee endorsed Dale's view that 'the gain to India from any such arrangement would be disproportionately small, as compared with the prestige which had accrued and would continue to accrue to that country from the maintenance of the present very fruitful scheme of international awards'.[97]

It came up for discussion again in 1951 when J. R. D. Tata met with the advisory committee. In addition to discussing the use of LTMT's accumulated income of £5,000, Tata raised issues about restricting the geographical scope of the Trust's activities and widening the ambit of medical research funded by it. Members of the committee argued that LTMT had established an international reputation in supporting research on leukaemia and other blood diseases for itself and that widening the research scope would only detract attention, making it similar to one of many international organizations funding medical research. Convinced that the objective of the international awards should not be altered, Tata insisted that more of the research supported by the Trust be conducted at the Tata Memorial Hospital (TMH), Bombay. In return, the committee assured that a good application would always be considered favourably. Tata also proposed establishing a new international award of value of £5,000–£10,000. However, the committee members were of the opinion that the Nobel Prize had already been in existence for over fifty years, and that a new award would only compromise the recipient's chance of a Nobel award; thus, it would not necessarily have functioned as an incentive in the way Tata might have imagined. Relatedly, the committee recommended recruiting a new Scandinavian member to the international community, in light of the growing research in the region.[98]

Bringing talk of Indianizing LTMT's philanthropy to a decisive stop, the international advisory committee concluded in its meeting later that year: (a) a change in objective, which remained of contemporary relevance, would 'detract from its individuality and its special memorial significance'; (b) further research could be undertaken, and applicants from TMH would be

---

[97] Minutes of the Meeting of the Scientific Advisory Committee of the Lady Tata Memorial Trust, dated 10 May 1949; file no. PP/DAG/D/2/2, WLA.
[98] The meeting was organized on 20 September 1951 and Note written on 1 October 1951. It was attended by H. H. Dale, F. James, J. R. D. Tata, and F. H. K. Green; Scientific Advisory Committee of the Lady Tata Memorial Trust: Minutes; from file no. PP/DAG/D/2/2, WLA.

eligible for support; (c) a financial award may not be the best way forward, but the Committee could recommend such an award to the trustees; and that (d) value of individual awards could be increased to utilize the available surplus income.[99] Sokhey's efforts notwithstanding, internationalization was deemed desirable both for its reputational capital it offered and the quality of scientific research it helped fund.[100]

Although of strategic importance to the nation, the international outlook of institutions such as TIFR and LTMT was never deemed to be counter to each other. Instead, both the national and international nature of such scientific institutions inhabited the same space.

*

The desire to build national institutions on the Tatas' part meant that they were confronted with, quite frequently, competing interests of state, even as the latter's patronage served a number of crucial functions. It was useful not just in terms of sharing the financial burden of founding these institutes of science and technology but also in imparting legitimacy, while retaining institutional autonomy. One can find evidence of various instances where the Tatas approached the governing regime of the day either prior or subsequent to the establishment of the institution to seek governmental sanction and support, without compromising on their own autonomous control over the institution's affairs. For example, undeterred by the colonial administration's reluctance to support the Tatas in the establishment of IISc, in 1915, Dorabji Tata once again approached them to enquire about the practicability of having the Institute included in the scope of the new scientific and industrial research scheme of the Board of Education.[101] Not always successful or smooth, such 'encounters' often led to acrimonious exchange, controversy, and contestation (as in the case of IISc, for example). More importantly though, the encounters between the Tatas and the contemporary government of the day are instructive as they bring into relief the differences between the elites' imaginaries of science and technology and how their respective roles in India's development differed from those of the ruling regime.

---

[99] Scientific Advisory Committee of the Lady Tata Memorial Trust: Minutes of the Meeting organized on 23 November 1951; from file no. PP/DAG/D/2/2, WLA.

[100] Elsewhere, tracing the history of the LTMT from 1932 to 1953, Kavadi argues that the international context of its work must be taken note of, and posits it as a 'highlight in Indian philanthropy and Western medicine in the late colonial period'; see 'Leukaemia Research', 74.

[101] From Tata's telegram to Burjorji Padshah dated 29 July 1915 from London; file no. 175/IISc-FP-History of Education; Tata Steel and Higher Technical Education in India: One Padshah Plan 1916–1921, TCA.

In 1913, Dorabji Tata initiated attempts at supporting research in tropical medicine in India. His desire was to support research that would have been 'valuable alike to the cause of science and the progress of India'. Although Tata's initial plans focused around endowment of research chairs, he wished to found a full-scale national-level school of research in tropical medicine. Even as invited experts favoured economy and cooperation across existing research faculties, medical hospitals, and endowed chairs in the country, Tata did not necessarily agree with their suggestions.[102]

In 1917, Tata renewed his efforts at launching a 'world class institute that would attract students from all over the world'. 'That could happen,' he believed 'only if it was staffed by the very best men obtainable "from anywhere in the world" and paid a salary that was commensurate with their qualifications'. The following year, Tata submitted his proposal to the colonial administration, inviting the latter to fund the building of the school and hospital and match his funding of Rs. 70,000 annually. In exchange, Tata promised to fund the school for an initial period of five years, prospectively raising his funding to Rs. 100,000 annually contingent on the satisfactory growth of the school. His intellectual ambition was to 'encourage Indian talent and to create round the School a scientific atmosphere'. Tata's scheme was met with scepticism within the colonial medical establishment which challenged both Tata's ability as a layperson to evaluate satisfactory progress in scientific research and his demands for control over the institute's governance and research work.[103]

In 1918, Tata was actively considering a further proposal, prepared by Colonel R. McCarrison of the Pasteur Institute of Southern India, Coonoor. Titled 'A Proposal for the Foundation of an "Indian Institute of Medical Research"', it proposed establishing six research-led departments of: epidemiology, physiology, pathology, protozoology, pharmacology and therapeutics, and radiography and electro-therapeutics, each with its own laboratory; a hospital with at least five wards and a total of hundred beds; an administrative block and other amenities such as a library, animal house, laundry, garage, and workshops for carpenters and blacksmiths. Expected to cost £150,000 with a recurring annual cost of £40,000, the institute was to be designed on the 'most modern principles and equipped in accordance with the most modern standards', and with provision for expansion if the progress of

---

[102] Cited from Kavadi, 'Medical Research', 296–302.
[103] Kavadi, 'Medical Research', 252–6.

medical science made it necessary. The hospital wards were planned to be constructed along 'the most approved principles of modern construction'.[104]

McCarrison's proposed institution was modelled on the Rockefeller Institute in the United States. 'America, where the science of Western medicine is of hardly older date than in India', he argued, 'has within the last twenty years forced her way into the very forefront of medical progress by methods which are characteristically her own'. The Rockefeller Institute for Medical Research was cited as the '*most perfect organisation* in the world'. It exhorted that like the United States, India could also engage in cutting-edge, modern, medical research by following a similar trajectory, financed by the Indian capitalists.[105] While the government supported the plans for a new training institution, Tata was more interested in founding a research-intensive institution. In a letter to the secretary, government of Bombay, Tata wrote that the government was wrong to presume that 'the Bombay School will be primarily for post-graduate study, and secondarily for research'. 'I am afraid there is some misunderstanding on that point', he added, 'for I have consistently felt and held that the object of my endowment should be to stimulate the spirit of research in tropical diseases, and not merely post-graduate study unconnected with research'.[106] Thus, even as the colonial administration was committed to overcoming the deficiencies in skilled manpower by training, the Indian elites conceived such institutions as sites of knowledge production that enabled India and Indian scientists to participate in cutting-edge medical research at par with leading institutions internationally.

There were still other differences. While Tata wished to recruit the 'best possible men' and made arrangements for commensurate remuneration to attract the best talent globally, the colonial administration viewed such salaries unduly excessive. A further point of contention related to the private practice by the Institute's staff. While Tata was keen that endowed professors dedicate their time to research work, with minimal consulting permitted provided it did not interfere with the professional duties of the staff, the

[104] From 'A Proposal for the Foundation of "An Indian Institute of Medical Research"' by R. McCarrison, dated 28 May 1918. File no. Home Department, Medical A, Proceedings nos. 86–88, January 1919, NAI.
[105] From 'A Proposal for the Foundation of "An Indian Institute of Medical Research"' by R. McCarrison, dated 28 May 1918. File no. Home Department, Medical A, Proceedings nos. 86–88, January 1919, NAI.
[106] Tata's letter to the secretary, Government of Bombay dated 11 July 1921; file no. FD 1/4197, TNA.

administration insisted otherwise.[107] Tata was also emphatic about retaining his autonomy over academic appointments at the School.[108]

Interpreting these differences, Kavadi has argued that the Tatas' approach challenged the 'official paradigm'. While the colonial government was willing to accept the Tatas' endowment, they wanted the gift to be made unquestioningly. Their differences over the primary purpose of the institution brought 'to the fore divergences in ideas, attitudes and perceptions between Tata and the collaborating agencies. The rhetoric seemed to indicate that both colonial officials and Dorabji were motivated by common views but their interests were not really compatible'. 'Unlike nationalists [such as Bose and Bajaj] who set up "nationalist institutions" the Tatas', Kavadi adds, 'appeared to view state-supported "national institutions" as essential'.[109]

*

The Tatas' desire to collaborate with the government without ceding control continued post-colonialism, leading to frequent 'encounters' with the Indian government, albeit less acrimoniously than in the past. During colonialism, Tatas' response was often dressed and characterized as a nationalist impulse— helping Indians take part in the global production of scientific knowledge by overcoming its historical deficits and not merely training skilled personnel; post-colonialism, their desire to retain control even when reducing or withdrawing their financial patronage altogether became more starkly evident.

In the early 1950s, for example, Rustum Choksi initiated discussions on SDTT's behalf with personnel in the health ministry of the Government of India to 'gift' the Tata Memorial Hospital (TMH) to the nation. Summarizing early discussion, Choksi outlined their initial 'understanding' of the conditions attached to the gift: that SDTT would continue to make a grant of Rs. 200,000 per annum for an initial period of three years; the Hospital's name will remain unchanged; the Tatas could nominate ten patients for free treatment and will be adequately represented on the governing board; and that no change will be made to the fundamental character of the agreement between SDTT and the government without the former's consent.[110]

---

[107] Kavadi, 'Medical Research', 325–354.

[108] Tata's letter to the secretary, Government of Bombay, dated 11 July 1921; file no. FD 1/4197, TNA.

[109] Kavadi, 'Medical Research', 483–5.

[110] Letter from Choksi to K. C. K. E. Raja dated 25 September 1951; file no. 207/DTT/PHIL/TMH/FP/2, TCA.

Despite attempts at producing a shared understanding, frequent contests emerged over several issues, particularly the functioning of TMH's governing board and the election of the board's chair. In 1956, Amrit Kaur, then health minister, wrote that while the government was happy to have SRTT's representative on the board, it was important that the government determine the board's chair especially as it was about to become the primary patron of the hospital shortly. 'My fear of politics creeping into ever[y] institution is really genuine', she wrote justifying her worry over an elected chair of the board, especially in 'medical and scientific institutions where things must be kept out of party politics if we are really to progress as we should'.[111] Countering her, John Matthai responded on behalf of the Tata Trusts that there was a clear case for the government to make an exception to its 'normal practice', as 'the founding of this Hospital was originally inspired by the desire to perpetuate an intimate personal memory and those of us who represent the Trust have a responsibility for seeing that the founder's feelings are not disregarded'. Although the Tatas had borne large capital expenditure, he reminded Kaur, it had made, after all, a free gift to the government.[112]

Hoping to reconcile differences, Kaur offered the position of the chair of TMH's Matthai, with the understanding that it will return to the government after three years, once the institute's functioning had stabilized. The government needed to adopt, she wrote, a 'uniform policy' with regard to institutions which received financial support from the government. 'Life is impermanent', she concluded, 'and circumstances change and governments have to protect themselves as far as humanly possible. I myself am sometimes alarmed at the rate at which so-called "democracy" is being followed with not quite the results that one would expect from democracy itself'.[113]

In search of institutional legitimacy, perpetuity (especially by securing governmental funds), and autonomy, the Tatas continued to engage in similar efforts at maintaining control over institutional governance. Their position was summarized in an internal exchange between Choksi and John Matthai from 1958. 'I think we need to keep stressing the point about autonomy whenever occasion arises in respect of the Hospital and the Cancer Centre as well', Choksi wrote. 'Though the Health Minister is inclined to treat institutions

---

[111] Copy of a letter from Amrit Kaur to Matthai dated 7 August 1956, no. M.479/56 H. M., and marked personal; file no. 207/DTT/PHIL/TMH/FP/2, TCA.

[112] Matthai's letter to Amrit Kaur dated 9 August 1956; file no. 207/DTT/PHIL/TMH/FP/2, TCA.

[113] Kaur's letter to Matthai dated 30 August 1956, no. M.508/56 H. M.; file no. 207/DTT/PHIL/TMH/FP/2, TCA.

connected with Tatas differently', he added, the 'general view appears to be that where Government pays the lion's share little purpose is served by so-called autonomy, since Government is answerable to the Parliament'.[114] It was, therefore, both in the interests of the institution itself and science and technology in general that the Tatas retained effective control of such institutions.

Examples of Tata's desire to control institutions it had endowed can be found elsewhere too. Following TMH's transfer, finally executed in 1957, and later the Cancer Research Institute—subsequently merged to form the Tata Memorial Centre—the Tata Trusts decided to sponsor a Tata Blood Bank and Transfusion Service to Bombay city in 1963. Its board was to be composed of no more than fifteen persons, the trustees proposed, of which five would have represented the Tata Trusts, and four further members with either special interest or knowledge of the subject nominated by the Trusts.[115]

Building 'national' institutions required navigating other pressures beyond the control of governing boards. The Tatas also worried about growing interference in the production of Indian science. At all times, though, they remained keen to preserve the international character of these supposedly 'national' institutions. Both J. R. D. Tata and Bhabha were worried that the government's Council of Scientific and Industrial Research and later the Atomic Energy Commission would regulate scientific research at TIFR in areas deemed essential to national security. Bhabha voiced his concerns early on. 'Fundamental research requires for its performance a free atmosphere', he began. 'The scientist must be free to think of what they like and to exchange their ideas with scientists in other parts of the world and it must be possible for the scientists themselves to move and to interchange between one country and another'. Hoping to demarcate science and technology, Bhabha argued that it was not possible to conduct fundamental research in 'an atmosphere with secrecy regulations as for example are found in commercial or strategic undertakings and it is for these reasons that the Atomic Energy Commission has to separate to some extent its fundamental research activities from its more technological activities which may perhaps be restricted by other consideration'. Advocating transparency, therefore, he concluded: 'There will be no secrecy at least in normal time except in times of emergency and everything will be free so that those who are genuinely interested can come and see

[114] From Choksi's letter to John Matthai dated 10 January 1958; file no. 207/DTT/PHIL/TMH/FP/4, TCA.

[115] Agreement between the governor of Maharashtra and the trustees of SDTT and SRTT, dated 25 June 1963; file no. 209/DTT/PHIL/TBB/FP/1, TCA.

what is being done and scientists from other parts of the world can come and work here and whatever we do will be published'. Hoping to allay his fears, Nehru promised that there was no need for secrecy in an institute such as the TIFR, that science did not flourish in secrecy; and if at all any such work needed to be done, it would be done elsewhere.[116]

During the course of negotiations over the future of the DCTR in 1957, John Matthai similarly advocated for 'an exchange of workers between our Centre and other population institutes abroad' before the Indian government. This, he noted, 'should be welcomed as a useful development conferring benefit on all the parties that are concerned'.[117] One of the many contentious areas that the Tatas and their appointed scientists remained concerned about was the government's crack-down on the international travel of Indian scientists. The former argued that international travel and training for staff were 'essential...especially [for] the younger ones to spend some time abroad and to learn many new techniques of biological and medical research in the well-equipped laboratories of Europe and U.S.A'.[118]

Such efforts were central to the Tatas' desire to continue to push scientific research in new directions, even as the institutes they founded were transferred to the government. In 1959, for example, a meeting was organized in Delhi between three Tata representatives, and the minister and secretary from the health ministry to discuss various matters relating to the affairs of TMH, ICRC, and DCTR. In the meeting, the Tata representatives indicated that their future contributions should not be used for everyday expenses, which the government has assumed responsibility for. Instead, funds provided by the Tatas should be dedicated to the development of new centres and departments: such as those of chemotherapy and research in radioactive isotopes. Hoping to push through with their proposals for new areas of scientific research, the Tatas' representatives complained about the frequent delays in soliciting the government's view on the proposals submitted for new developments. With regard to the ICRC, the representatives protested against the new practice of commenting on items on the minutes of board meetings by government personnel. They pointed out that until the recent past, all previous appointments on the board had been made in consultation with the Trust.

---

[116] Speeches made by Bhabha and Nehru at the foundation stone-laying ceremony of the Tata Institute of Fundamental Research, Bombay, 1 January 1954; from file no. 196/DTT/PHIL/TIFR/MIS/12, TCA.

[117] From Matthai's letter to Amrit Kaur, minister of health, Government of India, dated 4 February 1957; file no. 187/DTT/PHIL/IIPS/MIS/1, TCA.

[118] From file no. 209/DTT/PHIL/TMH/ICRC/APP/1, TCA.

The Tata representatives argued that this practice should be restored immediately. Finally, they argued that the Tatas were now under-represented on TMH's board, following Matthai's resignation. As the minister suggested revising the board's composition, the Tata representatives suggested nominating Sir Homi Mody (1881–1969) to the position of the chair. The minister promised to give all their requests sympathetic consideration.[119]

In subsequent correspondence, representatives of the Tata Trusts identified additional issues around the production of scientific knowledge at these institutes. These ranged from hygiene factors, institutional facilities, to training opportunities for Indian scientists. They identified specific concerns about the employment conditions of newly recruited personnel, the appointment of architects for the buildings' expansion programme, sanction for the above departments, and the selection of staff for training abroad. Despite the director's recommendation, the Government of India had been insisting on a separate process inviting applications to be re-submitted, the Tatas' representatives alleged.[120]

Raising them with the central government, Choksi alleged that the government's actions had curtailed the freedom of TMH's director. Citing the transfer agreement, the Tata Trusts argued that the government's role was to consider and approve the annual budget estimated by the TMH, which was an autonomous organization. Its director and the board, therefore, were free to make and implement decisions relating to expenditure, staff selection and promotion etc., and the interference of the government was seen as curtailment of powers, and that no benefits were to accrue from such action. There was, however, no resolution as the government appointed its director general of Health Services as the next chairman of TMH. Protesting vehemently, Choksi wrote that the government had violated the transfer agreement as its actions could hardly be considered consultative. Matthai's appointment, he added, had been a 'special case'.[121]

In their quest for legitimacy, excellence, control, and institutional autonomy, the Tatas' philanthropy for scientific development attempted to synthesize the

[119] From proceedings to the Meeting with the Minister of Health, Government of India on October 12, 1959; from file no. 209/DTT/PHIL/TMH/ICRC/APP/1, TCA.

Homi Mody joined the Tatas as a director in 1934 up to 1959. In between he was also appointed to the viceroy's Executive Council in 1941; and the governor of UP in 1949.

[120] Letter from J. C. Paymaster of TMH to Choksi of SDTT, dated November 10, 1959; from file no. 209/DTT/PHIL/TMH/ICRC/APP/1, TCA.

[121] Choksi's letter to D. P. Karmarkar, minister of health, Government of India on 18 April 1960; file no. 209/DTT/PHIL/TMH/ICRC/APP/1, TCA.

strengths of both state and private institutions without once ceding control. This careful balancing of patronage and interests in the making of 'national' and previously 'nationalist' institutions was deemed essential to their ultimate success—that is, contributing to India's development.

*

Albeit on a much smaller scale, others have also followed a similarly collaborative approach to scientific development, even if the governance and day-to-day control of such institutions remained with the elites and their representatives. Although heavily reliant on the patronage of philanthropists and the nation-state, these 'national' institutes remained avowedly international in outlook.

Founded by the Sarabhais' Karmakshtera Educational Foundation (KEF) in 1947, the Physical Research Laboratory (PRL) in Ahmedabad also partnered with government agencies and departments actively. It was initially dedicated to studies in cosmic rays—the area Vikram Sarabhai specialized in, having recently completed his doctorate in the subject at Cambridge. Its institutional growth, though, owed much to the involvement, first, of the Ahmedabad Education Society (AES) which funded PRL's expansion into atmospheric physics, and later governmental agencies.[122] By 1948, PRL had begun to collaborate with the India Meteorological Department, which helped catalyse its expansion.[123] PRL grew further under the quadripartite agreement between the two philanthropic organizations—AES and KEF, the Government of India's Department of Atomic Energy, and the state government from the late 1950s onwards. PRL was chaired by Kasturbhai Lalbhai (as the representative of AES) while Sarabhai served on PRL's management council as KEF's representative.

---

[122]   Hari K. Sen, 'The Progress and Present Status of Science in India', 26.
   Founded in 1935 at the behest of Vallabhbhai Patel, AES was established with a view to expanding higher education opportunities available to Gujarati youth. It was led by G. V. Mavalankar, later the first speaker of the Lok Sabha, Lalbhai, and Amrutlal Hargovandas who came together to fund the setting up of new educational institutions in the region. The Society has since founded educational institutions in the fields of architecture, commerce, engineering, management, pharmacy, and planning. See Ahmedabad Education Society, 'History', accessed 13 March 2020, https://www.aesahd.edu.in/history.shtml.
   AES's most recent initiative includes the Ahmedabad University. Founded in 2009, the University promises a liberal, research-led, and interdisciplinary education in order to prepare 'leaders of outstanding character' in their chosen fields, educate youth to become 'contextually literate global citizens', and to 'advance the social, economic, and ecological development of local, national, and international communities'. See Ahmedabad University, 'Purpose', accessed 13 March 2020, https://ahduni.edu.in/purpose.
[123]   Sikka, 'India Meteorological Department', 413.

As with the Tata institutions, visits by international scientists were encouraged, extensively. Between 1962 and 1963, for example, scientists from University College London (1) and NASA (3) gave seminars on space research, with particular attention paid to India's incipient rocket science programme. Five other scientists from India, the United Kingdom, and the United States were also invited to visit PRL and present their work. PRL's staff visited conferences in Cambridge, London, and Rome in Europe, in Peru, or as visiting scholars at MIT and NASA in the United States, France, Italy, etc.[124] In 1963, the Government of India handed over the operation and maintenance of its Equatorial Sounding Rocket Launching Facility at Thumba, Maharashtra to PRL with a further grant of Rs. 765,000 to the latter.[125] By 1964, though, PRL's expenditure had far exceeded the provisions under the third five-year plan. Recognizing the need for additional funds, the representative of the Government of India urged the philanthropic organizations— AES and KEF—to invest more and share the growing financial burden. Council members, though, were quick to point out that much of the growing financial burden on PRL was due to the rapidly expanding space research programme of the Department of Atomic Energy and therefore it was only right that the government agency continued to fund PRL.[126]

*

As with development, philanthropy for science and technology in the twentieth century was imagined primarily around ideas of *deficit*: institutional or individual. Most of the scientific and technological institutions subsequently founded by India's economic elites came to assume a national character— owing to their scale; patronage by the state including the colonial administration; their role in preserving and furthering national interests, national security, or economic development in one way or another; and in challenging colonialism in different ways. During colonialism, science and technology was nationalist as it was tied, intricately, to notions of autonomy and advancement. Even as the colonial administration remained committed to widening training institutions, elites such as the Tatas were convinced the funding of research was integral to achieving autonomy and excellence.

---

[124] Physical Research Laboratory, 'Annual Report, 1962–63', KL.
[125] Letter from R. Shroff, deputy secretary, Government of India to PRL's director dated 23 October 1963, KL.
[126] Minutes of PRL's management council's meeting, 10 February 1964, KL.

Such impulses intensified post-colonialism as Indian science and scientists embodied self-reliance and sovereignty. Despite their imbrication in the national question, science and technology remained paradoxically avowedly international in outlook. Notwithstanding the pushback from contemporary regimes including the post-colonial Indian government, philanthropy enabled the Indian economic elites to retain control over the governance of scientific and technological research institutions long after they had ceased to be its primary patrons.

5

Development

Elites' Pedagogic Reflex

'In every bit of work undertaken' by the Tata's Rural Welfare Board (RWB), 'the educative aspect [was] kept in mind and the work [was] planned in assimilable doses'.[1] It stressed 'gradual evolution', with a particular emphasis on the 'active and conscious participation of the local population, in the various economic, social and welfare activities undertaken to improve the conditions and quality of their living'. Crucial to modernizing rural Indian society, according to an internally commissioned evaluation report from 1986, was 'to mould the attitude and outlook of the villagers for this purpose and this is an ardous (*sic*) long term process'.[2] As elites founded new associations, boards, *sabhas*, and *sanghathans*, and later sponsored and partnered with NGOs, and still later founded 'cells' and think-tanks as part of the emergent realm of civil society, they assumed—I argue in this chapter—an educative role. The impulse to educate, like that of RWB, became crucial to their pursuit of national-modern development. This educating tendency, which I have chosen to designate as a 'pedagogical reflex' drawing on Chatterjee, can be witnessed in sites as disparate as: individual self, community, schools, institutions of science and technology, and markets; and in new and modern registers of citizenship, self-reliance, and merit, etc. they financed.[3] In the later parts of the chapter, I argue that fulfilling the *pedagogic reflex* necessitated both new forms of knowledge and cadres of foot-soldiers that traversed the many miles to the 'field' for the transmittal of national-modern; to which elites, once more, made extensive gifts.

---

[1] From a report titled, 'Devapur Project: Achievements of a Quiet, Persistent Effort by Tatas for the Development of a Drought Prone Area (1952–1984)'. File no. 185/DTT/PHIL/RWB/BO/1963/1, TCA.

[2] Y. S. Pandit, *A Survey of Devapur*, 1986. Tata Rural Welfare Board. File no. 185A/DTT/RWB/1986, TCA.

[3] Chatterjee, 'Civil and Political Societies', 165–78.

Philanthropy and the Development of Modern India: In the Name of Nation. Arun Kumar, Oxford University Press.
© Arun Kumar 2021. DOI: 10.1093/oso/9780198868637.003.0005

Educating the Masses

As the *Swadeshi* fever gripped the country, elites came forward—far more actively than before—to propagate nationalism. From khadi to Hindi and 'Indian' culture, elites financed civil society associations whose primary purpose was pedagogic. In 1930, for example, hoping to convince the masses to boycott foreign goods and support local industries, they launched the Swadeshi Prachar Association (or Association for Propagating Swadeshi). Despite the disagreement among the mill-owners, importers, distributors, and with the Congress Party, the postcolonial elites were clear in their pedagogic ambition. The Association's purpose was to carry on propaganda to induce Indians to 'use only Swadeshi cloth, meaning by that expression *Shudh Khaddar*, i.e., hand spun, hand woven Indian cloth or cloth produced by Mills in India in the manufacture of which no foreign yarn has been used and the Mills are under the control and management of Indians'. The Prachar Association was committed to spreading 'information among the people of the sources of supply of Swadeshi cloth'.[4]

The promotion of Hindi as a national language was also a popular cause, favoured particularly by the caste-Hindu elites. In the 1920s, for example, the Birlas supported the Kashi Pracharini Sabha (literally the Association for Propagating Kashi) for the propagation of Hindi.[5] They were soon joined by others, including Bajaj, Ramnath Goenka, and Padampat Singhania in the late 1930s and early 1940s. Actively involved in the propagation of Hindi in Southern India, Ramnath Goenka, the founder of the major daily newspaper *Indian Express*, was asked by Bajaj to devise a detailed financial scheme to sustain the operations of the *Hindi Rashtra Bhasha Prachar Samiti*, or the Committee for the Propagation of Hindi as a National Language, tapping into supposedly growing public support.[6] Elsewhere, fellow Marwari and leader of the J. K. Group, Padampat Singhania (1905–1979) pledged in 1937 to donate Rs. 15,000 each year for five years for the Samiti. It was to be used, specifically in the propagation of the language in non-Hindi speaking states, including Maharashtra, Sindh, Assam, Odisha.[7] Providing an overview of work conducted from monies donated by Singhania, Bajaj wrote: 'With the objective of

---

[4] From the Rules of the Swadeshi Prachar Association, 1930; from file no. 100, PT.
[5] Kudaisya, *G. D. Birla*, 71.
[6] Letter from Bajaj to Goenka dated 26 November 1937, Correspondence: Goenka, Ramnath, JB (1st inst.).
[7] From Correspondence: Singhania, Padampat, JB (1st inst.).

unifying India, Hindi Prachar Samiti has been actively promoting Hindi language'.[8]

Birla was also actively involved with the activities of Bharatiya Vidya Bhavan, founded by K. M. Munshi and his wife Lilawati. Among others, Birla sponsored the *Bharatiya Itihas Samiti* (or Indian History Society) at the Vidya Bhavan. It was tasked with preparing an eleven-volume history series on the 'History and Culture of the Indian People', under the leadership of the Indian historian R. C. Majumdar. In 1943, Birla agreed to donate Rs. 150,000 for the project and agreed to serve as the vice-chairman of the committee to oversee its publication.[9]

Framed as part of Hindu nationalism in colonial India, the proliferation of such civil society institutions—more often than not spawned by elites' money and networks—was driven by elites' impulse to educate the 'ignorant' masses and was built around strategies of persuasion and reform. Founded in 1932, the All-India Anti-Untouchability League adopted a two-pronged approach. It proposed employing two itinerant workers per revenue district or even for two districts depending upon the size of Dalit population in each district. While they were to educate the Dalits directly, their movement and mingling with them was expected to persuade other caste-Hindus to self-reform. Notwithstanding the criticism of such caste-reform initiatives (discussed in detail in chapter 2), the League hoped that the 'very existence of and the movement of these two workers in villages, and their joining freely with Harijans in order to know their needs and grievance', would have been 'propaganda by itself'. It would have served, the League's founders and financiers hoped, to influence the views, both public and private, of the orthodox caste Hindus by merely witnessing the inter-mingling of the workers with 'untouchable' communities.[10]

Similarly, in their support for prohibition and temperance movements throughout the 1920s–1930s (discussed in chapter 3 previously), the elites also adopted a pedagogic approach to persuade the masses. In April 1929, C. Rajagopalachari and Thakurdas designed a temperance programme on behalf of the Prohibition League of India. Costing Rs. 100,000, it was to be financed initially through the Madras Presidency's 'Temperance Programme'. Its aim was 'to develop active local feeling against the use of drink and drugs,

---

[8] Letter from Bajaj to Singhania dated 10 November 1938, Correspondence: Singhania, Padampat, JB (1st inst.). Such pedagogic efforts from the first half of the twentieth century involved the consolidation of linguistic, religious, and political interests as part of Hindu nationalism, see Mukul, *Gita Press*, 4–8.

[9] Kudaisya, *G. D. Birla*, 164.

[10] *The All-India Anti-Untouchability League: Aims and Objects, Scheme of Propaganda and Uplift Work, Budget and Constitution*, dated November 1932, file no. 121/1932, PT.

to foster and organize local effort wherever possible'. One hundred rural and five urban workers were tasked with conducting pedagogic work of cultivating this 'local feeling'; with twelve district and two urban inspectors, as well as a small central office to oversee accounts, clerical work, etc. In short, the programme sought to create a cadre of full-time workers 'devoting themselves to persuading people…against the use of Alcoholic drinks and drugs'.[11]

It is worth pointing out here that even as elites engaged in educating the masses, there was little sincere attempt at learning about India's masses themselves. The only exception to this was Gandhi who exhorted his patrons to learn about the poor. In 1927, for example, Birla was nominated by the Federation of Indian Chambers of Commerce and Industry to travel to Geneva as its representative for the tenth International Labour Conference. Although some of the orthodox members of his caste threatened ostracization, Birla decided to travel abroad and follow Gandhi's instructions on his travels. Along with his eleven-point code of conduct, Gandhi suggested that Birla meet the secretary of state or the British prime minister in London. He also encouraged Birla to familiarize himself with poverty and living conditions of the poor in England. This could be done, Gandhi suggested, 'by visiting jails and by walking through poor localities'. 'Station yourself near the bars in poor as also prosperous localities on Saturday nights', he directed, 'for making comparative study'.[12] In short, learn from the poor.

*

In the early 1950s, elites continued to champion *Swadeshi* as a way of invigorating indigenous industry for the economic development of the country. Business leaders such as S. P. Godrej and Naval H. Tata founded the Swadeshi League. Headquartered in Bombay, the League's aims were to 'propagate the cult of "Swadeshi" amongst our people and make them "Swadeshi-minded" in order to expand indigenous industry, commerce and services'. Tapping into their distribution and franchise networks, firms such as that of Godrej invited stockists, dealers, and showroom owners to join the League. '[Y]ou will materially benefit', they noted a circular from 1954, 'since the larger sale of "Swadeshi" products would mean greater income to all concerned'. Moreover, enrolment came with the added benefits of a free 'very informative journal'.[13]

---

[11] Scheme submitted to the Secretary of Government, Public Health Department, Government of Madras; file no. 64 (pt. IV), PT.

[12] Kudaisya, *G. D. Birla*, 95.

[13] Circular NDS/Cir/25417 dated 1 July 1954; Doc. 111, MS 08-01-419-306, GA.

Elites' pedagogic approach to development intensified, post-colonial, as development imaginaries gravitated firmly towards modernization. Responding to the drought and famine in Bihar in 1966–67, for example, TRC assumed the expected educational role—to help the poor peasants '*learn* scientific ways of agriculture and adopt self-help measures for an all-round uplift of the villages'. The potential recipients of such 'scientific' knowledge were often described as 'keen to learn better ways'. Through its efforts, TRC hoped to reorient the villagers' psychology to 'arouse the [c]o-operative team spirit and for taking up cleanliness drives in the villages'; and 'place the village economy on a sound basis by raising their standard of living to a dignified level'.[14]

It did not, however, yield expected results. A review of TRC's work in Bihar found that the villagers did not 'exhibit the requisite enthusiasm... They are constantly being persuaded to help themselves for their own benefit but their short sightedness often impedes the progress of the work'.[15] Noting the difficulties in *educating* the masses, a subsequent review of the RWB's interventions in Devapur similarly noted: 'Transformation in the attitude and outlook of the rural population which will goad it on for a sustained cooperative effort in the interest of the community as a whole, necessarily takes a long time'.[16] The pedagogic challenges were recognized elsewhere too. An evaluation report of the Tata Trusts' support to Auroville from 1987 noted that despite its programmatic success, Auroville had 'not been able to penetrate the family life so successfully'. 'The local villager's family units', the report argued, tended 'to continue [to be] isolated and firmly rooted in tradition with their old living and working habits'. And while, some families had benefited, materially, 'The new money has actually in many cases harmed the social fabric due to increasing social vices'. Such temporary setbacks, though, were not seen as shortcomings of their development imaginaries. On the contrary, they demonstrated conclusively the need for educating the people to 'awaken their consciousness––for hard work, a sense of understanding, spirit of cooperation,

---

[14] Work undertaken by Tata Relief Committee after drought and subsequent famine in Bihar, 1967. File no. 183/DTT/PHIL/TRC/BIHAR/1967/1–3, TCA; italicized for emphasis.

[15] Work undertaken by Tata Relief Committee after drought and subsequent famine in Bihar, 1967. File no. 183/DTT/PHIL/TRC/BIHAR/1967/1–3, TCA.

[16] Y. S. Pandit, *A Survey of Devapur*, 1986. Tata Rural Welfare Board. File no. 185A/DTT/RWB/1986, TCA.

feeling of optimism in their future and not only look for material and financial security'.[17]

*

Elites' pedagogic reflex was also evident in elites' philanthropy for population control, especially between the 1960s and 1970s. Unlike the government's coercive methods involving forced sterilization (most prominently used during the country's Emergency), India's economic elites placed their faith in science and medicine (discussed previously in chapter 4), and education and persuasion, which I discuss next.

In 1966, the Godrej group launched its family planning initiative as part of the Godrej Pragati Kendra (Godrej Centre for Progress). Primarily educative, the initiative sought to convince families to adopt family planning and persuade married couples to have no more than three children. Setting out the welfare aspects of family planning, an introductory note listed the benefits to the parents and children including enabling mothers to raise children only when they were ready to and fathers to work their jobs without the anxiety of raising a large family, thus becoming 'an asset not only to his family and his employer but also to the society'. Subsequent pamphlets sought to embed the benefits of family planning in the national question more directly. Pointing to the food situation in the country, a pamphlet noted that the recent cut of 12.5 per cent in rations was 'an indication of a grave food situation' confronting the country. Using folktales, it tried to educate the workers about their responsibilities and urged people to *voluntarily* adopt family planning 'so that the nation can conserve food and thus lead on to the path of self sufficiency'.[18]

Still other pamphlets used scare tactics to persuade couples to adopt family planning. Counting the current costs of raising a child to adulthood at current prices (1967) as Rs. 28,000, it pointed out that this was only a 'conservative estimate' with cost 'increas[ing] many times over'. Subsequent pamphlets pointed to the shortage of water in Bombay city, growing unemployment, and food availability as deleterious consequences of population growth. Following messages from religious leaders posted in their pamphlets, the Kendra published a more detailed pamphlet in October 1968 listing available services. In addition to contraceptives and sterilizations, they offered financial incentives to men and women undergoing sterilizations as well as to those who

---

[17] From S. R. Suratwala's Report on the visit to Auroville in July 1987; from file no. 180/DTT/PHIL/DON/18, TCA.

[18] From MS 06-10-11-1, GA.

convinced them to undergo the operation in the first place. By 1969, the Kendra was also distributing oral contraceptive pills free to women.[19]

J. R. D. Tata, similarly, made his position against coercion and for persuasion clear for 'population control' in several places. Following the conferment of an honorary doctorate, Tata spoke about the urgent need to control the country's population and accelerate economic development. Published widely in newspapers, Tata's speech elicited numerous letters seeking his urgent cooperation on finding the solution to the problem. One such letter held the 'common man' responsible for the problem and wrote, he 'is free to procreate to his heart's content and perhaps with revenge' in response to the forced sterilizations during the Emergency years. It argued that 'compulsory sterilization' was the only possible answer.[20] Tata strongly opposed coercion in his response. He cited the work of organizations such as the Family Planning Foundation, which was established in 1970, and later renamed as the Population Foundation of India in 1993. Founded by J. R. D. Tata and Bharat Ram, the leading industrialist and scion of the Sri Ram Group, with the objective of supporting 'path-finding scientific research' on population control, the Foundation focused on non-official efforts at population control, primarily through scientific research, which was 'innovative and experimental, developmental in orientation or had demonstration or replicative value' and action projects which had policy implications.[21]

The focus, therefore, was on exercising control not through coercion, but by funding scientific research (discussed previously in chapter 4) and educating the masses.

*

Throughout the twentieth century, India's economic elites gifted their money and lands, and volunteered their time and leadership to help support civil society organizations and found new ones. Although one might argue that propagandist associations from colonial India were distinct from developmental activities such as those of the RWB, post-colonialism, when it came to issues around which they sought to engage the masses and their mode for doing so, I would argue the opposite. They are less dissimilar than they appear to be. Both the nationalist associations and the nongovernmental development organizations sponsored through elites' philanthropy were, firstly, committed to crafting an autonomous developmental realm of the national-modern—distinct from colonial forms of modernity, carried out in the name of the nation: whether as part of different nationalisms from the first half of the twentieth century, or in the name of nation-building, later. Secondly, they were animated by a 'pedagogic reflex'.

As civil society was deemed central, intrinsic, and therefore universal, to the attainment of modernity, India's elites committed themselves to crafting this autonomous realm that was outside the regulation of the colonial state.[22] Propagandist, nationalist organizations such as the Swadeshi Prachar Association were part of the constellation of institutions that embodied the desire of the postcolonial elites to 'replicate in its own society the forms as well as the substance of Western modernity', while articulating its differences from it—more often than not by accommodating caste, religion, culture, etc.—which can be understood as 'circumscribed modernity' as I have suggested previously in chapter 2. Civil society in India, however, has remained an 'exclusive domain of the elite, that the actual "public" will not match up to the standards required by civil society'. The central function of the civil society, according to Chatterjee, therefore, has been 'one of pedagogy rather than of free association'.[23]

Building on this, I would argue that the postcolonial elites' commitment to educating the masses—that is, teach them about the assemblages, codes, conventions, attitudes, and behaviours of the national-modern—can be helpfully designated as their 'pedagogic reflex'. I use the term 'reflex' both in its physiological sense, as that which emerges instinctively or from pre-knowledge, and is, therefore, a default response or tendency; but also in its usage of reproducing essential features or qualities, i.e. essence.[24] This educative work was carried out in the newly constituted realm of civil society in the country. It was animated by the *pedagogic* ambition of the elites which used philanthropy, strategically and purposively, to educate the masses about the elites' formulations and formations of the national-modern.

*

---

[22]   Kaviraj and Khilnani, 'Introduction', 1–7.
[23]   Chatterjee, 'Civil and Political Societies', 174.
[24]   According to the Oxford English Dictionary, the word 'reflex' refers, in the physiological sense, to 'an action that is performed without conscious thought as a response to a stimulus'; but more widely 'an automatic, habitual, or instinctive action or response'. It also refers to 'an image, reproduction: a thing which reflects or reproduces certain essential features or qualities of an original' ('reflex', Oxford English Dictionary, accessed 7 August 2015; www.oed.com/view/Entry/160937?rskey=GNcPn6&result=1#eid).

The 'pedagogic reflex' has continued to animate elites' development imaginaries into the twenty-first century. SDTT's annual report from 2005–06, for example, outlined the need for training and building peoples' and organizations' capacities to participate in government-led decision-making processes. The Trust committed itself to 'building civil society' to ensure 'access of rights for the poorest of the poor and/or socially marginalized'.[25]

Unsurprisingly, then, synthesizing mainstream education and training with pedagogies of participation became the focus of twenty-first-century elites' philanthropy where education was increasingly seen as an amenable platform for changing lives, at scale.[26] The Bharti Foundation, for example, was founded with the aim of improving access and quality of education for children and youth across rural India. Launched in 2000, the Foundation's flagship Satya Bharti School programme currently runs nearly two hundred primary schools in six states, with a total outreach of nearly forty thousand children, a large majority of whom are Dalit.[27] It also runs partnership programmes with over seven hundred schools in fourteen states to improve students' and teachers' overall experience by providing supplementary curricular and extra-curricular resources. Particularly instructive here, is the Foundation's ultimate goal which is to make the rural children and youth it works with market-ready. The students must therefore grow to become 'educated, confident, *responsible and self-reliant employable citizens* of the country'.[28]

Similarly focused on the public education system, the Azim Premji Foundation is dedicated to the universalization of education in the country.[29] Launched in 2001, the Foundation was formed through a transfer of Premji's personal holding of shares in Wipro—one of India's leading IT and consulting firms with over a hundred and seventy-five thousand employees. In 2015, Premji had donated over 20 per cent of his personal stake in Wipro to the Foundation. Outlining his philanthropic motivation, Premji—once more,

[25] SDTT, Annual Report, 2005–06, file no. 210/SDTT/2005–2006, TCA.

[26] Sundar, *Giving with Thousand Hands*, 193.

[27] Bharti Foundation, 'Our work', accessed 18 December 2019, https://www.bhartifoundation.org/page/satya-bharti-school-programs.

[28] Satya Bharti School Programme, 'Objectives', accessed 18 December 2019, https://www.bharti-foundation.org/page/satya-bharti-school-programs; italicized for emphasis

[29] Premji (*b.* 1945) was born in Bombay where his father founded the Western Indian Vegetable Products Limited the same year. He was studying for an engineering degree at Stanford, United States, but had to return to India following his father's death, shortly before his graduation. Having taken over his father's business, Premji diversified the family business into soaps, shoes, and lightbulbs. He renamed the businesses to Wipro in 1977 before venturing into computer hardware, and later software, where he made extensive wealth as a leading provider of outsourcing services.

Azim Premji was the first Indian to sign up to the Gates's *Giving Pledge*; and by 2015, Premji alone accounted for nearly 80 per cent of total donations made by the top Indian philanthropists.

couched development within the national question—asking rhetorically, 'Do we feel connected to our country, to the people around us? Should not every Indian have the basic, bare necessities of a life of dignity? This is certainly not hoping for too much; its (*sic*) just basic safety, adequate food, a roof to sleep under, basic education and healthcare'.[30] Unlike others, the Foundation takes a comprehensive approach to education working on teacher training, curricular reform, assessment, measurement, etc. and at all levels of education (from primary to research within universities). Like the Tatas, it takes an institutional approach, having founded a number of demonstration schools (six in four states), district institutes (forty-six in six states), and a teacher learning centre. Each of these work closely with the public education system and offer 'on the ground support'. The Foundation's overall mission is to have 'deep, at-scale and institutionalised impact on the quality of education' in the country, which will in turn lead to a 'just, equitable, humane and sustainable society'.[31]

*

As elites have invested in fulfilling their pedagogic ambition of creating 'self-reliant employable citizens' through training and education, they have been confronted with the growing need for producing new fields of knowledge and cadres of professionally trained workers to carry out the pedagogic mission. 'India's problems', according to the Tatas, for example, 'were complicated and needed the study of social sciences, not only for a proper analysis, but also for achieving clearly defined objectives with modern methods and techniques'.[32] Their quest for such an applied knowledge in order to reform Indian society in ways that elites deemed important led them to funding and founding institutes of research and training in the social sciences, albeit on a much smaller scale than with science and technology. I turn to these in the rest of this chapter.

Reforming Society: Applied Social Sciences

Although largely dedicated to scientific research and training, Jamsetji Tata's initial plans for IISc, Bangalore, included provisions for teaching courses in

---

[30] Cited from Sundar, *Giving with Thousand Hands*, 154–5.
[31] Azim Premji Foundation, 'About us', accessed 18 December 2019, https://azimpremjifoundation. org/about/what-we-do#block-menu-menu-about-menu.
[32] From draft report of the history-writing of its philanthropy initiated from within the Tata Group; file no. 181/DTT/PHIL/MIS/3, TCA.

social sciences and humanities. Courses in education, psychology, history and archaeology, statistics, economics, and comparative philology, for example, were listed along with specialized courses in science and engineering subjects. With a view to widening the scope of social sciences and humanities departments at the Institute, Ratan J. Tata, then-deceased Jamsetji's younger son, initiated plans for establishing a new social science school. However, it led to a bitter contest between Morris W. Travers, the first director of the Institute, and Jamsetji's sons—Ratan and Dorabji—about the disciplinary orientation of the Institute. While the Tatas were committed to realizing the founding spirit of the Institute, their plans clashed with Travers's own vision for a scientific research centre in a country such as India. In a letter to Burjorji Padshah, Ratan J. Tata's then-trusted lieutenant, for example, Travers chided the former for his plans to apply proceeds from Jamsetji Tata's estate for 'anthropology'. 'The fault of all colleges in India', Travers wrote, 'is that they try to spread themselves too much. We [at IISc] require several additional departments in pure science and in applied science before we shall be able to consider the Institute strong, and, limited as we are, it is very difficult to decide in what direction we should start off'.[33]

In 1910, Ratan J. Tata again asked Burjorji Padshah to contact Travers outlining the plans for a postgraduate centre of research and teaching. Padshah's letter was accompanied by a note in which further details of the Tatas' scheme were laid out. Tata's proposal for an endowment for a School of Social Studies at IISc is particularly instructive in its imagination of the scope and place of social sciences in the development of the country. To be established alongside departments of science and technology at the Institute, the School was to benefit from its proximity to the latter departments 'because of the positive and comparative method to be applied to [their common] problems'. Departments of 'Heredity, or statistical methods' were to have offered their expertise to solving problems in the 'Physical and Social Wings'. The founding premise of the School, and it is worth citing at length, was as follows:

Within the last ten years, much has been done to rouse the people to the need of education in the sciences which are applicable to the development of

---

[33] Letter from Travers to Padshah dated 23 December 1906; file 86, UCL-SC. At the bottom of the page, Travers added later in pencil: 'Even at this stage I did not believe that Padshah was playing a crooked game with me'; such was the degree of animus between the Tatas and their representatives, on the one hand, and Travers, on the other. Also see Subbarayappa, *Pursuit of Excellence*; and Kim Sebaly, 'Tatas and University Reform', 117–36 for an account of the tussle.

industries. But a belief that a knowledge of these sciences will lead to their effective application to industries, presupposes a state of society which is ready and anxious to use every means in its power to improve its economic and general conditions. How far such an assumption is true of India, in what respects it fails and how in these respects the social life of the people may be corrected, are questions of the first importance to the statesman, the industrial leader and to the social reformer.[34]

The School was expected to 'do more investigation than teaching', 'deal with practical problems rather than theories and generalizations', and prepare students for both public and private careers. Included with the proposal was a detailed syllabus with twenty-five prospective areas of study, including: problems of heredity and environment, health and disease, marriage customs as contributing factors to social efficiency, police and the army, physique of the nation, deteriorating influences, strikes, trade unions, superstitions, etc. Drawing attention to the areas of 'public' life in the country that were seen as problematic, the proposal was expansive in terms of the breadth of social change the elites desired. It proposed conducting survey studies at the School to 'comprehend the whole life of man from cradle to the grave. The influence of Heredity on the one hand and that of theological and ontological beliefs on the other, will have to be included in this survey so that the studies really must extend prior to the cradle and beyond the grave'.[35]

In this way, social sciences—in elites' imaginings—sought to bring the 'social' world in its entirety under the 'gaze' of the trained researcher. It proposed training an 'army of journeymen investigators who will not argue what effects must take place, but point out that there are positive facts A, and positive facts B, and positive links seen as links between A & B'. Decrying what the proposal labelled as the 'deductive research' that went on in other contemporary institutions in the country, it argued that the research conducted at the School would be 'systematic' and based on 'the positive method'. The proposal thus envisioned methodological convergence between the physical and natural sciences on the one hand and social sciences on the other.[36]

The Tatas' efforts at establishing the School at IISc, however, remained unsuccessful. Committed to researching society in this way, Ratan J. Tata then

[34] Correspondence between Padshah and director, IISc regarding the establishment of Sir Ratan Tata School of Social Science, dated 19 May 1910; includes an outline of proposed school. File no. Passfield 10/2/1, London School of Economics Archives, London (LSEA).

[35] Correspondence between Padshah and director, IISc dated 19 May 1910.

[36] Correspondence between Padshah and director, IISc dated 19 May 1910; underlined in original.

offered his support to the University of London. His efforts culminated in the establishment of a research centre which later became the renowned Department of Social Science and Administration at the London School of Economics and Political Science. Attempts at establishing a School of Social Sciences in India, though, remained unfulfilled until the early 1930s, when they were revived by Clifford Manshardt.

A report on the possible areas of work for the Sir Dorabji Tata Trust recommended establishing a Bureau of Social and Industrial research for the 'continuous investigation of fundamental problems'. The Bureau was expected to tackle challenges relating to the 'Application of Science to Industry—an inquiry based upon recognition of the fact that unhealthy industries are a drain upon the economic health of the nation'. 'It might consider', the report added, researching 'the subject of Caste, both in production and distribution'. This was deemed particularly important for the following reason: 'while many employers pay attention to efficiency in production, they fail to recognise those inefficiencies in marketing which go far to blot out the savings accomplished through efficient production'. The proposal also outlined plans for the Bureau to study co-operative credit mechanisms to enhance the purchasing power of the masses, the economic condition of the Indian peasantry, and the economic and sociological results of unemployment.[37]

Echoing the 'scientific' study of the social realm from the earlier proposal from 1910, the Report's recommendation for establishing a Bureau finally took shape in the form of the Tata Institute of Social Sciences, Bombay (henceforth TISS). Approved in 1935, the Institute was initially called the Sir Dorabji Tata School of Social Work.[38] It was conceived, however, as a school of training with an unbridled emphasis on the *practical*—that is 'applying the best of social thought to our present-day social problems'.[39]

The idea of such a training institute was based on a growing recognition among the elites that realizing their pedagogic reflex required well-trained, often professionally certified, workers who were equipped with the necessary technical and social knowledge. As early as the 1920s, they realized that the lack of such trained human resources was a bigger constraint to their

---

[37] From a 'Preliminary Report for the Trustees of the Sir Dorabji Tata Trust Suggesting Methods of Utilising the Present Income of the Trust and the Broad Lines of Future Engagement'; file no. 198/DTT/PHIL/TISS/FP/4, TCA; underlined in original.

[38] Early approval to the Scheme, drafted by Manshardt, was given, and he was asked to develop the 'concrete details of organization'; from Minutes, 19th Meeting of the Board of Trustees, SDTT, dated 6 July 1935. File no. 178/DTT/DJT/PERS/PROP/LEG/WILLS/BO/OPT/1, TCA.

[39] From a note titled 'Proposed Sir Dorabji Tata School of Social Work'; from file no. 199/DTT/PHIL/TISS/MIS/1, TCA.

national-modern ambitions than financial capital ever could have been. Bajaj, for example, recognized that promoting khadi and boycotting foreign cloth (which as I have discussed in chapter 2 was crucial to envisioning community-based modes of production) needed an army of competent workers. It was not easy, he noted, 'to find able, energetic and reliable workers' for the All-India Spinners Association.[40] Demands for such workers were also raised by those closer to the field such as Manshardt. Recounting his experience of leading the Nagpada Neighborhood Society in his autobiography, Manshardt wrote about the lack of trained social workers in the country, especially in India's urban centres.[41] The desire for such professional training in the country, he believed, was huge; and enthusiasm among potential students was seen as an 'excellent commentary on the social spirit of the Indian student'.[42]

In a draft of his autobiography, Manshardt recalled his core idea behind TISS: 'As a graduate school, we maintained a high academic standard, but we also sought to be eminently practical and to apply the best of modern social thinking to the solution of India's social problems'. It needed to devise, though, new modes of training new cadres of social workers as contemporary training—which had been based on practical learning, through apprenticeships for example—was seen as 'unscientific' and 'limited in scope'. Such training lacked 'the modern scientific background necessary for rendering skilled and effective service for those in need'.[43] The School, therefore, needed to offer professional training based on modern 'scientific' social sciences.

While such 'scientific' social sciences were already available in the West—for example through research on poverty and social welfare funded by Ratan J. Tata at the LSE—it was not quite available in India. In orientating social work to the 'Indian' conditions, a proposal for the School suggested adapting Western social science knowledge to the specificities of the Indian context before it could be adopted at institutes such as TISS for professional training. This, the proposal noted, 'will place at the disposal of the Indian student the best social thought of the day and will encourage the Indian student to undertake fundamental research into Indian social and industrial

---

[40] Nanda, *In Gandhi's Footsteps*, 156.

[41] File no. 199/DTT/PHIL/TISS/MIS/1, TCA.

[42] From a chapter titled 'Bombay Days' from a draft of Manshardt's autobiography; from file no. 199/DTT/PHIL/TISS/MIS/1, TCA.

[43] From a chapter titled 'Bombay Days' from a draft of Manshardt's autobiography; from file no. 199/DTT/PHIL/TISS/MIS/1, TCA.

problems'. Thus, TISS sought to use Western social thought to understand the specifics of the Indian social condition.[44]

In an address at TISS's opening session, its founding director Clifford Manshardt outlined this task of 'translating' the scientific social science resources from the West to the Indian context. He acknowledged that even if the recommended books were from the West, the students could have been trained to think of them in the Indian context. Although this required 'modification', there was no need for an outright rejection of the West, a common impulse of some of the contemporary anti-colonial nationalists. Invoking the universality of human experience, Manshardt argued that 'Man's (*sic*) aspirations, strengths, and weaknesses,' after all, were 'pretty much the same the world over.'[45] Translating Western social science into the Indian context, Manshardt argued elsewhere: 'We recognized that the cultural, economic and social conditions of India differed from those of the West, and made every effort to adapt our materials to Indian conditions, and to interpret Indian problems in the light of the national social heritage'.[46] Thus, one finds that the modern social sciences needed to be modified, or translated to suit the Indian conditions, which were distinct from the West. Here, it is worth noticing how there was little effort at producing 'new' social thought based on the Indian experience; instead the emphasis was on tailoring and adapting Western ideas and educational material to Indian society, which needed to be reformed on account of its deficiencies and deviations.

TISS ultimately offered courses, which were broadly categorized into pre-professional courses (social origin, sociology, economics, and social psychology); orientation courses ('normal' human development, behaviour modification, family and child psychology, Indian industry and its workers); and practice courses (mental hygiene, delinquency, group work, recreation, etc.). Once trained, the graduates were expected to work as welfare workers for industries and municipalities, administrative officers in charity and welfare organizations, case workers [or what one might now call programme staff] of charities and trusts, statistical, economic, and industrial researchers,

[44] From file no.199/DTT/PHIL/TISS/MIS/1, TCA.
[45] From the Manshardt's address titled 'The School of Social Work and its Students' at the Opening Session of the Sir Dorabji Tata Graduate School of Social Work, 20 June 1938, Bombay. File no. 198/DTT/PHIL/TISS/FP/5, TCA.
[46] From a draft of Manshardt's autobiography, under the heading 'Bombay Days'; from file no. 199/DTT/PHIL/TISS/MIS/1, TCA.

industry inspectors and labour officers, social settlement workers, labour leaders, and adult education leaders, among others.[47]

Such a professionally trained social worker at TISS, Manshardt noted in his opening session at the institute in 1938, needed to possess scientific knowledge of society, as well as embody particular 'modern' behaviours and attitudes. They needed to 'speak and write in order to win the moral and financial support of the public', to 'learn to use time without dawdling', and that they were being 'trained for life, and life leadership demand[ed] thinking men *(sic)* of broad culture'.[48] Their training, accordingly, emphasized particular forms of multi-disciplinary knowledge (about society, history, psychology, economy, and industry), desirable behavioural traits (sincere, devoted, cultured), and key skills (such as effective writing and efficient use of time). Notwithstanding such lofty expectations, the truth was far from it. The early graduates, Manshardt noted, lacked the necessary English language skills. They needed to be trained, therefore, in speaking and writing English first in order to overcome the 'linguistic difficulties' of a pan-Indian institution.[49] The trained development professionals, it was noted elsewhere, always displayed 'a spirit of devotion and service but it also implies a good up-to-date knowledge of how societies are born and grow; what capacities human individuals bring to the service of society; how defects in human individuals corrode the life of societies; how economic factors affect civilizations; how high ethical ideals give a tone to civilizations'.[50]

*

As the irresolutions of modernity in the country became more glaring post-colonialism, the received and 'translated' social sciences from the West came under challenge. An institution-wide review at TISS, conducted in 1953, questioned the earlier attempts at translation or indigenization of social theories and knowledge. The reviewers J. Matthai, A. Wilkins and E. Younghusband argued that the institute's students were being set an arduous task when they are asked to 'study in an alien tongue the practices of an alien culture and then try to apply these in situations which in any event make

---

[47] From a note titled 'Proposed Sir Dorabji Tata School of Social Work'; from file no. 199/DTT/PHIL/TISS/MIS/1, TCA.

[48] Address delivered by C. Manshardt titled 'The School of Social Work and its Students', at the Opening Session of the Sir Dorabji Tata Graduate School of Social Work, 20 June 1938, Bombay. File no. 198/DTT/PHIL/TISS/FP/5, TCA.

[49] File no. 199/DTT/PHIL/TISS/MIS/1, TCA.

[50] From the Souvenir released to mark the Silver Jubilee of TISS 1936–1961, file no. 206/TISS Silver Jubilee Souvenir, TCA.

demands upon all their resources of knowledge and personality'. Such borrowed curricular resources ran a further risk that 'teachers who have been trained in the West and who have not practised in India will seek to plaster Western methods on to the Indian situation'. Cautioning against the use of Western social work theory and teaching material given the differences in conditions in the West and in India, they argued, 'what is universal should be distinguished from what is applicable only in local circumstances'. Revealing of the tensions that inhered when universal forms of modernity were received into a context different from which they had emerged, the three reviewers called for moving past mere translations. Instead, they argued for developing 'local' social science resources that were careful to the contexts they sought to describe.[51]

The need for 'local' resources became even more glaring as the Tatas' philanthropy to ameliorate poverty began to move past the large urban industrial centres into the rural hinterlands. In 1974, an institution-wide review of TISS was commissioned to Malcolm S. Adiseshiah, where he urged the institution to consider the 'question of meeting the social work needs not only of the urban-industrial complex', as had been the case starting from TISS's founding; but of 'the rural programmes and rural institutions which ha[d] been set up to serve the majority of our poverty-stricken people, particularly the small, marginal and drought-prone farmer, the landless labourers, the Scheduled Castes and Tribes, the pre-school child and the lactating mother etc'. He recommended that TISS develop a 'rural orientation in training', in which there was greater emphasis on the 'Social Developmental role of social work'. An attached note on 'Social Work Education' by S. N. Ranade further emphasized the differences between the Indian and US contexts, as well the challenges confronting social work in the two countries. He argued that 'Social work here is not confronted with a small segment of the population of the physically disabled or the mentally incapacitated but with a large body of people who have no access to basic services necessary for civilized existence'.[52] The orientation recommended by the review led to the establishment of TISS's rural campus at Tuljapur in Marathwada region of Maharasthra subsequently in 1986. Designed as an alternate rural campus, Tuljapur focused on combining 'development of the social/human component with physical resource

[51] File no. 195/DTT/PHIL/TIFR/MIS/1, TCA.
[52] Adiseshiah's letter dated 20 April 1974 to J. J. Bhabha, chairman, TISS and attached report; file no. 204/DTT/PHIL/TISS/Report of the Review Committee–2, TCA.

management, the fusion of relevant science and technology with local resources, and people's development, organisation and action'.[53]

As the demand for new knowledge of Indian society grew so did the recognition that the tasks confronting the professional development workers were far from easy or even straightforward.

In a review of RWB's activities, Y. S. Pandit, a statistical superintendent with Bombay's Labour Office who was later involved with the Tatas from 1940 to 1968, outlined the challenges confronting development professionals. 'In order to influence the attitude of the villagers', he argued, it was 'essential for the voluntary agency [and its workers] to establish close contacts with them, to understand their customs, traditions and other forces which determine their behavioural pattern and to secure their confidence. This is possible only if the agency [and its workers] digs in its toes'. He cautioned the development professional against excessive spoon-feeding of communities they worked with; and that the professionals' role, mainly, was to provide the financial and technical input. They must encourage the community to make the maximum possible effort. Such workers, Pandit wrote, needed to be idealists, devoted, efficient, and honest field workers, who were willing to stay in the villages, to obtain a 'true picture' and identifying the 'specific problems'.[54]

The newly trained development professionals, though, were up to the task. Responding to the earthquake in Koynanagar in 1967, for example, TRC's professionals displayed genuine sympathy and a personalized approach to dealing with the masses. 'Talking to each family head and offering aid after a sympathetic and detailed inquiry of his family', they 'appeared to make a very deep impression on these unfortunate simple folk'. Writing at the end of her field visit, Leela Moolgaokar, chair of the Relief Committee, shared her guilt in 'returning to the comforts of Bombay leaving you boys (sic) to work so hard and also to brave the rigou[r] of the local weather and living conditions'.[55] She believed that the professionals were setting 'an example in leadership by insisting on staying with your boys in the dilapidated house (...) with a working day of over 12 hours and sharing with them all their hardships. It was indeed a surprise to me to find your team so happy and not at all concerned about the hard work, the heat, dust and lack of good food'.[56]

[53] 'Perspectives for the Future', file no. 200/TISS Golden Jubilee 1936–86 brochure, TCA.
[54] Y. S. Pandit, *A Survey of Devapur*, 1986, Tata Rural Welfare Board. File no. 185A/DTT/RWB/1986, TCA.
[55] From a letter dated 7 May 1968 written by Leela Moolgaokar to Kulkarni; from file no. 184/DTT/PHIL/TRC/KOYNA/1967/6, TCA.
[56] Work undertaken by Tata Relief Committee after earthquake in Koyna. File no. 184/DTT/PHIL/TRC/KOYNA/1967/5, TCA.

Having shared her experience with her husband [who headed TELCO, which later became Tata Motors], Moolgaokar reported that 'he was really happy and proud that his Telco boys (*sic*) (...) [were] capable of doing excellent work at a place where their tools are mostly their ingenuity and where there was no trace of normal facilities of living to which they are accustomed'. Exhorting the team to push further to ensure all deadlines are met, Moolgaokar sought an assurance from the team on this and offered her help to achieve the deadlines. Within this seemingly quotidian correspondence relating to project management in development work, one finds the defining of yet another attribute of the development professional: his (in most cases) ability to complete one's work in a time-bound manner irrespective of one's external conditions. Despite her sympathy for the professional workers' living conditions, Moolgaokar emphasized the need for timely completion of work.[57]

Young and energetic, another reviewer of RWB's Devapur programme, Dr. Allie C. Felder Jr. noted elsewhere, development professionals possessed the 'ability to work well together and ha[d] a great respect for work (dignity of labour)'. Their quality was 'exemplified by the initiative and sincerity of purpose shown'. 'The social worker was just as curious and interested in learning what insects were attacking wheat crops as was the agricultural technician. Similarly, the agricultural technician was interested in the group dynamics displayed', he added. 'Each of the staff members appeared to know everyone elses (*sic*) job in general and was an expert in his own specific job. Each appeared to have had sound training', Felder Jr. concluded. Their cross-disciplinary training of personnel had given them 'a quest for knowledge and new ideas'. It had resulted in 'respect for the dignity of labour and encouraged them to come to the level of the people in order to have their knowledge accepted'. Without an apparent feeling of seniority among the team, Felder Jr. noted that their mutual relationships were 'remarkably harmonious'. He described individual development professionals as exceptional, 'unafraid to act, and to try out new ideas in difficult situations', perceptive, who possessed 'sufficient missionary spirit to tackle various complicated problems' and a 'degree of humbleness', and 'respected for his (*sic*) sincerity of purpose'.[58]

---

[57] Work undertaken by Tata Relief Committee after earthquake in Koyna. File no. 184/DTT/PHIL/TRC/KOYNA/1967/5, TCA.

[58] Report on Rural Welfare Board by Dr. Allie C. Felder Jr. representing the Co-operative League of USA and the American International Association of Economic and Social Development. File no. 185/DTT/PHIL/RWB/PROJECT/1, TCA.

Such a commitment to the cause of development was also found among the NGOs supported by the Tata Trusts. Evaluating a proposal for funds from Auroville in 1984, for example, J. R. D. Tata wrote that its distinctive feature was that 'unlike any other similar programme in India, it has at its command the services of a hundred or more highly educated and dedicated workers, many of whom are professionally qualified and all of whom work with their own hands'. He added: 'I don't think there is, or can be, a single rural and educational project in India which can command such a large team of high grade, educated and devoted workers'.[59] Elsewhere, considering making a gift to the Arpana Research and Charities Trust, Haryana, the internal communication noted the 'sacrifice' of medical doctors in giving up their professional work to serve development. It commended the professionals for 'Giving up their professions and dedicating their lives to the service of rural India, they work with missionary zeal. They live in a community, share their private means, generate their own income, and work in a voluntary capacity, setting a splendid example'. A memorandum from 1986 called the work of the doctors a 'remarkable experiment in harnessing the urban intelligentsia for serving the rural population'.[60]

*

As I have argued previously, Indian economic elites were quick to recognize the potential dangers of the neoliberal global capitalist order that threatened the poor peasants, artisans, workers, etc. in the country at the turn of the twenty-first century—even if their responses were merely to invest in building individual capacities to manufacture market-ready citizens.

Like the Tatas' philanthropy from the twentieth century, 'new age' Indian philanthropists have similarly invested in funding the research of 'applied' social sciences and training of professional development workers in their pursuit of the modernization of Indian society. Reflecting the movement of the disciplinary burden of reforming society from sociology (at IISc) to social work/administration (TISS) to management (again at IISc, TISS, and IIMs), and most recently public policy, the Bharti Foundation founded the Bharti Institute of Public Policy at the Indian School of Business, Hyderabad.

[59] From the Memorandum for appeal, written by D. K. Malegamvala, director, SDTT dated 13 March 1984 to request SDTT to make a further three-year grant to Auromitra—Friends of Auroville Research Foundation; from file no. 180/DTT/PHIL/DON/11, TCA.
[60] Memorandum on appeal from Arpana Research and Charities Trust, Haryana, dated 29 May 1984; from file no. 180/DTT/PHIL/DON/13, TCA.

Partnered with the Fletcher School of Law and Diplomacy at Tufts University in the United States, the Institute hopes to 'impact public policy by delivering cutting-edge education, research and engagement'. It has identified agriculture and food, environment, education, finance, and governance and digital identity as the main domains of its work.[61]

Similarly, the Azim Premji Foundation launched the Azim Premji University in 2010. Organized around five schools of education, development, policy and governance, arts and sciences, and continuing education, the university offers a range of undergraduate and postgraduate programmes in the above areas. Eschewing a narrow utilitarian view of knowledge and itself, the University is nonetheless committed to the Foundation's stated social purpose to 'develop a deep understanding of the role of education in creating awareness of moral and ethical issues in debates on development and social policy'.[62]

*

'Science,' the historian Gyan Prakash noted, could not 'orchestrate India's industrialization on a systematic basis without organization'.[63] The burden of orchestrating social re-organization in the country, I have been arguing thus far, fell to the social sciences to fulfil the needs of modern industry and a modern nation which required a pre-existing modern society. As part of which, the bodies and lives of the masses were brought under the expert gaze of the scientists (including the doctor, public health officers, and sanitation experts) and the social scientists (including the statistician, the social worker, and the sociologist). While others have attributed such governing 'technics' to the realm of the state,[64] I would argue that the economic elites have played an influential role in funding the production of social science knowledge to modernize Indian society, and ultimately accelerate the modernization of Indian industry. Towards this end, not only was new disciplinary knowledge needed but equally, India's youth needed to be trained in these new social sciences to equip them with the necessary knowledge and skills in order to apply the latter in the field. In addition to possessing the 'right' kind of knowledge, they were expected to display 'modern' attitudes in their work.

---

[61] Bharti Institute of Public Policy, 'About', accessed 3 January 2020, https://www.isb.edu/bipp/about.

[62] Azim Premji University, 'Origin and Purpose', accessed 18 December 2019, https://azimpremjiuniversity.edu.in/SitePages/origin-and-purpose.aspx.

[63] Prakash, Another Reason, 193.

[64] See, for example, Prakash's Another Reason; and Chatterjee's 'Beyond the Nation?', 30–4.

The emphasis on the professionalization—and later managerialization—of development work has only intensified and continued since.[65]

Postscript

For those of us from the so-called Third World, modernity—and its pursuit in the form of development—is conceived and narrated, by and large, in relation to the West—its past, our present; and its present a sign of what our future might look like. Whether we choose to reject or embrace it, it is almost always in relation to Western forms of modernity. Here, Kuan-Hsing Chen's suggestion in his magisterial *Asia as Method* is worth considering. Chen invites us [from Asia] to 'become each other's points of reference, so that the understanding of the self may be transformed, and subjectivity rebuilt'.[66] 'Diverse historical experiences and rich social practices of Asia,' he argues, 'may be mobilized to provide alternate horizons and perspectives.' Developing such alternates, however, requires shifting our frames of reference. Following Chen, therefore we need to stop thinking of postcolonial development as a deviation, a laggard, or even hybrid, in order to rethink our development. This book is, hopefully, one such attempt to theorize development in postcolonial India—as imagined by its elites—on its own terms. After all, modernity is 'not a normative drive to become modern', but as Chen concludes 'an analytical concept that attempts to capture the effectiveness of modernizing forces as they negotiate and mix with local history and culture'.[67]

---

[65] See, for example, contributions to Sadhvi Dar and Bill Cooke's edited *The New Development Management*.

[66] Kuan-Hsing Chen, *Asia as Method*, 212.   [67] Kuan-Hsing Chen, *Asia as Method*, 244.

Coda

The Calculus of Development

In a telling rebuke, Jyoti Basu, the chief minister of West Bengal's democratically elected Marxist government remarked: 'All the activities of the Birlas are aimed at personal enrichment'. 'Even the educational and religious trusts set up by Birla', he said 'were established merely to evade taxes'. 'Profit', Basu concluded, was 'the Birlas's (*sic*) primary objective'.[1] Given Basu's scathing but unsurprising assessment of Birlas' philanthropy, how might we explain elites' extensive record of philanthropy for India's development despite the setbacks and irresolutions of national-modern? Was it driven by elites' narrow calculus of making and protecting profits as Basu suggests?

Or, did it have to do with 'enchantments' of modernity?[2] One possible way of explaining their enduring, even stubborn, commitment to modernity would be in the form of elites' ethical commitment to modernity. 'Building a modern society', the British anthropologist Frederick Bailey wrote, 'is not a routine process in which all the steps are known and all contingencies anticipated. On the contrary: it is a world of mistakes, frustrations, disappointments, anxiety and conflict'. Only those 'who have a moral commitment to a modern society', he concluded, 'will persist in the face of disappointment and failure'.[3]

Or was it, as hagiography and historiography suggest, driven by elites' love for the country? Jamsetji N. Tata's industry and philanthropy, we are told for example, were driven by his love for the country, for Bombay city, and the intense desire to add to this wealth. The pursuit of wealth, though, was not an end in itself as it had no value for him except to use it to make India great: industrially, and to give its men and women the education that could make the country great.[4] He has been described variously and frequently as a nationalist, humanist, patriot, one 'who helped India take her place in the

---

[1] Cited from Kudaisya, *G. D. Birla*, 382. [2] Dube, 'Enchantments of Modernity', 729.
[3] Bailey, 'Peasant View', 312.
[4] Behroze Cursetjee's talk delivered at the Tata Staff College on 22 February 1956; from file no. 174, TCA.

Philanthropy and the Development of Modern India: In the Name of Nation. Arun Kumar, Oxford University Press.
© Arun Kumar 2021. DOI: 10.1093/oso/9780198868637.003.0006

league of industrialised nations'.[5] Such descriptions and representations are not limited to corporate communication or hagiographic accounts written by sympathetic insiders.[6] His son, Dorabji's philanthropy was similarly impelled, we are told, by the desire to develop Indian industry, wealth from which was used to 'pioneer for India the study of social sciences; of fundamental sciences; the treatment of and research in cancer; integrated rural development; and more recently, preservation of the country's rich heritage of the performing arts'. It helped build the first atomic reactor in Asia and sponsored the higher education of hundreds of Indians abroad.[7]

In this coda, I suggest that India's postcolonial elites used their philanthropy *for* power—which involved challenging, collaborating, seeking approval from, supporting, and sometimes even by-passing contemporary governing regimes from time to time. In so doing, they deployed their capital: both financial, social, and cultural to protect their own class interests. Their mode of philanthropy also varied greatly: from donations to political parties to strategic use of their access to political leaders to influence political and economic decisions.

*

That Indian elites used their philanthropy, pragmatically, as they mediated the changing political landscape of twentieth century India is hardly surprising.[8] While I demonstrate their use of philanthropy in building collaborative governing regimes from the twentieth century in this coda, I have a further purpose in mind. I have chosen to include it here—in a book that is primarily 'a' history of development—in order to bring into relief how development was used, even if not always, to legitimize elites' philanthropy to shore up their own class interests. That is, the pursuit of India's national development through elites' philanthropy provided the moral basis to preserve and further accumulate their capital—be it economic, political, speculative, or even symbolic—and ultimately power. Elites' pursuit of capital and power—dressed as

---

[5] 'The Giant Who Touched Tomorrow', Tata Group, accessed 25 June 2013, http://tata.com/aboutus/articles/inside.aspx?artid=AapOEYsYNwI=.

[6] For example, Tata was said to be driven by an 'abiding passion to lift India from a predominantly agricultural, subdued nation to a modern, industrialized one—a nation able to hold its own in the emerging twentieth century'; see Lala, *Love of India*, xviii. Such claims of Tata's nationalism can also be found in contemporary historiography such as Harris, *Tata: A Chronicle* and more recent scholarly accounts such as Luhrmann, *The Good Parsi*, 92; and Sivakumar, 'Business Ethics of Tata', 354.

[7] Lala, *Heartbeat of Trust*, vii.

[8] Haynes notes this in relation to Surati merchants as they lived through the decline of the Mughal empire and the rise of the East India Company and later Indian nationalism; see 'Tribute to Philanthropy', 339–60. Palsetia makes a similar point in relation to Jamsetji Jejeebhoy's philanthropy from the nineteenth century; see '"Honourable Machinations"', 55–75 and 'Merchant Charity', 197–217.

development—was therefore somehow acceptable, I argue, because it was carried out in the name of the larger national interest. Differently from much of development studies then, where elites are often characterized as anti-development or captors of scarce resources and therefore detrimental to development,[9] I argue that India's postcolonial elites longed for development because it was ultimately favourable to their own interests. In so doing, I comment—although belatedly in the book—on elites' enduring, even obstinate, engagement with the national-modern despite its many setbacks and irresolutions.

As I have argued previously, unlike the more familiar forms of post-colonial national development commonly found in many Third World countries, national-modern has shared a prior and more complicated relationship with colonialism. National development was frequently conceived of in opposition to colonialism; even where it drew heavily on colonial forms of modernity, it sought to re-fashion them in its own national spirit. The national-modern, however, often sought to—at least in the first three decades of the twentieth century—operate *within* colonial modernity and did not necessarily stand in opposition to it. Reflecting which, India's postcolonial elites were characteristically pragmatic in their approach towards the colonial administration, nationalism, and later the post-colonial nation-state, using their philanthropy strategically.

In addition to their entrepreneurial collaborations starting from as early as the nineteenth century,[10] Tatas were almost always willing to support or collaborate with the colonial administration in their gift-making, which helped them accumulate reputational capital. In addition to their active efforts at partnering (or proposing to at the very least) with the imperial in the endowment of scientific and technological institutions the Tatas' founded and funded that I have outlined in chapter 4, the Tatas were forthright in their support of the colonial administration during wars. During the World War I, for example, the Tatas made its resources available for the use of the colonial administration. In 1917, the India Office sought the use of Tata House, Navajibai Tata's Bombay residence then, as a non-residential Nurses' Club—promising that her valuables would be stored safely and no damage would be done. She responded from the York House in Twickenham expressing her pleasure in placing the House at their disposal. The then governor of Bombay,

---

[9] DiCaprio, 'Introduction', 12–3.
[10] Jamsetji N. Tata was known to have profited extensively through cotton trade when the American Civil War had disrupted the supply of raw material to the Lancashire cotton mills. Soon after, they joined a merchant syndicate as military contractors to the British Abyssinian expedition. See Majumdar, *India's Industrial Revolution*, 108.

Lord Willingdon was 'deeply grateful' for this.[11] Similarly, during the World War II, the Trustees of SDTT agreed to give their land at Sewri, Bombay to the military establishment of the colonial government from 12 June 1942 for up to six months after the end of the War, at a nominal price of Re. 1 each year.[12] Such gestures led to the accumulation of reputational capital for the Tatas, and the colonial administration was quick to repay the favour. On the occasion of her husband, Dorabji Tata's proposed visit to Japan en route to America and England in 1917, for example, internal communication between the governments of Bombay and India recorded that Dorabji Tata was 'thoroughly loyal in his sympathies and deserves every honourable treatment at the hands of His Britannic Majesty's representatives in Japan'.[13]

Such use of philanthropy to build bridges with the ruling state continued, post-colonialism. The Tata Trusts were quite transparent about their philanthropic mode in an internally commissioned report from 1965 on SDTT's activities. The Trust's grants, it noted 'do not go to support the ordinary conventional type of institutions, but which tend to encourage neglected aspects of service, new trends in social thought, and all that advances the social, intellectual and industrial life of the country'. Following from which, the Trust 'has adopted the policy of initiating and maintaining new projects till they can be *conveniently* passed on to the state, and in place of those taken over initiate other pioneering ventures'.[14] Despite their collaborative mode, the Tatas were equally cautious to distance themselves from the governing regime and retain their autonomy in order to 'turn at will in unexplored directions', unlike most Third World nation-states that were bogged down by their bureaucracy. Setting out their case for autonomy, they noted that 'Experience has shown that private effort can get going quicker, for it is not circumscribed and encumbered by procedures that are inevitable where State finances are involved'. And further that, 'In the immediate relief of human distress, in giving a hand to struggling yet promising institutions, in spotting and nurturing talent, in setting free scholars and creative workers at all levels and giving them a modicum of security and independence, the personal touch and the Private Foundation comes into its own and plays an essential part. The wheels of the State move slow and on [set] tracks'.[15]

In *Nucleus and Nation*, Robert Anderson called this the 'Tata model of development', which was 'officially sanctioned and well supported, but

---

[11] File no. L/MIL/7/18879, IOR.   [12] File no. 179/DTT/PHIL/PROP/AGR/1, TCA.
[13] From file no. L/PS/11/106, IOR.
[14] From file no. 182/DTT/PHIL/HISTORY PROJECT/3, TCA; italicized for emphasis.
[15] From SDTT, Biennial Report, 1998–2000; from file no. 182/DTT/AR/1998–2000, TCA.

relatively autonomous from the state machinery'.[16] Like the Tatas, in his stew-
ardship of IIM, Ahmedabad, Lalbhai was also clear about maintaining institutional autonomy. He always distinguished between 'government support and
government interference'.[17] Examples of the collaborative mode of doing philanthropy was not limited to endowment of large institutions of research and
training and can also be found in smaller scale (at least in monetary terms) of
grant-making. TRC's relief work after the Koyna earthquake in 1967, for
example, was initiated after 'establish[ing] contact' and with government's
'concurrence'.[18] Similarly responding to the floods in Gujarat in 1968, TRC
initiated its work after 'interviews with the Revenue Minister and other officials of the Gujarat Government'.[19] The state government's involvement was
useful in obtaining land for the construction of the houses in four selected
villages of Navsari.[20] They were also approached by the Navsari municipality
to construct 450 additional houses in the town, or at least 150; the TRC
refused to do so since the expenses involved were too high, but also because
doing so would result in the TRC deviating from its 'uniform pattern' of
houses constructed in the four villages.[21]

*

Despite subsequent claims to the contrary, the Tatas were also pragmatic
enough to distance themselves from supporting nationalism to avoid con-
frontations with the colonial administration. While sympathetic insiders have
cited Jamsetji N. Tata's support to Pherozeshah Mehta, founding member of
the Indian National Congress, as indicative of his nationalist support,[22] others
have been more circumspect. Harris, for example, noted that Tata was no
more than a 'warm supporter' of Congress and never participated actively in
its activities; and that 'a well-reasoned loyalty to British rule was part of Mr.
Tata's political faith'. He wanted England, Harris adds, to 'point the way to
freedom, and to carry out the finest traditions of the Liberal creed'.[23] Such was
Tatas'—and Parsis', more generally—opposition towards nationalism that it

[16] Anderson, *Nucleus and Nation*, 531.
[17] From a brochure of the IISc, from 1957; from file no. 190/DTT/PHIL/IISC/MIS/8, TCA.
[18] From file no. 184/DTT/PHIL/TRC/KOYNA/1967/4, TCA.
[19] From file no. 183/DTT/PHIL/TRC/GUJARAT/1968/2, TCA.
[20] From file no. 183/DTT/PHIL/TRC/GUJARAT/1968/1, TCA.
[21] From file no. 183/DTT/PHIL/TRC/GUJARAT/1968/3, TCA.
[22] With Mehta, Lala notes, Tata started the Ripon Club in 1880 and then the Bombay Presidency
Association to discuss political issues. And that Mehta noted that even though Tata 'could never be
induced to appear and speak on a public platform, the help, the advice, and the cooperation which he
gave to political movements never ceased'; see *Love of India*, 40.
[23] Harris, *Tata: A Chronicle*, 267, 276–7.

led Gandhi to worry that 'Tata and the Parsis might become oblivious to the wants and aspirations of the multitude of their countrymen, as the "Rockefeller spirit" seemed to be overtaking the great house of the Tatas'.[24] Between 1909 and 1913, his son, Ratan J. Tata, though, was more forthcoming in his support of Gopal Krishna Gokhale's Servants of India Society (founded in 1905) and Gandhi's agitation in South Africa against racial discrimination. There are no further records of Tatas' benefaction to other nationalist leaders, subsequently. Thus, there was comparatively little by way of difference from colonialism articulated in Tatas' philanthropy from the early part of the twentieth century; thus, maintaining its distance from nationalism.

Like the Tatas, the Birlas were also careful about how their industry and philanthropy might be perceived by the colonial administration, despite their support to Hindu nationalism. In 1920, for example, following the purchase of the newspaper *Empire* by the Birla Group, Ghanshyam Das Birla only went as far as to rename it as the *New Empire*. Signalling continuity and not anti-colonialism, Birla was also reluctant to openly support the Tilak Memorial Swarajya Fund in 1921. It was only under growing pressure from his own community that the Birlas finally came forward to contribute Rs. 1 lakh to the Fund.[25]

Others such as Thakurdas, however, were more forthcoming in expressing their willingness to build collaborative governing regimes with the British. Against the backdrop of the non-cooperation movement in January 1922, a small group of influential people including Thakurdas and Ambalal Sarabhai called for a conference to be organized later that month. Sending out public invitations, they argued that a large majority of 'thoughtful people' in the country believed that India's 'full national development [was] *within* the orbit of the British Commonwealth'. Calling for a representative conference, they suggested dedicating efforts to exploring avenues for an 'honourable settlement' among nationalist factions calling for civil disobedience on the one hand, and the imperial government's heavy-handed use of legislative action that had led to large-scale imprisonment of political leaders on the other hand.[26] In preparation of the conference, Sarabhai wrote to Thakurdas providing details of his recent meeting with Gandhi. Reporting Gandhi's 'very friendly' attitude and his promise to attend the conference with 'an open

---

[24] Palsetia, *Parsis of India*, 316.   [25] Kudaisya, *G. D. Birla*, 61–71.
[26] Their letter dated 3 January 1922 was published in the *Indian Social Reformer* of January 08, file 24, PT. Other signatories of the letter included Madan Mohan Malaviya and Mohammed Ali Jinnah; emphasis added.

mind', Sarabhai suggested that they push for the following resolution to be adopted at the conference: 'This conference is of the opinion that the N. C. O. [non cooperation] movement will not cease as a result of the repressive policy of the Govt & that the only means to restore peace in the Country & good will between the Govt & the people, is by the Govt following a conciliatory policy & by meeting the wishes of the people'.[27] Far from isolated, such efforts are indicative of how India's economic elites frequently dedicated their time and effort to ending political and economic instability in the country notwithstanding the anti-colonial nationalist sentiment.

Similar strategic use of philanthropy to build collaborative regimes of power with the British can also be found in Thakurdas's active involvement with the Welfare of India League. Founded as a bi-racial platform involving Indians and Europeans alike, it promoted India's place as an equal partner within the British Commonwealth. It focused on representativeness of different races and communities and encouraged intellectual and cultural cooperation among them.[28] Under Thakurdas's presidency, the League frequently distanced itself from the political tumult of the early 1930s. Setting out the challenges confronting the League, a note outlined its difficulties in trying to 'steer a middle course at a time of great political excitement, and when the country is passing through such a phase that the still small voice of reason is heard indistinctly'.[29] Emphasizing that it was not started for the purposes of political propaganda, the League undertook various welfare causes such as the treatment of political prisoners in Bombay Presidency in 1933, including their housing with ordinary convicts, women's safety and privacy during their transfer from one jail to another, and the unsatisfactory conditions of toilets and bathrooms in the prisons.[30]

Frequently taking a conciliatory tone, Thakurdas appealed for the maintenance of close ties between the Indians and the British. Speaking at Chatham House in London on 4 July 1933, Thakurdas spoke of India's continued and special connection with Britain. Denying that any of the Indian participants at the Round Table Conferences desired severing this connection, he called for political reform in India. Attending the conference at a 'considerable self-sacrifice', Indians' loyalty to Britain should not have been questioned only

---

[27] Sarabhai's letter to Thakurdas dated 9 January 1922, file 24, PT.
[28] Draft rules of Welfare of India League, file 109/1931, PT.
[29] From an undated note, file 109/1931, PT.
[30] From the League's submission to the secretary, Home Department, Government of Bombay, dated 24 January 1933; file 109/1931, PT.

because they now wished to govern themselves. While making a case for self-governance, Thakurdas's remarks both acknowledged Indian elites' desire to hold more power over the country, as well as the role of Great Britain, which he said, had 'undoubtedly done a great deal for the masses of India, but it was out of date to say that Indians whose brothers and sisters the masses were should not have full voice in governing them'.[31] As the political fortunes began to shift more decisively in the 1940s, the elites were no longer anxious about how their actions might be perceived by the colonial administration. In 1940, for example, Bajaj released a note in English, Hindustani, and Marathi arguing that it was wrong to support the British war effort either with men or money. Non-violent resistance, he noted, was the only worthy pursuit against all wars.[32]

*

Haunted by the spectre of communism, Indian economic elites were quick to turn to their philanthropy to counter it. Here also they mobilized 'development' extensively and frequently, both to consolidate their own class interests and obfuscate their intent. As early as 1929, for example, Dorabji Tata attempted to organize a new political party comprised entirely of capitalists: both Indian and European, to protect their interests against the perceived dangers of growing influence of the leftists in the Indian trade unions. Both Thakurdas and Birla, though, differed with Tata. They argued that instead of reacting and rushing into a collaboration with European capitalists, it would have been more useful to attack the root causes behind the growth of communism in the country. Reminiscent of American 'scientific philanthropy',[33] Birla and Thakurdas argued that Indian capitalists also needed to scrutinize their own roles in the Left's growing appeal. Unconvinced by Tata's plans for collaboration across racial lines between Indian and white European capitalists, Birla suggested a new partnership between the then-newly established Federation of Indian Chambers of Commerce and Industry and the Congress Party to support their candidates in the upcoming Assembly elections. With

---

[31] Thakurdas's remarks at a meeting at Chatham House, London on 4 July 1933, file 1, PT.

[32] From Bajaj's papers dated 20 December 1940; correspondence: Gandhi, M. K., JB (1st inst.).

[33] In Sealander's formulation, scientific philanthropy involved in-depth study of society and understood the dangers of industrialization. It prompted the elites to engage in systematic gift-making to causes that attacked the roots of poverty instead of its symptoms. It took various forms but involved extensive gifts to scientific research and training in selected disciplines, especially in the first half of twentieth-century United States; see Sealander, 'Curing Evils', 222.

Relatedly, Guilhot has argued that earlier investments in scientific research and training 'were trying to reduce the opposition between capital and labor by investing in progressive scientific ideologies promising to overcome it'; see 'Reforming', 474.

Thakurdas, he formed a committee of Motilal Nehru, Malaviya, and himself to raise Rs. 4 lakhs to assist handpicked candidates.[34]

Throughout the 1930s, Birla also worked actively with Congress's right-wing leaders such as Vallabhbhai Patel and C. Rajagopalachari to challenge Nehruvian faction's socialism. Although previously reluctant to partner with British capitalists, Birla was not averse to lobbying with British politicians to discredit Nehru's supposedly left-leaning, socialist views. This included the use of the rhetoric to challenge contemporary 'socialist' solutions and point to the urgent need of managerial (and so, businesses') capacity to meet India's developmental needs. Outlining his support for rural community development, for example, Birla wrote: 'The masses will ask themselves: "Have we been able to get more nourishment than before?…Are we any the better in respect of our standard of living?".' 'A man needs 3,000 calories of balanced diet…40 yards of cloth, a decent hut to live in', the masses will soon start asking, he added, '"Are we getting all this?" And the answer will definitely be "NO".' What India needed 'for such vast constructive work', therefore, was 'experience, efficiency, proper planning and administrative capacity'. 'Few among the Congress men', according to Birla, possessed any such skills despite their enthusiasm and excitement. What was needed, therefore, was a turn to constitutionalism, organization, and management, and not a left-wing revolution. Arguing for modernization of economic production, Birla was also quick to discredit growing calls for abolishing the *zamindari* system in order to alleviate agrarian distress, increase production, and address the challenges of hunger and poverty among the peasantry. Elsewhere, he added: 'people will demand more bread and the bread is not going to come out of the confiscation of zemindaris (*sic*)'. The Indian ministers, then, will need to decide 'what they are going to do for ameliorating the condition of the people. If they think that the amelioration depends on the confiscation of the properties, then I think they are deceiving themselves'.[35]

Although Birla identified poverty and hunger as a crucial problem afflicting the peasantry in the country that needed to be 'solved', he was convinced that abolition of the pre-existing socio-economic relations within rural communities such as the exploitative *zamindari* system or land reforms to re-constitute rural communities were not part of the solution. Instead, he turned them into problems that needed administrative solutions and experience, which

---

[34] Kudaisya, *G. D. Birla*, 123.
[35] Cited from Kudaisya, *G. D. Birla*, 173, 184.

economic elites such as himself possessed in abundance. Thus, even as Birla supported a programme of reform in order to bring modernity to Marwaris with their superstitions, taboos, and dated rituals, it refused to extend this to modernize similarly dated social systems of economic production, such as the *zamindari*. Modernizing these, he argued, served no developmental purpose whatsoever. In this way, Birla exercised his influence to shape development imaginaries rendering certain development trajectories wholly unacceptable, while arguing for the economic modernization of agriculture.

*

Birla continued to exercise his influence, post-independence, as the jostling between economic elites (given their interests in protecting and expanding private capital, investment, and enterprise) and the Nehruvian government— which favoured a mixed economy with key strategic sectors under government ownership or control—intensified. In this, he deployed development in all kinds of ways to protect the interests of the capitalists' class. Just as development imbued nationalism's critique of colonialism with positive intent, it functioned as a shorthand for a supposedly universally desirable form of social, economic, and political change that was somehow over and above all forms of ideology, beyond contest as it were (its content, as I have been arguing throughout the book, though, has been far from stable or shared). Such a formation of development manifests itself widely in Indian elites' exchanges with their post-colonial political leaders.

On a trip to the United States in 1954, for example, Birla spoke at venues around the country including at the Council for Foreign Relations, the prominent American foreign policy think tank notorious for its influence on US foreign policy and committed to its global expansionism, the American Institute of Pacific Relations, and at informal lunches and dinners where he said Indians 'had no "ism". We were all united in one common ground to improve the standard of our people'. In which, India's economic elites such as himself supported the Nehru government.[36] Elsewhere in another letter to Nehru from 1955, Birla wrote that capitalists such as himself and socialists such as Nehru shared the same destination even if their routes might have been different. The latter wanted 'more food, more cloth, better houses, better sanitation, better medical facilities, better education and so on and so forth for every person. You also add that this objective could be achieved only

---

[36] Birla's letters to Mathai dated 11 and 17 September 1954; file 3, 1043.

through increased wealth and its better distribution'.[37] Setting out the case for the involvement of private capital in India's development, Birla argued that neither could they by themselves increase wealth and distribute it fairly. After all they were 'only the common limbs of the national sector', each with its own strengths. To operationalize such a partnership, Birla welcomed Nehru's proposal for India's capitalists and political leaders to meet regularly to carry forward their shared commitment to development.[38]

Even as Birla continued to denounce ideology outside, he continued to make a case for private capital and enterprise in his private correspondence with Nehru, albeit in a somewhat roundabout way. Instead of arguing against socialism, Birla relentlessly pointed Nehru to India's urgent need for foreign exchange for financing its development, especially in implementing its second and later third five-year plans. Securing these monies as aid or as a loan, Birla reasoned on several instances, required that potential creditors (mainly the First World countries) perceive India favourably—which in turn meant securing space for private capital and enterprise (such as his own).[39] Needless to mention that such lobbying was impelled by the wider Cold War anxieties within the United States—which Nehru was quick to point out to Birla was less an ideological war, but more about global dominance, the failures of US foreign policy and its persistent efforts at aggravating other countries, and that what India needed, far more than American money, was goodwill.[40]

Despite Nehru's downplaying of Indian need for foreign exchange, Birla continued to make a case for foreign exchange that it needed, and how it could have only come if India appeared firm in its denunciation of communism and support for private capital, property, and enterprise. During his trip to the United States, for example, Birla met a wide range of political and business leaders, as well as newspersons in the United States. In his report to Nehru, Birla noted that he had actively defended India's choice of a socialist, mixed economy. It was meant, he wrote, to minimize inequality and raise the standard of living in the country. 'My conception of socialism', Birla argued, 'is a system under which everyone will be a small capitalist in the sense that he will have the necessary comforts of life and some surplus for rainy days'.

---

[37] G. D. Birla's letter to Nehru dated 8 April 1955; file 3, 1043.

[38] Nehru's letter to G. D. Birla dated 3 April 1955; file 3, 1043.

[39] For example, before departing on his trip later in 1956, Birla wrote a letter to Nehru in August 1955 listing what India needed most, which was foreign exchange; followed by a managerial cadre, transport, equilibrium between heavy, large-scale industry and small, cottage industry, and finally an able bureaucracy; Birla's letter to Nehru dated 25 August 1955; file 3, 1043.

[40] In response to Birla's letter seeking Nehru's counsel on India's international relations' principles and policies, Nehru outlined twelve main points; letter from Nehru to Birla dated 6 February 1956; file 3, 1043.

Notwithstanding Nehru's tepid response to the prospect of development aid from the United States, Birla actively made a case during his trip to the United States in 1956 for foreign exchange in order for India to finance its second five-year plan, especially in securing the necessary technology and equipment. Seeking to allay their fears about the role of private capital and enterprise, Birla pointed them to the private investment outlined in selected sectors as part of the first five-year plan, with more to follow. This demarcation, he noted, was flexible and amendable as per the demands of India's industrialization.[41]

On his trip to England in 1956, Birla repeated his message about the need for foreign exchange and aid to finance India's development, and that it was contingent on international perceptions of its economic policies. Speaking to bankers, financiers, and political leaders, he reported encountering growing worries over the Indian government's economic policies. They were, he recounted for Nehru's benefit, less worried about the turn to socialism but more about economic instability in the country. Hoping to put pressure on Nehru over his economic policies, Birla argued that the nationalization of banks, insurance, and minerals worried their British counterparts. The Nehru government's demand for majority investment in Burmah-Shell, Birla informed the former, worried the British greatly. All this, Birla concluded, undermined India's case for foreign exchange, which it needed badly to fulfil the financial requirements of its second five-year plan. 'In future', he continued, 'our needs shall be greater and greater. And a prospective borrower can hardly afford to prejudice the lending market. Whether the prejudice is right or wrong is not the point'. Thus, he sought to exert pressure on Nehru that India's chosen model of economic development required, first and foremost, foreign capital to meet its demands for development and that it could ill afford to rub those it hoped to raise money from the wrong way, by continuing with the Nehru government's nationalization programme.[42]

On his trip to the United States of America in 1957, Birla again raised the matter of American aid to finance India's development, which he estimated to be in the region of 1,000 million US$. Relaying his conversation with Ellsworth Bunker—the US ambassador to India from 1956 to 1961—to Nehru, Birla noted that Bunker believed that a long-term loan of three-quarters of India's assumed needs could be arranged, provided incoming

---

[41] Birla's note dated 15 May 1956, attached with his letter to M. O. Mathai dated 19 May; file 3, 1043.
[42] Birla's note dated 20 April 1956, attached with his letter to M. O. Mathai dated 21 April; file 3, 1043.

foreign investment was allowed without hindrances. Wholly agreeing with Bunker, Birla attempted to assure Nehru that it was a sentiment with which Birla was in complete agreement. To Nehru, Birla wrote: 'if a good economic climate was created, money from the States would be forthcoming', notwithstanding some 'upsetting factors'.[43] The latter of these, expectedly so, referred to the victory of the Communist Party of India in the elections to Kerala's state legislature. From the American standpoint, according to Birla, it had raised the spectre of a communist India, which endangered Indian demands for development aid: official or otherwise. Eugene Black, then president of the World Bank, Birla wrote elsewhere, had remarked that India could not 'expect "a capitalist institution to finance socialization" (sic)'. Similarly, George Humphrey, US treasury secretary, enquired, Birla reported, if the Indian government was going to take over all private property. Seeking to allay their fears, Birla continued to argue that the 'only way to meet Communism is to make the country economically a strong one'. Hoping to persuade the US foreign policy establishment to curtail its military aid to Pakistan, he reasoned that it 'shall not help anyone (…) mak[ing] its Government unpopular and unstable without any advantage to the U.S.A.'[44]

*

Philanthropy also served more immediate and less strategic objectives—such as saving on taxes. In 1965, for example, Kasturbhai Lalbhai and Vikram Sarabhai led the effort, on behalf of the textile mill-owners in Ahmedabad, to fund the construction of buildings for the Indian Institute of Management in Ahmedabad. Hoping to raise nearly Rs. 20 lakhs, Lalbhai wrote to numerous business leaders from the city. In a letter to Madhav Prasad Birla, Lalbhai requested his Digvijay Woollen Mills and Jiyajirao Cotton Mills Ltd. to contribute Rs. 250,000, deductible as revenue expenditure from income tax. Not only would it help save taxes, Lalbhai wrote, but the Institute was going to be 'of tremendous advantage for creating managerial staff to the Industrial Units in the country'.[45] To Neville Wadia, scion of the Wadia Group, Lalbhai was even more pointed in seeking donations of Rs. 50,000 each from National Peroxide and Bombay Dyeing. If Wadia agreed to donate the money, Lalbhai pointed out—in effect—it would have been the Government of India that was

---

[43] Birla's note following his lunch with the Bunkers on 1 April 1957; file 4, 1043.
[44] Birla's note dated 15 May 1956, attached with his letter to M. O. Mathai dated 19 May; file 3, 1043.
[45] Lalbhai to Madhav Prasad Birla on 1 September 1965, SL17, Potla126, KL.

paying close to 60 per cent of it.[46] Philanthropy, therefore, became a crucial but unsurprising outlet of elites' pragmatic pursuit of profits.

Elites' pragmatism also manifest itself in more confrontational tactics of funding right-wing think tanks and political parties to counter the Indian government's economic policies under Nehru's prime ministership. J. R. D. Tata, for example, believed that Nehru's economic policies had 'drift[ed] to the extreme left; the private sector [was] being tolerated as long as it serve[d] the purpose'. He suggested, therefore, withholding all financial support to the Congress and lobbying allocation of a small number of seats in the Indian Parliament to economic elites.[47] Political funding, lobbying, and establishment of free-market think tanks soon became part of Tatas' growing philanthropy to counter socialism in the mid 1950s, notwithstanding their later self-claims that cite their philanthropy as evidence of their 'socialist outlook'.[48]

In 1955, the Tatas funded the establishment of the Forum of Free Enterprise, an anti-socialist think tank.[49] Led by Ardeshir D. Shroff, the Forum was founded as the 'ominous clouds of socialism were gathering strength', which caused growing concern within the business fraternity that resources would be moved away from the private to the public sector, including the means of production.[50] Active since the Forum works to 'give impetus to advocating, protecting and promoting liberal economic thinking and imperatives of private enterprise and free markets'.[51] Following its involvement with the founding of a think tank, in 1959, the Tatas supported the founding of the Swatantra Party (literally Freedom Party), a conservative party comprising mainly erstwhile princes, feudal landlords, and leading businessmen that espoused free market and dismantling of the License Raj.[52] Their support to the party, JRD Tata wrote to Nehru, was in India's larger interest. Despite switching

---

[46] Lalbhai to Neville Wadia on 27 December 1965, SL14, Potla126, KL.

[47] G. D. Birla's letter to M. O. Mathai dated 26 April 1955; file 3, 1043.

[48] 'A Tradition of Trust', Tata Group, accessed 25 July 2014, http://tata.com/aboutus/articlesinside/A-tradition-of-trust.

[49] Markovits, *Merchants, Traders, Entrepreneurs*, 162.

[50] A. D. Shroff had joined the Tatas in 1940 as a financial advisor and had retired from the Group's services in 1960. See TCA, 'AD Shroff (1899–1965)', accessed 19 March 2015, http://www.tatacentralarchives.com/history/biographies/12%20adshroff.htm.
From Forum of Free Enterprise, 'Forum Journey', accessed 19 March 2015, http://www.forumindia.org/forum_journey.htm.

[51] Forum of Free Enterprise, 'Genesis', accessed 19 March 2015, http://www.forumindia.org/about-usmain/about-us/genesis.

[52] Markovits, *Merchants, Traders, Entrepreneurs*, 162.

allegiance, going forward, the Tatas hoped to contribute to the political funds of both the Congress and the Swatantra Party.[53]

Such gift-making played a crucial role in helping economic elites such as the Tatas resist the economic policies of the Indian government from the 1950s to the 1970s, including those of Nehru, and later his daughter Indira Gandhi. Development, here, was mobilized to build legitimacy for elites' attempts at countering the Indian government. That is, such philanthropy had become necessary to save the developmental prospects of the country as its own government's economic policies had led to underdevelopment, and needed immediate correction. Looking back, J. R. D. Tata noted in a letter from 1981, the causes of India's underdevelopment lay 'largely in the economic policies adopted for the last thirty years by successive Governments and Parliaments in the pursuit of a misconceived interpretation of socialism'. The solution, Tata offered, was to search for an alternate: a 'fundamental change in Government's approach' to the national economy.[54]

*

While at the time of India's independence, the Tata Trusts claimed to be committed to ending 'poverty, and ignorance and disease and inequality of opportunity', development challenges remained:

> In education, (...) one out of every two Indians is still illiterate. Although basic education is being introduced as a fundamental right under the Constitution, the current scenario is dismal (...) In livelihoods, while the per capita net national product has doubled since Independence, disparities have increased with 35 crore [or 350m] Indians still below the poverty line. In health, life expectancy of the average citizen has increased, but annually 34 lakh [or 3.4m] children do not reach their fifth birthday on account of poor access to basic health services, poor maternal health, and malnutrition.[55]

As the twentieth century drew to a close, elites continued to justify their developmental philanthropy in the name of wider national interest.

---

[53] Khare, Harish. 'Liberals, This Is the Time to Keep the Faith', *Outlook*, 17 November 2014; available online at: http://www.outlookindia.com/article/Liberals-This-Is-The-Time-To-Keep-The-Faith/292510; retrieved 19 March 2015.

[54] Letter from J. R. D. Tata to S. Sitaram, All India Manufacturer's Association, dated 21 October 1981, from file no. 319/JRDT/Cor/Gen/22, TCA.

[55] SRTT, Annual Report, 1996–97. File no. 213/SRTT/1996–97, TCA.

Acknowledging the significant work undertaken by the nation-state through the singular linear narrative of progress, the report was not hesitant to point to the limits or the failures of this narrative. In so doing, the Tatas sought to carve out the role for elites' philanthropy and civil society organizations founded and funded by them.

With the demise of communism in Eastern Europe, civil society came to be conceptualized as an 'alternative to or as independent of the state'. This, Neera Chandhoke argues has never been India's case. Similar to what my research suggests, she argues that civil society in India, instead, was always premised on the failures of the Indian state in providing a 'minimum standard of life to its people'.[56] Such failures in India, it is worth emphasizing here, are not simply a result of the space vacated by the state as it adopts neoliberal economic policies, but the gaps arising out of or despite its presence: that is, its own inefficiencies. The Tata Trusts admitted as much as they went on to argue in the above report: 'Government allocations for the social sector have increased considerably over successive Plan periods, yet leakages in the delivery system coupled with poor quality implementation have not yielded the desired results. It is apparent that the State is unable to cope with the complex problems associated with reversing these trends. The non-profit sector or the Third Sector now needs to take on a more visible role'.[57]

Claims that the post-colonial nation-state—which emerged from nationalism's critique of colonialism and how it impeded India's development and subsequently drew its legitimacy from the promise of social justice[58]—could no longer be entrusted with the task of developing the nation were repeated elsewhere. Delivering the Jawaharlal Nehru birth centenary lecture at a meeting of the Indian Science Congress Association in Calcutta in 1993, Sohrab P. Godrej argued that 'A recent evolution in Indian society, in a rapidly changing world, is a growing awareness that responsibility for the development and security of our vast and complex country cannot be left to government alone'. 'A variety of resources and talents have to be harnessed to promote development of diverse dimensions of Indian society', he added, 'way beyond the goodwill and even the capacity of democratic governments'. Invoking Hindu scriptural traditions of giving and Carnegie's generosity, philanthropy—guided by Gandhian trusteeship, according to Godrej—enabled 'a

---

[56] Chandhoke, *Conceits of Civil Society*, 11–20.
[57] SRTT, Annual Report, 1996–97. File no. 213/SRTT/1996–97, TCA.
[58] Chatterjee, *Nationalist Thought*.

peaceful yet revolutionary adjustment' in society between the forces of the markets and those of the state.[59]

'In the continuum of *samaaj* (society), *bazzar* (market) and *sarkaar* (government)', Rohini Nilekani wrote elsewhere, 'only a strong society can keep markets and state accountable to the public good'.[60] Notwithstanding her deliberate but problematic conflation between society and civil society—in building which elites such as Nilekani invest—to mitigate against the failures and check the deleterious consequences of both the markets and the state.

It meant, Godrej concluded in his address quoted above, that the elites can be entrusted with the 'hopes, aspirations, interests and anxieties of the disadvantaged and the less privileged'.[61] Because, we are told, it is in the national interest to do so.

---

[59] Transcript of Godrej's address delivered on 23 March 1993 at Calcutta; from MS09-16-54-5, GA.
[60] Rohini Nilekani Philanthropies, 'Perspective', accessed 11 June 2021, https://rohininilekani.org/.
[61] Transcript of Godrej's address delivered on 23 March 1993 at Calcutta; from MS09-16-54-5, GA.

Elites' Historiographic Anxieties: A Methodological Caution

Archives are not the most popular of places to *do* development studies from. That place is often reserved for the 'field'—more often than not distant, where the poor reside, to which the researcher travels, and from which we hope to learn. Like most people, I also started in the field. But spending my time working through why contemporary development looked the way it did on the ground convinced me more and more that I must do two things. Firstly, in order to think about development now, one needed to understand its historical trajectory. Secondly, it was not enough to write about development from below—as more often than not agendas and choices were being shaped elsewhere, in spaces where one was either not necessarily welcomed or was loathe to become part of.

And so I decided to look at development from above and historically, or 'history "from above"' as Srirupa Roy calls it; which brought its own methodological challenges.[1]

'Mainstream development discourse', Kothari has argued, 'is silent about its history, legacy and genealogy. It rarely acknowledges its historical antecedents', she adds, 'and in particular its roots in a colonial past'.[2] But this was only partly true in my case. Yes, the elites were silent about profiting from colonial trade in the nineteenth and even twentieth century, including their reprehensible involvement in the opium trade—proceeds from which they later gave away in charity.[3] But they were not silent about the other historical force from twentieth-century India that had shaped and was shaped by their philanthropy—nationalism. In fact, if anything, they were always quick to parade gifts from the past that they had made in service of the nation. According to business historians, elites have always been concerned about the uses and abuses of history, and would like, very much so, to control history and its institutional devices (archives, cataloguing, memory and memoirs, etc.). Not only does this enable elites to build their reputation and political influence; but consolidating cultural capital in this way leads to further accumulation of wealth.[4] This simultaneous—but expected (why wouldn't they?)—forgetting and memorizing that characterized the history of elites' philanthropy has resulted in what can be called their historiographical anxieties. These anxieties manifest themselves in the archives and in historiography itself.

Launched in January 1991, the Tata Central Archives (or TCA) were the first private business archives in the country, which collected 'letters, documents, images, printed books, group publications and ephemera of potential historical and critical significance to

---

[1] Roy, *Beyond Belief*, vii.   [2] Kothari, 'History, Time, Temporality', 65.

[3] Wacha was unequivocal about the Tatas' involvement in the opium trade. He wrote: 'Opium and cotton were the two staple commodities in which it [Tata's father's firm] traded, and young Mr. Jamsetji's attention was soon engaged on them. The trade in the former took him to Hongkong (*sic*) first and that in the latter to London, and Liverpool later on'. Jamsetji, Wacha adds, 'completed his training in respect of the China trade and developed his native instinct of shrewdness and commercial sagacity' in Hong Kong; see *Life and Work*, 3.

[4] See, for example, Suddaby et al., 'Rhetorical History', 147–73 on the use of history as a strategic resource; and Harvey et al., 'Entrepreneurial Philanthropy', 429–30 on the elites' ability to transform one form of capital to another using philanthropy.

the Tata group'.[5] The desire to archive historical artefacts can be understood as part of a modern historical consciousness that Habermas described as 'the consciousness of an epoch that relates itself to the past of antiquity, in order to view itself as the result of a transition from the old to the new'.[6] It enables the articulation of their central role in the transition to modernity—which in India's case, is invariably wound up with the national question. TCA, for example, presents itself to prospective researchers as a repository of material that pertains to not just the history of Tatas but also makes claims about its wider relevance. 'Apart from Tata history', TCA holds—it claims, 'a sizeable number of documents on Indian industrialisation and correspondence with national leaders such as Dadabhai Naoroji and Mahatma Gandhi. This material is of tremendous use to researchers and historians who are able to view preserved records from a number of years past'.[7]

While gesturing towards their significance, archives are also careful to distance themselves from any attempts at persuading how histories should be written. They do so, for example, by emphasizing their passivity. TCA, for example, claims that 'history lies treasured in these carefully preserved files at the archives'.[8] In this way, archival material is rendered passive, lying in wait for the historian's interpretation to flesh out their significance for the benefit of the rest of the world—not that they are ordered, catalogued, stored, etc. in particular ways.

This purported passivity or neutrality of archives, though, belies elites' active attempts at shaping historiography. Such attempts varied from enlistment—for example, I was once asked—or maybe, instructed by an archivist—'we know you will not say anything "critical," will you? But in any case, we must take all precautions'—to regulating access and availability of archival material, and even in its destruction, not to mention the power embodied in the archival texts itself.

Elites' historiographic anxieties took its most extreme form in Tatas' destruction of sources, notwithstanding TCA's subsequent attempts at systematically preserving historical records, are well documented. Harris's biography of Jamsetji Tata acknowledged that there was only very limited material available. It was based, primarily, on Tata's papers in English and oral accounts from his son, Dorabji.[9] These papers, we are told, were procured from Dinshaw E. Wacha, who had written an earlier account of Tata's life in 1915.[10] All this material was subsequently destroyed once Harris had completed writing his book.[11] A third account of Tata's life was written in 1970 which was based on material from his letters, diary, and articles and which is no longer available for research.[12] Others have noted that whatever material has survived is not made readily available to researchers for 'fear

[5] TCA became a division of the Tata Services Limited in 1997 and was moved to Pune in 2001. Tata Central Archives, 'Homepage', accessed 24 July 2014, http://tatacentralarchives.com/default.htm.

[6] Habermas, 'Modernity', 163.

[7] 'Tata Central Archives', Tata Group, accessed 30 July 2014, http://tata.com/aboutus/articlesinside/Tata-Central-Archives.

[8] 'Tata Central Archives', Tata Group, accessed 30 July 2014, http://tata.com/aboutus/articlesinside/Tata-Central-Archives.

[9] Harris, Tata: A Chronicle, xv. See Lala for retrospective details on material on which Harris based his chronicle; Love of India, xvi.

[10] From a letter from Dinoo S. Bastawala, granddaughter of Dinshaw E. Wacha, dated 7 April 1960; from file no. 174/JNT/HISTORY/PROJECT/COR/Research by Mr. R Salivati/1; also see Wacha, Life and Work.

[11] Benjamin and Rath, 'Modern Indian Business History', 1.

[12] Lala, Love of India, xv–xvi confirms that material on which Saklatvala and Khosla's Jamsetji Tata, published in 1970, was based is not available any longer.

that it may result in adverse remarks'.[13] From that which is left behind, access in the private archives is regulated, often in ad hoc ways. TCA, for example, does not make any catalogues, digital or otherwise, available to researchers at any stage of negotiating access. The archivist *determines*, based on the researcher's presentation of the subject, the relevant material that can be accessed. This, I later found, was standard practice at TCA, and was told that it was on account of *bad* experiences in the past where researchers would come to TCA on one pretext and asked for unrelated material. There was no access to private papers for fear of potential 'problems', the nature of which was not made clear to me. From the material made available, conditions of photocopying were ad hoc and had little to do with copyright regulations.[14]

Such tactics serve dual purposes: while preventing, or impeding at the very least, attempts to write differently by silencing selective aspects of history, they help crystallize particular kinds of historical claims from above. It enables elites to make claims about a 'long tradition' of service to the nation, that is still ongoing.[15] The Tata Group, for example, claims that its philanthropy and wider social concerns are an integral part of its 'founding DNA'.[16] And so, while Gandhi's endorsements of Tatas are highlighted to mark the significance of the archives as well as Tatas' benefactions to the nation and its history, Gandhi's chiding is duly forgotten in elites' archives.

---

[13] Benjamin and Rath, 'Modern Indian Business History', 1.

[14] For example, while I was not allowed to photocopy from the digitized files of minutes of SDTT's board meetings (file no. 637/SDTT BO Meetings, 1932–2005, TCA), duplicate printed copies of minutes of selected years had been boxed elsewhere (perhaps accidentally), whose photocopies I was able to obtain.

[15] The corporate website of the Godrej Group, for example, presents a seemingly continuous narrative of manufacture of quality products by the Group. It is instructive to note that the historical story re-presented on the website is markedly nationalist in orientation; and where businesses and nation-building were not necessarily at cross-purposes but symbiotic. For example, the production of Cinthol soap in 1918 is introduced as produced 'against the tide of the Raj'; that in 1951, it produced ballot boxes for India's first elections 'when we think of how long we've been dancing with history, we are humbled'; about the refrigerator in 1958, it says 'Godrej is here to dazzle the desis'; see Godrej Group, 'About Us', accessed 24 July 2014, http://www.godrej.com/godrej/Godrej/aboutusstories.aspx.

Similarly, the Aditya Birla Group, of the now-divided Birla family, describes its history as starting from the earliest cotton trade in the nineteenth century. It follows a similar pattern of grounding its history within the wider context of nation-building, by saying:

> In the early part of the 20th century, the Group's founding father, Mr. Ghanshyamdas Birla, set up industries in critical sectors such as textiles and fibre, aluminium, cement, and chemicals. As a close confidant of Mahatma Gandhi, he played an active role in the Indian freedom struggle. He represented India at the first and second round-table conferences in London, along with Gandhiji. It was at Birla House in Delhi that the luminaries of the Indian freedom struggle often met to plot the downfall of the British Raj. Mr. Ghanshyamdas Birla found no contradiction in pursuing business goals with the dedication of a saint, emerging as one of the foremost industrialists of pre-independence India. The principles by which he lived were soaked up by his grandson, Mr. Aditya Vikram Birla, the Group's legendary leader.

See Aditya Birla Group, 'About Us', accessed 30 July 2014, http://www.adityabirla.com/about-us/heritage. Thus, one finds that large businesses in India use their history to re-present their present as part of a longer, historical continuity; and have tended to ground it within a markedly nationalist context.

[16] 'Tata Group, "Leadership with Trust", accessed 11 August 2014, http://tata.com/aboutus/sub_index/Leadership-with-trust.

In the 1920s, for example, Gandhi supported the world's first anti-dam movement against the Tata Electric Supply Company. The Company proposed constructing dams for electricity generation which were expected to result in the submergence of fifty-two villages, and thousands of acres of fertile soil, affecting the peasants from the Malva community. Later, without giving any prior notice or intimation, the company officers started various preparatory works such as construction of temporary camps, laying of roads etc. They evicted peasants from their land. The farmers were abused, threatened, terrorized, and forcibly evicted from their lands. Consequently, there was widespread unrest among the masses. It led to mass mobilization and the organization of a *satyagraha*, led by Senapati Bapat, under the popular slogan *Jaan athava jamin* (our lives or land).[17] Gandhi was forthcoming in support for the *satyagrahis*. In 1921, he wrote in *Young India* that 'My heart goes out to these poor people. I wish the great house of the Tatas, instead of standing on their legal rights, will reason with the people themselves (. . .) What is the value of all boons that the Tata scheme claims to confer upon India, if it is to be at the unwilling expense of even one poor man?' He suggested that 'the custodians of the great name that they would truly advance India's interest if they will defer to the wishes of their weak and helpless countrymen'.[18] Speaking at Bassein, Gandhi repeated his support of the peasants: 'I hope that our Tata Company will take no steps against the satyagrahis of Mulshi Peta. It is welcome to acquire the land even without payment with people's goodwill, but I hope it will make no move to obtain it so long as even one owner is unwilling'.[19] Despite running for four years, the campaign was not successful in stalling the peasants' eviction from their lands. More recently, others have written about the Tata Dharangrastha Kruti Samiti (or the Tata Dam-affected Action Committee), which under the leadership of Medha Patkar, has been supporting the tenant framers, which a few generations later are still waiting for their compensation and rehabilitation benefits. According to activist Medha Patkar in May 2007, theirs was 'the oldest case of forcible land acquisition in the history of the country'.[20]

*

And so, writing histories of development from above involves negotiating power—perhaps more acutely and extensively than elsewhere—and working past elites' historiographic anxieties. Even if it is germinative in bringing into relief the continuities in our ideas of development, it must be approached, therefore, with extreme caution.

---

[17] Bhuskute, 'Maharashtra Rehabilitation Act', 170–1.
[18] From Gandhi's article in *Young India* dated 27 April 1921; Collected Works of Gandhi (henceforth CWG), vol. 23, 90.
[19] From Gandhi's speech at Bassein on 7 May 1921; CWG, vol. 23, 118.
[20] Anosh Malekar, 'The Mavlas of Mulshi: Displacement's Earliest Victims', *Infochange News*, July 2008, http://infochangeindia.org/agenda/migration-a-displacement/the-mavlas-of-mulshi-displacements-earliest-victims.html.

Bibliography

Collected Works

AWS Writings and Speeches of Dr. B. R. Ambedkar [volumes 1–17], http://drambedkar-writings.gov.in/content/.

CWG Collected Works of M. K. Gandhi [volumes 1–100], https://www.gandhiserve.net/about-mahatma-gandhi/collected-works-of-mahatma-gandhi/.

Monographs and Edited Collections

Alvares, Claude. *Science, Development and Violence: The Revolt against Modernity*. Delhi: Oxford University Press, 1992.

Amsden, Alice H., Alisa DiCaprio, and James A. Robinson, eds. *The Role of Elites in Economic Development*. Oxford: Oxford University Press, 2012.

Anderson, Robert S. *Nucleus and Nation: Scientists, International Networks, and Power in India*. University of Chicago Press, 2010.

Appadurai, Arjun. *Modernity at Large: Cultural Dimensions of Globalization*. Minneapolis: University of Minnesota Press, 1996.

Bassett, Ross. *The Technological Indian*. Cambridge, MA: Harvard University Press, 2016.

Bhabha, Homi K. *The Location of Culture*. London: Routledge, 1994.

Brown, Wendy. *Edgework: Critical Essays on Knowledge and Politics*. Princeton: Princeton University Press, 2005.

Chambers, Robert. *Whose Reality Counts?: Putting the Last First*. London: Intermediate Technology Publications, 1997.

Chambers, Robert. *Rural Development: Putting the Last First*. London: Routledge, 2013.

Chambers, Robert, Arnold Pacey, and Lori Ann Thrupp, eds. *Farmer First: Farmer Innovation and Agricultural Research*. London: Intermediate Technology Publications, 1989.

Chandhoke, Neera. *The Conceits of Civil Society*. New Delhi: Oxford University Press, 2003.

Chatterjee, Partha. *Nationalist Thought and the Colonial World: A Derivative Discourse*. London: Zed Books, 1986.

Chatterjee, Partha. *The Nation and its Fragments: Colonial and Postcolonial Histories*. Princeton: Princeton University Press, 1993.

Chatterjee, Partha. 2004. *The Politics of the Governed: Reflections on Popular Politics in Most of the World*. New York: Columbia University Press.

Chatterjee, Partha. *Empire and Nation: Essential Writings, 1985–2005*. Ranikhet: Permanent Black, 2010.

Chatterji, Joya. *Bengal Divided: Hindu Communalism and Partition, 1932–1947*. Cambridge: Cambridge University Press, 1994.

Chen, Kuan-Hsing. *Asia as Method: Towards Deimperialization*. Durham: Duke University Press, 2010.

Chowdhury, Indira, and Ananya Dasgupta. *A Masterful Spirit: Homi Bhabha, 1909–1966*. Delhi: Penguin India, 2010.

Cooke, Bill and Uma Kothari, eds. *Participation: The New Tyranny?* London: Zed Books, 2001.

Crush, Jonathan, ed. *The Power of Development*. New York: Routledge, 1995.

Dar, Sadhvi, and Bill Cooke, eds. *The New Development Management: The Dual Modernization*. London: Zed Books, 2008.

Deshpande, Satish. *Contemporary India: A Sociological View*. New Delhi: Viking, 2003.

Edelman, Marc. *Peasants against Globalization: Rural Social Movements in Costa Rica*. Stanford: Stanford University Press, 1999.

Edelman, Marc, and Angelique Haugerud. *The Anthropology of Development and Globalization*. Oxford: Blackwell Publishing, 2005.

Elwin, Verrier. *The Story of Tata Steel*. Bombay: Commercial Printing Press, 1958.

Escobar, Arturo. *Encountering Development: The Making and Unmaking of the Third World*. Princeton: Princeton University Press, 1995.

Ferguson, James. *The Anti-politics Machine: 'Development', Depoliticisation and Bureaucratic Power in Lesotho*. Cambridge: Cambridge University Press, 1994.

Ferguson, James. *Expectations of Modernity: Myths and Meanings of Urban Life on the Zambian Copperbelt*. Berkeley: University of California Press, 1999.

Gandhi, Leela. *Postcolonial Theory: A Critical Introduction*. New York: Columbia University Press, 1998.

Guha, Ranajit. *Dominance without Hegemony: History and Power in Colonial India*. Cambridge, MA: Harvard University Press, 1997.

Gupta, Akhil. *Postcolonial Developments: Agriculture in the Making of Modern India*. Durham: Duke University Press, 1998.

Habib, Irfan S. *Indian Nationalism: The Essential Writings*. New Delhi: Aleph, 2017.

Harris, Frank R. *Jamsetji Nusserwanji Tata: A Chronicle of his Life*. London: Oxford University Press, 1925.

Harris, Frank R. *Jamsetji Nusserwanji Tata: A Chronicle of his Life*. 2nd edition. Bombay: Blackie and Sons, 1958.

Hennessy, Jossleyn. *India Democracy and Education: A Study of the Work of the Birla Education Trust*. Bombay: Orient Longman, 1955.

Jaffrelot, Christophe, eds. *Hindu Nationalism: A Reader*. Princeton: Princeton University Press, 2007.

Karaka, Dosabhoy Framjee. *The Parsees: Their History, Manners, Customs, and Religion*. London: Smith, Elder and Co., 1858.

Karaka, Dosabhoy Framjee. *History of the Parsis Including their Manners, Customs, Religion, and Present Position*, vol II. London: Macmillan, 1884.

Knight, Barry, Hope Chigudu, and Rajesh Tandon. *Reviving Democracy: Citizens at the Heart of Governance*. London: Earthscan, 2002.

Kohler, Robert E. *Partners in Science: Foundations and Natural Scientists 1900–1945*. Chicago: University of Chicago Press, 1991.

Kuber, Girish. *Tatas: How a Family Built a Business and a Nation*. Delhi: Harper Collins, 2019.

Kudaisya, Medha. *The Life and Times of G. D. Birla*. New Delhi: Oxford University Press, 2003.

Kudaisya, Medha (ed.). *The Oxford India Anthology of Business History*. New Delhi: Oxford University Press, 2011.

Lala, Russi. M. *The Heartbeat of a Trust: Fifty Years of the Sir Dorabji Tata Trust*. New Delhi: Tata McGraw-Hill, 1984.

Lala, Russi. M. *Beyond the Last Blue Mountain: A Life of JRD Tata*. New Delhi: Penguin Books, 1993.

Lala, Russi. M. *The Joy of Achievement: Conversations with JRD Tata*. New Delhi: Penguin Books, 2003.

Lala, Russi. M. *Creation of Wealth*. New Delhi: Viking, 2004.

Lala, Russi. M. *For the Love of India: The Life and Times of Jamsetji Tata*. New Delhi: Penguin Books, 2006.

Lee, David and Howard Newby. *The Problem of Sociology*. London: Routledge, 1983.

Luhrmann, Tanya M. *The Good Parsi: The Fate of a Colonial Elite in a Postcolonial Society*. Cambridge, MA: Harvard University Press, 1996.

Majumdar, Sumit K. *India's Late, Late Industrial Revolution: Democratizing Entrepreneurship*. Cambridge: Cambridge University Press, 2012.

Markovits, Claude. *Indian Business and Nationalist Politics: The Indigenous Capitalist Class and the Rise of the Congress Party*. Cambridge: Cambridge University Press, 2002.

Markovits, Claude. *Merchants, Traders, Entrepreneurs: Indian Business in the Colonial Era*. London: Palgrave Macmillan, 2008.

Moraes, Frank. *Sir Purshottamdas Thakurdas*. New Delhi: Asia Publishing House, 1957.

Mukherjee, Rudrangshu. *A Century of Trust: The Story of TATA Steel*. New Delhi: Portfolio, 2008.

Mukul, Akshaya. *Gita Press and the Making of Hindu India*. Noida: HarperCollins, 2015.

Murphy, Jonathan. *The World Bank and Global Managerialism*. London: Routledge, 2008.

Nanda, Bal Ram. *In Gandhi's Footsteps: The Life and Times of Jamnalal Bajaj*. Delhi: Oxford University Press, 1990.

Palsetia, Jesse S. *The Parsis of India: Preservation of Identity in Bombay City*. Leiden: Brill, 2001.

Payton, Robert L., and Michael P. Moody. *Understanding Philanthropy: Its Meaning and Mission*. Bloomington: Indiana University Press, 2008.

Piramal, Gita. *Business Maharajas*. New Delhi: Penguin Books, 1996.

Piramal, Gita. *Business Legends*. New Delhi: Penguin Books, 1999.

Prakash, Gyan. *Another Reason: Science and the Imagination of Modern India*. Princeton: Princeton University Press, 1999.

Rahnema, Majid, with Bawtree, V. *The Post-development Reader*. London: Zed Books, 1997.

Roy, Srirupa. *Beyond Belief: Indian and the Politics of Postcolonial Nationalism*. Durham: Duke University Press, 2007.

Roy, Tirthankar. *A Business History of India: Enterprise and the Emergence of Capitalism from 1700*. Cambridge: Cambridge University Press, 2018.

Saklatvala, B., and K. K. Khosla. *Jamsetji Tata*. New Delhi: Publications Division, Ministry of Information and Broadcasting, Government of India, 1970.

Schumacher, Ernst F. *Small Is Beautiful: A Study of Economics as if People Mattered*. London: Blond and Briggs, 1973.

Scott, James C. *Seeing Like a State: How Certain Schemes to Improve the Human Condition Have Failed*. New Haven: Yale University Press, 1998.

Sehgal, Rashme. *Basant Kumar and Sarala Birla: Life Has No Full Stops*. New Delhi: Amaryllis, 2011.

Sen, Sunil Kumar. *The House of Tata, 1839–1939*. Calcutta: Progressive Publishers, 1975.

Shiva, Vandana. *Staying Alive: Women, Ecology and Development*. London: Zed Books, 1989.

Subbarayappa, B. V. *In Pursuit of Excellence: A History of the Indian Institute of Science.* New Delhi: Tata McGraw-Hill Publishing Company, 1992.

Sundar, Pushpa. *Beyond Business: From Merchant Charity to Corporate Citizenship, Indian Business Philanthropy through the Ages.* New Delhi: Tata McGraw-Hill Publishing, 2000.

Sundar, Pushpa. *Business and Community: The Story of Corporate Social Responsibility in India.* New Delhi: Sage, 2013.

Sundar, Pushpa. *Giving with a Thousand Hands: The Changing Face of Indian Philanthropy.* Delhi: Oxford University Press, 2017.

Tripathi, Dwijendra Nath, and Jyoti Jumani. *The Concise Oxford History of Indian Business.* New Delhi: Oxford University Press, 2007.

Wacha, Dinshaw E. *The Life and Life Work of JN Tata.* Madras: Ganesh, 1915.

Witzel, Morgen. *Tata: The Evolution of a Corporate Brand.* New Delhi: Penguin Books India, 2010.

Book Chapters and Articles

Agrawal, Arun. 'Dismantling the Divide between Indigenous and Scientific Knowledge.' *Development and Change* 26, 3 (1995): 413–39.

Bailey, Frederick G. 'The Peasant View of the Bad Life.' In *Peasants and Peasant Society*, edited by Teodor Shanin, 299–21. Harmondsworth: Penguin, 1968.

Bhuskute, R. V. 'The Maharashtra Rehabilitation Act 1989.' In *Rehabilitation Policy and Law in India: A Right to Livelihood*, edited by Walter Fernandes and Vijay Paranjpye, 169–91. New Delhi: Indian Social Institute, 1997.

Birla, Ritu. 'C=f(P): The Trust, "General Public Utility", and Charity as a Function of Profit in India.' *Modern Asian Studies* 52, 1 (2018): 132–62.

Charnovitz, Steve. 'Two Centuries of Participation: NGOs and International Governance.' *Michigan Journal of International Law* 18, 2 (1997): 183–286.

Chatterjee, Partha. 'Beyond the Nation? Or within?' *Economic and Political Weekly* 32, 1, 2 (1997): 30–4.

Chatterjee, Partha. 'On Civil and Political Societies in Postcolonial Democracies.' In *Civil Society: History and Possibilities*, edited by Sudipta Kaviraj and Sunil Khilnani, 165–78. Cambridge: Cambridge University Press, 2001.

Chowdhury, Indira. 'Fundamental Research, Self-reliance and Internationalism: The Evolution of the Tata Institute of Fundamental Research, 1945–47.' In *Science and Modern India: An Institutional History, c.1784–1947*, edited by Uma Das Gupta, 1095–129. New Delhi: Pearson Longman, 2011.

DiCaprio, Alisa. 'Introduction: The Role of Elites in Economic Development.' In *The Role of Elites in Economic Development*, edited by Alice H. Amsden, Alisa DiCaprio, and James A. Robinson, 1–16. Oxford: Oxford University Press, 2012.

Dube, Saurabh. 'Introduction: Enchantments of Modernity.' *The South Atlantic Quarterly* 101, 4 (2002): 729–55.

Ferguson, James. 'Decomposing Modernity: History and Hierarchy after Development.' In *Postcolonial Studies and Beyond*, edited by Ania Loomba, Suvir Kaul, Matti Bunzl, Antoinette Burton, and Jed Esty, 166–81. Durham: Duke University Press, 2005.

Fox, Richard G. 'Communalism and Modernity.' In *Making India Hindu*, edited by David Ludden, 235–49. Delhi: Oxford University Press, 1996.

Guilhot, Nicolas. 'Reforming the World: George Soros, Global Capitalism and the Philanthropic Management of Social Sciences.' *Critical Sociology*, 33 (2007): 447–77.

Guru, Gopal. 'Dalits in Pursuit of Modernity.' In *India: Another Millenium?*, edited by Romila Thapar, 123–36. New Delhi: Penguin, 2000.

Habermas, Jürgen. 'Modernity—An Incomplete Project.' In *Contemporary Sociological Thought: Themes and Theories*, edited by Sean P. Hier, 163–74. Toronto: Canadian Scholars' Press, 2005.

Habib, Irfan S, 'Introduction.' In *Indian Nationalism: The Essential Writings*, edited by S. Irfan Habib, 1–36. New Delhi: Aleph, 2017.

Harvey, Charles, Mairi Maclean, Jillian Gordon, and Eleanor Shaw. 'Andrew Carnegie and the Foundations of Contemporary Entrepreneurial Philanthropy.' *Business History* 53, 3 (2011): 425–50.

Hatcher, Brian A. 'Imitation, Then and Now: On the Emergence of Philanthropy in Early Colonial Calcutta.' *Modern Asian Studies* 52, 1 (2018): 62–98.

Haynes, Douglas E. 'From Tribute to Philanthropy: The Politics of Gift Giving in a Western Indian City.' *Journal of Asian Studies* 46, 2 (1987): 339–60.

Helleiner, Eric. 'Reinterpreting Bretton Woods: International Development and the Neglected Origins of Embedded Liberalism.' *Development and Change* 37, 5 (2006): 943–67.

Jennings, Michael. '"Almost an Oxfam in Itself": Oxfam, *Ujamaa* and Development in Tanzania.' *African Affairs* 101 (2002): 509–30.

Kavadi, Shirish N. 'Lady Tata Memorial Trust and Leukaemia Research in Europe, 1932–53.' *Economic and Political Weekly* 49, 45 (2014): 69–74.

Kavadi, Shirish N. 'The Founding of the Tata Memorial Hospital, 1932–1941.' *Indian Journal of Cancer* 56, 3 (2019): 282–4.

Kaviraj, Sudipta. 'An Outline of a Revisionist Theory of Modernity.' *European Journal of Sociology* 46, 3 (2005): 497–26.

Kaviraj, Sudipta, and Sunil Khilnani. 'Introduction.' In *Civil Society: History and Possibilities*, edited by Sudipta Kaviraj and Sunil Khilnani, 1–7. Cambridge: Cambridge University Press, 2001.

Kothari, Uma. 'History, Time and Temporality in Development Discourse,' in *History, Historians and Development Policy: A Necessary Dialogue*, edited by C. A. Bayly, Vijayendra Rao, Simon Szreter, and Michael Woolcock, 65–70. Manchester, Manchester University Press, 2011.

Kumar, Arun. 'Book Review, Business and Society: The Story of Corporate Social Responsibility in India by Pushpa Sundar.' *Management Learning* 44, 5 (2013): 563–6.

Kumar, Arun. 'Pragmatic and Paradoxical Philanthropy: Tatas' Gift-giving and Scientific Development in India.' *Development and Change* 29, 6 (2018): 1422–46.

Kumar, Arun and Sally Brooks. 'Bridges, Platforms, and Satellites: Theorizing the Power of Global Philanthropy in International Development.' *Economy and Society*, 50, 2 (2021): 322–45.

Kumar, Deepak. 'The "Culture" of Science and Colonial Culture, India 1820–1920.' *British Journal for History of Science* 29, 2 (1996): 195–209.

Kumar, Prakash. '"Modernization" and Agrarian Development in India 1912–52.' *Journal of Asian Studies* 79, 3 (2020): 1–26.

Kumar, Ravinder. 'Gandhi, Ambedkar, and the Poona Pact, 1932.' *South Asia: Journal of South Asian Studies* 8, 1–2 (1985): 87–101.

Lobo, Lancy. 'Adivasis, Hindutva and Post-Godhra Riots in Gujarat.' *Economic and Political Weekly* 37, 48 (2002): 4844–9.

McRobie, George. 'Intermediate Technology: Small Is Successful.' *Third World Quarterly* 1, 2 (1979): 71–86.

Mishra, Srijit. 'Farmers' Suicides in Maharashtra.' *Economic and Political Weekly* 41, 16 (2006): 1538–45.

Mohanty, B. B., and Sangeeta Shroff. 'Farmers' Suicides in Maharashtra.' *Economic and Political Weekly* 39, 52 (2004): 5599–606.

Mukherjee, Sraman. 'New Province, Old Capital: Making Patna Pataliputra.' *Indian Economic Social History Review* 46, 2 (2009): 241–79.

Nayak, Ajit, and Mairi Maclean. 'Co-evolution, Opportunity Seeking and Institutional Change: Entrepreneurship and the Indian Telecommunications Industry, 1923–2009.' *Business History* 55, 1 (2013): 29–52.

Nederveen Pieterse, Jan. 'After Post-development.' *Third World Quarterly* 21, 2 (2000): 175–91.

Niranjana, Tejaswini. 'Nationalism Refigured: Contemporary South Indian Cinema and the Subject of Feminism.' In *Subaltern Studies: Community, Gender and Violence*, vol XI, edited by Partha Chatterjee and Pradeep Jeganathan, 138–66. Delhi: Permanent Black, 2001.

Osella, Filippo. 'Charity and Philanthropy in South Asia: An Introduction.' *Modern Asian Studies* 52, 1 (2018): 4–34.

Palsetia, Jesse S. '"Honourable Machinations": The Jamsetjee Jejeebhoy Baronetcy and the Indian Response to the Honours System in India.' *South Asia Research* 23, 1 (2003): 55–75.

Palsetia, Jesse S. 'Merchant Charity and Public Identity Formation in Colonial India: The Case of Jamsetjee Jejeebhoy.' *Journal of Asian and African Studies* 40, 3 (2005): 197–217.

Porter, Michael E., and Mark R. Kramer. 'Philanthropy's New Agenda: Creating Value.' *Harvard Business Review* 77 (1999): 121–31.

Porter, Michael E., and Mark R. Kramer. 'The Competitive Advantage of Corporate Philanthropy.' *Harvard Business Review* 80 (2002): 56–68.

Portes, Alejandro. 'On the Sociology of National Development: Theories and Issues.' *American Journal of Sociology* 82, 1 (1976): 55–85.

Ramanathan, Malathi, and Subbarayappa, B. V. 'Indian Institute of Science: Its Origin and Growth, *c.*1909–1947.' In *Science and Modern India: An Institutional History, c.1784–1947*, edited by Uma Das Gupta, 871–926. New Delhi: Pearson Longman, 2011.

Ramdas, Kavita N. 'Philanthrocapitalism: Reflections on Politics and Policy-making.' *Society* 48 (2011): 393–6.

Schneider, Leander. 'Freedom and Unfreedom in Rural Development: Julius Nyerere, *Ujamaa Vijijini*, and Villagization.' *Canadian Journal of African Studies* 38, 2 (2004): 344–92.

Sealander, Judith. 'Curing Evils at their Source: The Arrival of Scientific Giving.' In *Charity, Philanthropy, and Civility in American History*, edited by Lawrence J. Friedman and Mark D. McGarvie, 217–39. Cambridge: Cambridge University Press, 2003.

Sebaly, Kim P. 'The Tatas and University Reform in India, 1898–1914.' *History Of Education* 14, 2 (1985): 117–36.

Seth, Sanjay. '"Nehruvian Socialism", 1927–1937: Nationalism, Marxism, and the Pursuit of Modernity.' *Alternatives: Global, Local, Political* 18, 4 (1993): 453–73.

Seth, Sanjay, Leela Gandhi, and Michael Dutton. 'Postcolonial Studies: A Beginning . . . ' *Postcolonial Studies* 1, 1 (1998): 7–11.

Sikka, D. R. 'The Role of India Meteorological Department, 1875–1947.' In *Science and Modern India: An Institutional History, c.1784–1947*, edited by Uma Das Gupta, 381–426. New Delhi: Pearson Longman, 2011.

Sivakumar, N. 'The Business Ethics of Jamsetji Nusserwanji Tata––A Forerunner in Promoting Stakeholder Welfare.' *Journal of Business Ethics* 83, 2 (2008): 353–61.

Smith, Elta. 'Imaginaries of Development: The Rockefeller Foundation and Rice Research.' *Science As Culture* 18, 4 (2009): 461–82.

Srinivas, Nidhi. 'Mimicry and Revival: The Transfer and Transformation of Management Knowledge to India, 1959–1990.' *International Studies of Management and Organization* 38, 4 (2008): 38–57.

Suddaby, Roy, William M. Foster, and Chris Quinn Trank. 'Rhetorical History as a Source of Competitive Advantage.' *Advances in Strategic Management* 27 (2010): 147–73.

Suri, K. C. 'Political Economy of Agrarian Distress.' *Economic and Political Weekly* 41, 16 (2006): 1523–9.

Tripathi, Dwijendra Nath. 'Book Review. Business and Society: The Story of Corporate Social Responsibility in India.' *Journal of Entrepreneurship* 23, 2 (2014): 334–7.

Wallerstein, Immanuel. 'The Concept of National Development, 1917–1989: Elegy and Requiem.' *American Behavioral Scientist* 35, 4/5 (1992): 517–29.

White, David L. 'From Crisis to Community Definition: The Dynamics of Eighteenth-century Parsi Philanthropy.' *Modern Asian Studies* 25, 2 (1991): 303–20.

Reports

Blake, Simon, Tara Chand, Nilanjana Dutta, Adrain Fradd, and Gaurav Gupta. 'Giving in India: A Guide for Funders and Charities.' London: New Philanthropy Capital, 2009.

Government of India. 'Report of Fact-finding Team on Vidarbha: Regional Disparities and Rural Distress in Maharashtra with Particular Reference to Vidarbha.' 2006, http://planningcommission.nic.in/reports/genrep/rep_vidarbha.pdf.

Mishra's 'History's Waiting Room.' *The Guardian*, 28 February 2015.

Sen, Hari K. 'The Progress and Present Status of Science in India,' Research Report. Hanscom: Air Force Cambridge Research Laboratories, Office of Aerospace Research, US Air Force (1963).

Working Papers and Theses

Benjamin, N., and Prabhash Narayana Rath. 'Modern Indian Business History: A Bibliographic Survey.' GIPE-WP-06. Gokhale Institute of Politics and Economics, Pune (2005).

Chowdhury, Indira. 'The Laboratory and its Double: The Making of the Scientist-Citizen at TIFR.' CASI Working Paper Series, 12–01. Center for the Advanced Study of India, University of Pennsylvania, Philadelphia (2012).

Kavadi, Shirish N. 'State Policy, Philanthropy, and Medical Research in Western India, 1898–1962.' Unpublished thesis for PhD (Arts) in History. Asiatic Society of Mumbai, Mumbai (2011).

Kumar, Arun. 'Organizing Tataland, the Modern Nation: A History of Development in Post/Colonial India.' Unpublished thesis for PhD in Organisation, Work and Technology. Lancaster University, Lancaster (2015).

Index

For the benefit of digital users, indexed terms that span two pages (e.g., 52–53) may, on occasion, appear on only one of those pages.